Why the Law Is So Perverse

Why the Law Is So Perverse

LEO KATZ

THE UNIVERSITY OF CHICAGO PRESS   CHICAGO AND LONDON

LEO KATZ is the Frank Carano Professor of Law at the University of Pennsylvania Law School. He is the author of *Bad Acts and Guilty Minds: Conundrums of the Criminal Law* and *Ill-Gotten Gains: Evasion, Blackmail, Fraud, and Kindred Puzzles of the Law*, both published by the University of Chicago Press.

The University of Chicago Press, Chicago 60637
The University of Chicago Press, Ltd., London
© 2011 by The University of Chicago
All rights reserved. Published 2011.
Printed in the United States of America
20 19 18 17 16 15 14 13 12   2 3 4 5

ISBN-13: 978-0-226-42603-7 (cloth)
ISBN-10: 0-226-42603-3 (cloth)

Library of Congress Cataloging-in-Publication Data

Katz, Leo.
   Why the law is so perverse / Leo Katz.
      p. cm.
   Includes bibliographical references and index.
   ISBN-13: 978-0-226-42603-7 (cloth : alk. paper)
   ISBN-10: 0-226-42603-3 (cloth : alk. paper)   1. Law—Interpretation and construction.
2. Law—Social aspects. 3. Law and ethics.   I. Title.
   K290.K38 2011
   340'.11—dc22

                                                          2010049618

FOR CLAIRE,

With whom so many things began
that have not stopped beginning

Contents

Acknowledgments

I have worked on this book about as long as I have been married, a round decade, and my wife, Claire Finkelstein, has thus not had any chance to escape thinking it through with me. If there be readers who, having read something else of mine, find signs of progress and maturation here, the credit, I suspect, belongs to her, and it is to her that, in small recompense, I dedicate this book.

As with my other books, one of the first to read and react to it was Skip Bean, who managed to make time for it while running a legal practice and a business at the same time. I received another very complete early reading from Peter Huang, whose expertise in social choice theory and the mathematics behind it protected me from many a howler. (But please don't blame him for any that crept back in *after* he read it.) Bruce Chapman, one of the pioneers on whose work this book builds, gave me the benefit of multiple readings, and I got to spend some of the most stimulating days of my professional life with him at the University of Toronto as he patiently went through every one of the book's major arguments with me.

One of the easily overlooked pleasures of completing a book is that one gets to call on, and occasionally strike up a friendship with, people one otherwise had no legitimate reason for imposing on. Such pleasures were particularly ample for me in connection with this book. In the course of seeking out the reactions of economists to what I had to say, I got to know Alvaro Sandroni at the University of Pennsylvania's economics department, now (sadly for me) at the Kellogg School at Northwestern University, who read and commented on the manuscript and whose interests turned out to be so astonishingly convergent with mine that we are now determined to write something together. Gabriela Chichilnisky came to a conference I organized called "Sharp Boundaries and the Law," and we got the benefit of having Chichilnisky's theorem explained to us by its originator. Matthew Spitzer, probably the first scholar to forge a connection between social choice and the law, invited me to his law and economics workshop at the University of Southern California, where I also met Alan Miller, then a graduate student at Cal Tech, now a professor at the University of Haifa, who is in the process of opening up all kinds of new avenues between law and social choice. Melvin Hinnich and Larry Sager at the University of Texas offered memorably trenchant comments on the loophole section of the book when I presented it there. Lewis Kornhauser came over from NYU to give a detailed critique of the book's penultimate draft and to participate in a workshop on it, hosted by Cary Coglionesi and Howard Kunreuther's Seminar in Risk Regulation, which escalated into something close to a six-hour event. Andy Postlewaite's vigorous participation in that same workshop, pressing me on the exact connection between Arrow's theorem and loopholes was a particular bonus of that event.

At an earlier stage in the book's evolution, I derived great inspiration from a seminar I cotaught with my colleague Ed Rock on the philosophy of corporate law. It was Ed who first taught me about the profound significance of the Kornhauser-Sager discursive paradox.

Many others, colleagues as well as family, read and commented on large portions of the manuscript (or its predecessor articles). With no pretense at completeness, they include, in no particular order: Charles Silver, Mitch Berman, Claire Hill, Dan Shaviro, Michael Moore, Heidi Hurd, Greg Keating, Eric Posner, Howard Chang, Douglas Husak, Matthew Adler, Stephen Morse, Ken Simons, Jacqueline Ross, Friedrich Katz, Jana Katz, Larry Solum, Joseph Bankman, Brant Hellwig, Michael Knoll, Michael Finkelstein, Chris Sanchirico, Larry Solan, David Weisbach, Saul Levmore, Richard Arneson, Larry Alexander, Stephen Perry, Roy Sorensen, Eviator Zerubavel, Michael Abramowicz, Peter Schuck, Paul Robinson, Stephanos Bibas, Joachim Hruschka, Sharon Byrd, Maimon Schwarzschild, Emily Sherwin, Richard McAdams, Richard Ross, Sandy Kadish, George Fletcher, Jim Jacobs, Peter Cane, Jane Stapleton, Geoffrey Brennan, Yochanan Shachmurove, Larry Temkin, Christoph Engel, and several successive classes in my law and morality seminar at the University of Pennsylvania.

I had the help of two excellent research assistants, Vadim Cherepanov, a graduate student in the Penn economics department, and Levent Kutlu, a graduate student of the Rice University economics department.

I had the benefit of being able to present portions of the book at workshops at the University of Toronto, the University of Minnesota, Temple University, Rutgers University (Camden), the Australian National University, the University of Southern California, the University of Illinois, the Max Planck Institute for Common Goods in Bonn, and New York University.

One of the luckiest breaks of my publishing career has been to fall early on into the hands of John Tryneski, my editor at the University of Chicago Press. John's astute reactions to my work, his choice of readers, and his warm encouragement are what every academic author dreams of.

Early versions of some of the arguments in this book appeared in several articles: "Villainy and Felony: A Problem Concerning Criminalization," *Buffalo Criminal Law Review* 6, no. 100 (2002): 451–82; "Choice, Consent and Cycling: The Hidden Implications of Consent," *Michigan Law Review* 104 (2006): 627–70; and "A Theory of Loopholes," Journal of Legal Studies 39, no. 1 (2010):1–31.

I began this book under the auspices of a Guggenheim Fellowship, and I thank the Guggenheim Foundation for its support. I largely completed it during a stay at the Berlin Wissenschaftskolleg, and I thank that institution for a memorable year. Last, but hardly least, there is my professional home, the University of Pennsylvania Law School, whose students, faculty, dean, and generous alumni have been the indispensable mainstays of my professional support system.

Philadelphia 2010

Introduction

There are ideas that are preposterous on their face, and yet one is hard pressed to say why. This book is about such ideas.

Here is an example. Let us imagine a maverick legislator who advances a proposal for reforming our penal system, which he says will cut prison costs by 99 percent. What he would like to introduce, he says, is a system he refers to as "voluntary torture, but with the emphasis on voluntary." "The point of punishment is pain," he begins the speech in which he unveils his idea. "Without pain, there is neither deterrence nor retribution." Then he gets to the point: "If you think about it, prison is just one of many possible pain-delivery systems and unfortunately one of the most expensive. We could accomplish the same thing much more cheaply if instead of making a prisoner's life moderately painful for a prolonged period of time, which is what prison does, we made it intensely painful for a very short period of time: a lot of pain, but for a short duration—that should give us as much retribution and deterrence as before, but at a fraction of the cost."

Seeing the expression on your face, he adds: "I know, I know, you're going to say this is hardly new, and civilized countries have gotten beyond it. But my system is really very different from what we had in the Middle Ages: it is entirely voluntary. No one will be tortured unless he asks to be and unless we are sure that he is of sound mind and knows what he is doing. In other words, everyone will continue to have the option of serving his regular prison term, but whoever doesn't want to can opt for the torture alternative instead. And if you are wondering why anyone would opt for torture, my idea is that we make the torture alternative just slightly more attractive than the prison sentence. We will make it not quite long enough and not quite severe enough to be judged by most prisoners the exact equivalent of a long sentence. What we are offering them is a 'torture discount,' a little like the prepayment discount you get for paying your real estate taxes by a certain date. Although the discount is slight, prisoners will come to view torture much like a very painful medical procedure for curing paralysis—the paralysis of jail. The amount of deterrence and retribution we get out of the new system is virtually the same as before, but it will come so much more cheaply. Torture doesn't cost much; that's why they could afford it in the Middle Ages. As you can see, it's a win-win situation."

Is there anything wrong with this proposal? If there is, it isn't easy to say what. The system is voluntary. Society is a lot better off because it costs so little, and the prisoner is slightly better off because he gets the torture discount. That's why the legislator sees this as a win-win transaction. Despite all that, we would not dream of adopting it. Nor am I suggesting that we should. But there is something perverse here that requires explanation. We have the possibility of an all-round beneficial reform but are adamantly refusing to avail ourselves of it. Why?[1]

In this book I seek to explain why the law is full of perversities of this kind: strange and counterintuitive features that one cannot justify but that one would not want to eliminate either. They all have, I will try to show you, a common cause.

The cause turns out to be not, as one might have thought, historical or political or psychological but, rather, logical in nature. Creating laws that do not suffer from such problems turns out to be logically impossible. Oliver Wendell Holmes famously said that the life of the law is experience, not logic. He was more wrong than right. Historical experience surely counts. But some of the most fundamental as well as fundamentally strange features of the law are rooted in logic rather than experience.

What are those fundamentally strange features? Here are a few more examples:

1. The law is replete with loopholes. No one seems to like them, but somehow they cannot be made to disappear. Why?
2. The law answers almost every question in an either/or fashion: guilty or not guilty, liable or not liable. Either it's a contract or it's not. But reality is rarely that clear-cut. Why aren't there any in-between verdicts?
3. There is a lot of conduct that we intensely dislike—ingratitude, for instance—but refuse to make illegal. Why? There are ingrates who strike us as much worse than, say, a petty thief. We have no compunction about punishing petty thefts. Why not also ingratitude?

What we shall find in the course of this book is that all of the problems I just listed, as well as many others I did not, closely resemble problems in another area that are much better understood and that are known to be essentially logical in character. That area is the theory of voting. Voting rules are notorious for exhibiting innumerable logical paradoxes. What I will try to show you is that many of the things that vex us about law are presentations of those same paradoxes in a different garb.

To really understand why this is true, one will have to read the book, but by way of introduction I will offer a glimpse of why it might be true. That will require, however, that I first provide you with a little bit of background on the paradoxes of voting.

A Brief Tour of the Voting Paradoxes

The eighteenth-century French mathematician Jean-Charles de Borda, much like academics today, was preoccupied with rankings. Ranking students is of course what academics are expected to do, but the habit quickly generalizes to ranking their colleagues, their colleagues' departments, and the universities to which these departments belong. They rank them by publication record, citation count, honorary degrees, memberships in learned academies, prizes, their students' credentials, their students' first jobs, their students' ratings of the quality of their teaching, their reputation among others in their field, and various weighted combinations of all or some of these. Borda's particular preoccupation apparently was with making sure that only the right people were elected to various elite academies, and this preoccupation led him to an interesting discovery.[2]

A common way to make such elections was by majority vote. Borda imagined a case in which the electors of such an academy have to choose among three candidates. Which candidate should be chosen, he asked, if a majority prefers Candidate Bertrand to Candidate Cecil, and a majority prefers Candidate Alain to Candidate Bertrand? One would think that, Bertrand being superior to Cecil, and Alain in turn being superior to Bertrand, Alain is the one who should prevail. In other words, one would be inclined to reason that the electors have directly and unequivocally expressed their collective judgment that Alain is better than Bertrand and that they *indirectly* expressed their judgment that Alain is better than Cecil when they collectively declared Cecil to be less good than Bertrand. If, therefore, we hold a vote in which Bertrand prevails over Cecil and then another vote in which Alain prevails over Bertrand, we should then declare Alain the overall winner.

The problem with that, Borda showed, is that if we asked the electors to choose between Alain and Cecil, we might well find out that a majority actually prefers Cecil. That's right: a majority might prefer Alain to Bertrand, a majority might at the same time prefer Bertrand to Cecil, and yet it might also be the case that a majority would prefer, not as one would expect, Alain to Cecil, but the reverse. Majority voting, as the matter is usually put, is not transitive. (We shall see later how this comes to happen.)

Actually things could get even worse. If there are four candidates— Alain, Bertrand, Cecil, and Daniel—it might happen that while a majority prefers Cecil to Daniel, and Bertrand to Cecil, and Alain to Bertrand, so that it really looks as though Alain is top dog, if we then hold a vote between Alain and Daniel, every single vote might be cast for Daniel, not Alain. In other words, if we aren't careful we might end up selecting Alain even though every single elector thinks Daniel is better.

Borda suggested what he thought was a far superior method because it did not have these problems. It came down to this: ask the electors to rank each of the candidates from first to last. Then calculate each candidate's average rank, and the one with the highest average wins.

Unfortunately, it was soon pointed out to Borda by a younger colleague, one Marie-Jean de Condorcet, that this method had a different kind of flaw. Suppose that Alain comes out the winner, with Bertrand second, and Cecil last. Just as Alain is about to be given his appointment, someone brings to the academy's attention that it was grossly misinformed about Bertrand: much of the work he is renowned for has been attributed to him mistakenly! That might seem like a complete irrelevancy, since Bertrand was not chosen. The problem under Borda's method, however, is this: Suppose the information about Bertrand had come out before a vote was taken. Needless to say the electors' estimation of Bertrand would have plummeted, and he would have become everyone's last choice, ending up with the lowest average rank. But what about the average rank of Alain and Cecil? No elector has changed his mind about their relative merits compared with each other. Nevertheless it might well turn out that their average ranks would now be the reverse of what they were before. That's right: with Bertrand having fallen to the bottom of everyone's list, Cecil might end up with a higher average rank than Alain and would thus end up with the appointment. But that seems absurd.

Voting theorists like to drive home the full absurdity of this sort of thing with a joke about a man who goes into a restaurant, sees chicken, steak, and fish on the menu, and thinks he would prefer the chicken. But before he even has a chance to place his order, the waitress informs him that the fish that day is not as fresh as it should be, whereupon he changes his mind and orders steak instead. That's right—he decides to have steak rather than chicken, having heard that the fish isn't so fresh. If the academy used Borda's system for choosing among Alain, Bertrand, and Cecil, it would be doing the exact equivalent: Between Alain, Bertrand, and Cecil, it first opts for Alain. Then, having heard that Bertrand isn't as appealing a candidate as he seemed at first, it changes its mind and opts for Cecil instead. This seems utterly irrational—and hardly an improvement on the intransitivity of majority voting.

For nearly a century and a half after Borda's and Condorcet's discovery of these voting paradoxes, no one much cared to think further about the logic of voting—which is more than a little surprising, given our constant resort to voting as a way of finding out what a collectivity really wants. In the late 1940s a Columbia PhD student in economics named Kenneth Arrow was inspired to ask a question that seems totally natural in retrospect but which neither Borda nor Condorcet nor anyone since had bothered to ask: Can one come up with a voting system that does not suffer from these flaws? Specifically, a voting system that is not incoherent (i.e., intransitive) the way majority voting is, is one that would respect the unanimous preferences of the voters (which majority voting does not do either: recall that Daniel was able to beat out Alain, even though voters unanimously preferred Alain) and one that would not fall prey to the chicken-steak-fish problem the way Borda's method does. Arrow's answer is perhaps the most surprising finding in all of twentieth-century social science: such a thing cannot be done. Any even vaguely democratic voting system is going to suffer from at least one of these flaws.[3] Arrow's impossibility theorem, as it is generally known, is thus the biggest voting paradox of them all. (Later I will give a very simple rendition of the logic that gives rise to it.)

Further similarly startling discoveries followed in its wake, such as the finding that different voting systems can generate wildly different results. This seems to make it impossible to speak coherently about a group having a "collective will" of some sort, which of course flies in the face of what political philosophers have believed since antiquity. Then there was the discovery by Amartya Sen that any voting system that tries to respect people's rights is bound to override their unanimous wishes on at least some occasions. Much more recently, there was the discovery by Graciela Chichilnisky that all voting methods are bound to be weirdly discontinuous. For instance, suppose we want to rank all candidates by the extent of the support they command from the electorate. There are of course many different ways of measuring that support. I already mentioned Borda's method, which would have each voter rank the candidates, and averages those rankings for a final, overall ranking, but that is just one way of doing it. What Chichilnisky found is that whatever method we use, something quite odd will happen at times: if only a few voters change their minds very slightly, perhaps moving one candidate up a notch and another down, it might be enough to turn the end result completely upside down, and suddenly a candidate who was near the top might drop to the bottom and vice versa.

The outpouring of strange results about voting systems has not so far abated. An entire new field has come into being, known as the theory of social choice, devoted exclusively to exploring the perverse ins and outs of voting systems.

The Law Takes Account of Arrow's Theorem

It was not until about thirty years after Arrow's discovery that legal scholars began to think about the implications Arrow's insight might have for law, and a formidable body of scholarship resulted.[4] That makes a lot of sense: after all, a good deal of lawmaking and of judging is a collective enterprise, and therefore Arrow's theorem should have interesting implications for this aspect of law. A wide variety of questions were investigated and many long-held shibboleths discarded. For instance, people used to think of interpreting statutes as being not very different from interpreting a will. Just as a judge interpreting a will should try to get into the testator's head to resolve any ambiguity in the will, a judge interpreting a piece of legislation should try to get into the legislature's collective "head" to resolve an ambiguity in the law. Arrow's theorem and its progeny tell us, however, that we cannot think about a legislature as having anything like a collective head. There not being a collective head, how, then, should one go about resolving statutory ambiguities?

Soon the legal literature began to generate collective choice paradoxes of its own. One of the more startling results was something Lewis Kornhauser and Larry Sager found that has come to be called the discursive paradox.[5] Consider a contracts dispute in which one of the parties seeks to get out of a contract on the grounds that (1) it was made under duress and (2) it is too indefinite. The issue is to be decided by a panel of three judges, on the basis of majority vote. Judge A does not think the contract is too indefinite, but he thinks there was duress and therefore the contract is invalid. Judge B does not think there was duress, but he does think that the contract is too indefinite and therefore he too would hold the contract invalid. Judge C does not think there was duress and does not think there is indefiniteness and therefore thinks the contract is valid. Now let's count up the votes. Two judges believe the contract is *not* too indefinite; two judges believe the contract was *not* made under duress; two judges believe the contract is invalid. Those three things of course don't fit logically together. If on the basis of majority vote we decide that there was no duress and no indefiniteness, then the logical implication is that the contract is valid. But a simple majority vote of the judges is to the contrary. Should the case ultimately be decided on the basis of the issue-by-issue majority vote of the judges or on the basis of their overall majority vote? Who knows. That's why it's a paradox.

What This Book Does

Thus one way of connecting the theory of social choice with law is to focus on the collective character of law creation. But there is another way, yielding insights of a different kind, that has only recently begun to be explored. To see what it is about requires some further background.

It was understood from early on that Arrow's theorem is not just about voting but can be extended to tell us something far more general about all decision making, whether it involves collectivities or not. Most decision making is of the type decision theorists like to call multicriterial. It was soon realized that when you are synthesizing a multiplicity of criteria into a final decision, you are doing something very similar to synthesizing the preferences of a multiplicity of voters into a final selection among candidates. To be painfully explicit about it, suppose you are trying to decide which of several cars you should buy. You rank the cars along a variety of relevant dimensions: price, safety, looks, and so forth. In the end, you have to somehow aggregate these various rankings into a master ranking that dictates which car you will actually buy. Whether you do this formally in the way I describe or with only vague awareness of what you are doing is unimportant. The fact is that your decision is fairly analogous to that of aggregating the preferences of voters into a master ranking. It is therefore subject to a version of Arrow's theorem and a version of the voting paradoxes.[6]

What several legal scholars came to realize—chief among them Bruce
Chapman and Matthew Spitzer—is that this makes for another interesting and hitherto unexplored connection between Arrow's theorem and
the law.[7] Legal decision making can be thought of as a kind of multicriterial decision making, and therefore Arrow's insights should be relevant.
Spitzer used this approach to show why the decisions of administrative
agencies will inevitably turn out to offend against one or another relatively
basic requirement of justice that legislatures try to impose on them. He
gives as an example the process by which the Federal Communications
Commission used to award broadcasting licenses. Congress gave the commission a list of criteria that it was to consider in making its decisions,
having to do for instance with the applicant's financial soundness and control over other media outlets in the area. Congress insisted that the stated
criteria and no other factors enter into the commission's decision. Using
the social choice perspective, Spitzer was able to show that (under some
very basic assumptions) the commission would not be able to avoid being
influenced by certain other factors Congress considered irrelevant—not
because of any cognitive shortcomings on the part of the commissioners,
but purely as a matter of logic. What Congress had asked the commission
to do turned out to be logically impossible.

Bruce Chapman has used this way of looking at law to explain a long-
standing puzzle about the structure of legal rules. Here is an example. The
criminal code contains a long list of specific offenses (murder, theft, rape,
etc.) as well as a separate list of defenses (self-defense, insanity, etc.). This
kind of division into offenses and defenses is characteristic of most areas
of law. Usually the prosecutor, or the plaintiff, has the burden of proving
that the defendant is guilty of the offense, and it then falls to the defendant
to show that he was acting in self-defense or out of insanity or whatever.
Now, one might wonder why things are set up that way. One might for
instance define murder not as it currently is, as an intentional killing, but
as an intentional killing *other* than in self-defense or while insane. One
might then require the prosecution to make the case not merely that the
defendant killed intentionally but that he was not acting in self-defense
and that he was sane. The law generally does not do it that way. Using the
social choice perspective, Chapman is able to explain why.

This, then, is the groove into which I will be stepping, the perspective
from which I will be proceeding—legal doctrines thought of as instances
of multicriterial decision making. Specifically, what I aim to do is take four
particularly vexing peculiarities of the law and explain them as inevitable

by-products of the fact that legal doctrines are multicriterial. Each of these four peculiarities will turn out to be the counterpart of a certain well-known insight from the theory of social choice.

Why these particular problems? First, because they lend themselves superbly well to this kind of an explanation and, second, because they are so very fundamental. To see just how fundamental they are, let's consider briefly what makes up the bulk of the typical hour in a law school class. A new case introducing the students to a new legal doctrine is taken up. One of the principal things the professor will do is to explore the purpose, or justification, of the doctrine. A commonplace way of doing this is to ask whether the doctrine is one the parties would have voluntarily imposed on themselves had they thought about it long before doing whatever it was that got them into a conflict with each other. For instance, if the dispute has to do with whether a seller can rescind his offer only up until the buyer has mailed his acceptance, or up until the acceptance has actually reached him, the instructor might then ask what most of us would want to happen long before we ever became embroiled in litigation over this question. If the doctrine corresponds to what we would want, that represents a strong justification for having it. But if it does not, that raises the question of why the law is so perverse as to impose such a doctrine on us. Wouldn't everyone be better off if the law did not do this? More colloquially put, wouldn't it be a win-win solution if the law let the parties have things the way they wanted them? Answering this question is closely wrapped up with the first perversity this book takes up, the one embodied by the title of part I, "Why Does the Law Spurn Win-Win Transactions?"

The second thing the law teacher does is ask his students to picture themselves as lawyers planning to do the most for a client who finds that the doctrine somehow does not let him do what he wants to do. "Say your client is a doctor who has made some unfortunate investments in some real estate partnerships," he might say. "Creditors will soon be at his doorstep. He might lose everything he owns in repaying them. Is there any way he can avoid that?" The perceptive student might reply: "I'd tell him to move to Florida, buy a house there, and invest his money in some special kinds of pensions and some special kinds of insurance until all his money is spent. Then he should declare bankruptcy. Creditors will have to content themselves with whatever is left and leave him alone forever after. Later he can sell the house and cash in his pension and his insurance, but they can no longer touch it." In this way students learn about the myriad ways in which they can "restructure" someone's affairs so as to circumvent a pesky law. What we seem to be teaching our students here is how to take advantage of the law's loopholes, which raises the question of why laws should be so replete with loopholes that the teaching of their exploitation is a mainstay of legal training. I take up this issue in part II, "Why Is the Law So Full of Loopholes?"

The third thing the law teacher does is explore the doctrine's boundaries—the hard-to-categorize cases that are most likely to give rise to litigation: Is it an assault for a man to kiss a sleeping woman? Has the hunter acquired ownership of a wild animal when one of his bullets has been lodged in it, whereupon the animal stumbles into another hunter's trap? Is the alumnus's promise of a donation a binding contract? Posing these kinds of questions may be the activity law professors most often indulge in, often to excess.

The problem this raises—dealt with in part III, "Why Is the Law So Either/Or?"—is why the law is so disturbingly rigid when dealing with such boundary cases, why it paints in black and white when reality seems to come in shades of gray. The law insists that something either is an assault or is not, either gives rise to ownership or does not, either is a binding contract or is not. There are no in-betweens. The trouble is that many of the actual cases seem like in-betweens. In fact a case would never reach the courts if it did not seem to be in between. But why not let the court say that while this is not a clear-cut case of an assault, it is sort of an assault and that therefore we will award the victim a fraction of the damages, or impose on the perpetrator a fraction of the punishment, that would be appropriate if this were a clear-cut case? Wouldn't that avoid a lot of unnecessary hairsplitting? That's what many legal scholars have come to believe. Are they right? Would it be better if the law were less either/or?

Finally, the law teacher is likely at some point to inquire into the relationship between the doctrine and morality. Is this doctrine what morality would call for, he will ask, or is it the opposite, or does morality not speak to it at all? Part IV concerns itself with one particularly tantalizing aspect of this issue, succinctly captured by its title, "Why Don't We Punish All We Condemn?" Consider the doctrine that says that there is no duty to aid a stranger. Think about the expert swimmer who stands by while someone drowns. Trivial effort would have saved the victim's life. This is something we morally condemn but somehow are very reluctant to punish. In general, the law lets bad Samaritans get away with being bad Samaritans. To see just how strange that is, let's compare how we feel about this bad Samaritan to how we feel about a purse snatcher. The bad Samaritan seems far worse than the purse snatcher; nevertheless we wouldn't hesitate to punish the purse snatcher, whereas we will only very reluctantly, if at all, punish the bad Samaritan. Why should that be? Why is our criminal law so out of sync with our moral sentiments?

My surmise is that the legal perversities I consider in this book are only the most interesting of a much larger set of legal peculiarities that can all be explained as indirect manifestations of one or another well-known voting paradox (such as Arrow's theorem). A promising strategy for understanding any legal perversity might thus be to search for its "doppelgänger" in the theory of social choice.

An Aside

I want to clear up a possible misapprehension on the part of some readers before proceeding any further. My frequent references in this introduction to the theorems of social choice theory might leave readers with the off-putting impression that this book is somehow mathematical or formal in character. It is not. While the theory of social choice on which it draws is largely the creation of mathematicians and mathematical economists, fortunately for this author, who is neither of those, understanding its insights or using its arguments requires no such background. This book is written in prose and devoid of anything resembling a formula by one who thinks in prose, not formulas, and is meant for all who read prose, whether or not they also relish formulas.

PART I

Why Does the Law Spurn Win-Win Transactions?

CHAPTER ONE

Things We Can't Consent To, Though No One Knows Why

Why Do We Forbid Voluntary Torture?

What is wrong with torturing a prisoner when he consents to it to shorten his sentence? This is the problem with which I began this book and to which I now want to return. *Volenti non fit iniuria*—consent cures the wrong—is a hallowed maxim of the law. But the prisoner's consent to torture does not cure the wrong. Why not?

To be sure, consent does not always cure the wrong. It does not do so when coercion or deception are involved or the consenting person is too incompetent to know what he is doing, or if what the consenting parties are up to affects others—third parties, as the law likes to call them—who never gave *their* consent. (If two people want to conduct a drag race on a public highway, *that* obviously that can't be up to just them.) These are long-standing, well-established, almost self-evident limitations on the validity of consent. It makes sense that consent doesn't work if the consenting person didn't "really" consent—which he did not do if he was coerced, deceived, incompetent, or, like the third-party bystander in a drag race, was never even asked. The ultimate reason for these limitations presumably is that consent is worth respecting only when it gives rise to a win-win transaction—the consenting parties benefit and others aren't injured—which isn't true when coercion, deception, incompetence, or risk to a third party are involved.[1]

The problem is that our prisoner does not come within any of these well-established limitations on consent. He obviously is not deceived, incompetent, or consenting to something that might injure a third party. Is he being coerced? Yes, in the sense that he is being pressured by the situation, as it were, into volunteering for torture. But that's not really the kind of coercion that bothers us, because it is no different than being "coerced" into buying a car by the need to get around. No one is threatening to do something wrongful to him if he doesn't let himself be tortured. And so the question remains: what is wrong with letting him volunteer for torture?

Over the years, a number of more controversial suggestions have been made about when consent should not be allowed to cure a wrong. Could these help with our torture case? The least controversial of these suggestions is paternalism, which could be summed up as saying: "When someone is doing something harmful to himself, we are entitled to stop him whatever his ostensible wishes." Sometimes this is justified by saying that, although not actually deceived, he lacks the insight required to see that he is harming himself. Using drugs and playing Russian roulette often are put into this category. Sometimes paternalists take an even more radical stance: when someone is harming himself, they say, then even if he fully understands what he is doing, that is an inherent wrong we are entitled to stop. As one would expect, this more extreme kind of paternalism has fewer defenders than the first.

Does this help with our torture case? Not much. It is hard to argue that the prisoner is in any way lacking in insight when he makes such a deal. He seems to be making a perfectly enlightened choice. Is it possible to argue that it is simply wrong for someone to be tortured, regardless of how he feels about it? This kind of paternalism comes close to being argument by fiat.[2] True, sometimes that might be enough. If someone were simply agreeing to have himself tortured for the masochistic pleasure it affords him, in other words, for the sake of a benefit most of us don't think a benefit at all, we might feel all right in saying, "This is an inherent wrong, however much you like it, and we won't let you do it." But in our torture case someone is making a choice we could easily see ourselves making: some torture in exchange for no imprisonment really might be a benefit (depending on the amounts involved of course); in fact it almost surely is. So how can we pronounce it to be inherently wrong?

Two more suggestions are worth considering, but before we do, there is something I ought to clarify. When I say that consent does or does not count, I am speaking quite loosely. So far that hasn't mattered, but it is about to. There are actually different ways in which consent can count, and sometimes one needs to distinguish between them. When I asked whether the prisoner's consent in my torture case counts, I was simply asking whether the person who tortures him would still be guilty of a wrong if he proceeded to torture him. But there is a related question one might ask. Suppose the prisoner says yes and we release him on condition that he come back a week later to receive his torture-punishment. The week passes, and when he comes back he says he has changed his mind. He would rather go back to jail than be tortured. Does his previous consent bind him? Can we force him to follow through? Can we ask him to pay damages for not following through? In other words, *does his consent only count to cure the wrong, or does it also create a binding contract?* Often we won't have to distinguish between these two ways of counting, but sometimes we will.

Let's consider, then, a further ground sometimes offered for disregarding consent. Some people have said that consent shouldn't count—it shouldn't cure *and* it shouldn't bind—if the consenting party is being exploited. What would be an example of that? Think about the survivors of a shipwreck who encounter a passing boat that is willing to take them on board, but only if they promise to give the rescuers all of their life savings. This is very much a win-win transaction. The survivors are neither coerced nor deceived nor incompetent; they are making a perfectly sensible decision to give up their wealth in return for their lives. Still, many people would condemn this bargain as exploitative, refuse to enforce it, and maybe even punish the rescuers for making it. What exactly makes the bargain exploitative? The most persuasive suggestion I have heard, offered by the philosopher Alan Wertheimer, is that the rescuers are charging more than the "market price" for the rescue.[3] What Wertheimer means is that the rescuers are charging a higher price than they could charge if some other rescue ships had been in the vicinity as well. In other words, it is not wrong for the rescuers to charge something for the rescue; what makes it exploitative is that they are charging too much. They are taking advantage of their uniquely advantageous position in relation to the victims' uniquely vulnerable position. Unfortunately, it is hard to see this kind of exploitation in the situation of our prisoner: here there is no exploiter overcharging his victim. If anything, the "victim"—the prisoner—is being undercharged, since he is offered a punishment somewhat lighter than the one he deserved.

There is one last reason I should mention why consent is sometimes not given effect: the so-called commodification problem. Many people feel that certain things should never be bought or sold: kidneys, corneas, sex, and babies, for instance. Such things, they feel, just don't belong in the world of commerce. They can be given away but not traded. They shouldn't be treated as commodities. Legal scholar Margaret Radin explains why. Look at what would happen, she says, if childless couples could pay willing birth parents to give up their baby. "If a free-market baby industry were to come into being," she writes, "with all of its accompanying paraphernalia, how could any of us, even those who did not produce infants for sale, avoid measuring the dollar value of our children? How could our children avoid being preoccupied with measuring their own dollar value? This measurement makes our discourse about ourselves (when we are children) and about our children (when we are parents) like our discourse about cars."[4] Her point is an interesting one, but it does not help with our torture case. There is no conventional buying or selling going on here of the kind that might make us think of prisoners as selling their bodies like a commodity.

Is voluntary torture perhaps sui generis—so singular and oddball as not to be worth worrying about? No, it is not sui generis. There are many more cases like it, as we shall see in the next section—cases where we strongly feel that consent should not count but that cannot be explained on the grounds of coercion, deception, incompetence, or effects on innocent third parties (like the unwitting bystanders of a drag race). Some—but not all—of these cases might conceivably be explained by invoking paternalism, exploitation, or "commodification," but it is time I admitted that I feel very wary of those. There is a reason these categories are so controversial. Whereas the idea that consent does not count when there is coercion, deception, etc., is firmly woven into our morality, intuitively compelling, and clearly reflected in our laws, the idea that consent shouldn't count on grounds of paternalism, exploitation, or commodification is much less firmly rooted or intuitively compelling. It is an idea that has a hard time standing up to the countervailing intuition that if two people want to do something and no one else is the worse for it, we should let them. To really feel satisfied that one understands why the selling of corneas, or babies, or sex tends to be disallowed, one would like to have it explained on the basis of principles that are as firmly rooted and as intuitively compelling as those about deception and coercion. Can that be done?

Before trying to solve this problem, let me show you that it really is worth solving—by giving you examples of some of the most important categories of cases we feel as puzzled about as the torture case.

Why Is There No Specific Enforcement of Most Promises?

Every year patients who need kidney transplants die because they cannot get one. That's ironic because kidneys are in such abundant supply.

Nearly everyone of us is born with two of them, even though we could do perfectly well with just one. If only a few of us donated their redundant kidneys, the shortage would end. Maybe you don't believe me when I say our second kidney is redundant. You might think that if one of your kidneys fails it would be nice to have a spare. But that's not true, because most diseases that could ruin your kidneys would ruin both at once. To be sure, there is the small matter of having to undergo major surgery.

Suppose now that on seeing that voluntary kidney donations aren't going to be forthcoming in sufficient number, someone embarks on a new scheme to solve the problem. He announces the formation of a kidney club. Members of this club, he declares, are guaranteed a kidney if they should ever need one. Becoming a member requires only one thing: that you sign a contract stipulating that when any member of the club should need a kidney, you will participate in a "kidney lottery," by which the club will randomly select a member who must then donate one of his kidneys to his needy fellow club member—and that if you are selected, that is what you will do. Would you join such a club? I know I would. I am guaranteed that I will not die for lack of an available kidney. In return I run the small risk of having to donate one of my own, which will be onerous, but not inordinately so. And if you are rational, you will feel the same way.[5]

Imagine next that my number is drawn: I am chosen as someone who has to donate one of his kidneys. At this point, however, I balk. I simply don't want to submit. Is there anything the club members can do? Can they get a court to order me to submit? Can they take matters into their own hands and force me at gunpoint to submit? The answer is that the law won't let them do any of those things. They might be able to sue me for monetary damages of some kind on the ground that I have breached a contract, but that is as far as the law will let them go. The court will not order "specific performance"—there will be no literal enforcement of the promise. But why? Is it because I did not explicitly say in advance that I can be forced to comply if I don't do so voluntarily? No, that doesn't matter. As the law stands, even if I had said so, I could not be forced. The result is of course that such clubs will probably not be formed. Yet everyone, myself included, would be eager for them to be formed, to sign up for them, and to agree to being forced to comply in case we should refuse to. What good reason could the law have for frustrating such a win-win transaction?

Indeed what makes the nonenforcement of the promise so very baffling, and important, is that the law proceeds this way not just in unusual cases like the kidney club but whenever someone promises to render some kind of personal service. A painter refusing to paint the portrait he promised or an actor refusing to act in the movie to which he committed will never be compelled to actually follow through, even though they said, when they first made their promises, that they fully expected to be compelled in case they should ever try to renege. But in fact all the law does, in case of reneging, is make them pay damages. Anything further is viewed as tantamount to enslavement—self-enslavement, to be sure, since the "slaves" here volunteered for the arrangement, but it is impermissible all the same. This of course suggests the further question, What exactly is wrong with self-enslavement, especially when it is temporary? Self-enslavement might sound exotic and unreal, but only because its real-life incarnations go by other names, like indentured servitude and debt peonage. The law no longer allows either of these, but if both parties desire them, then absent coercion, deception, etc., why not?

Why Do We Feel Uneasy about Tradable Emission Rights?

For some time now, many economists have touted a system of tradable emission rights as being a particularly desirable form of environmental regulation, better than the more traditional "command-and-control" approaches, whereby the government simply mandates specific emission devices and emission limits for every polluter. This new kind of licensing system—now actually in wide use, its best-known example being "carbon trading"—works roughly like this: The government decides on a certain tolerable maximum for emissions of a given type. It then allocates to each manufacturer a license to produce a certain amount of such emissions. Finally, it permits those licenses to be traded. This is regarded as an especially efficient form of environmental control because it gives each manufacturer an incentive to develop the most cost-effective, emission-reducing technologies and because it ensures that those who have the greatest need for such licenses are able to buy them from others who have less need for them. Nevertheless, this kind of market-based environmental regulation has remained very controversial. Despite having become quite common, it continues to produce great unease. Most of those who object, however, have had great trouble pinpointing exactly what they find so objectionable about it, since none of the traditional reasons for banning such sales seem to apply: no coercion, no deception, and no ill effects on third parties.[6] Is there any defensible basis for the critics' unease?

Why Do We Prohibit Unorthodox Property Rights?

If I own some land and want to sell you a part of it, there are many different ways in which I might carve you a piece out of it. I might just draw a simple boundary around a part of the land and give that to you. That would be to divide the land *physically*. But I might also divide it up *temporally*—by giving it to one person up until a certain date and having it go back to me thereafter. (I am not talking about renting it out to someone for a certain period, with him being the tenant and me being the landlord, but actually letting him own it outright for the designated period—with all the rights and privileges of an owner, who is unbeholden to any landlord, because for the designated period he *is* the landlord.) There are yet more complicated ways of parceling out the land: I might sell you the land but prohibit you from using any of its lumber, keeping that right to myself. Or I might retain for myself the right to travel across the land whenever I need to. (People usually do this when it is the only way to gain access to some other nearby property they continue to own.) To understand how it is that property can be divided in these various often unorthodox ways, first-year law students are told to think of the owner as holding not merely one thing—his land—but actually a bundle of things, namely a set of rights with respect to that piece of land (the right to use it today, the right to use it tomorrow, the right to use its lumber, the right to exclude others, and so on) of which he can give away as large or small a subset as he chooses.

All of this should sound reasonable, and might even seem self-evident. But there is a less self-evident aspect to it that is easily missed. Suppose the person to whom I sell the land, subject to my right to the exclusive use of its lumber, then sells it to someone else. Does the new owner have to respect my right to the exclusive use of its lumber? He never had any dealings with me and he never made such a promise. It doesn't matter. The law requires him to respect whatever rights I retained, and it does so on the basis of a very simple but compelling sort of logic. Since the person to whom I sold the land never actually acquired whatever rights I did *not* give him—like the exclusive use of the lumber—he cannot sell such rights to anyone else. The new owner cannot make use of its lumber, because he never acquired that right from the seller, who could not sell it to him because it was not his to sell, any more than he could sell him the Brooklyn Bridge. That right continues to be my property—a slightly unusual type of property, to be sure, but my property all the same.

Given what I have just said, you might think that I could just take any subset of my bundle of property rights and sell them to a willing buyer.

Mysteriously, though, the law won't allow that. I am in fact only allowed to sell certain kinds of subsets. The law of property provides a fixed menu of legitimate subsets, and whatever I want to give to someone must be on that menu or it won't count. Suppose what I would like to sell to someone is a time-share in some land I own. (I keep using land as an example, but property of course can consist of many other assets than real estate.) Specifically, I would like to give him ownership of the land for the first half of every year and keep ownership for the remaining half for myself. It turns out such an arrangement is not on the menu of legitimate property types. What does that mean? Well, suppose I did try to give such a time-share to X. And suppose that sometime later I decided to sell my own remaining time-share to Y. What is it that Y now gets? Does he only get the time-share that I kept to myself, or does he get all of the land, 100 percent of the time? Remarkably enough he gets all of the land, 100 percent of the time. This is true even if I told him that I couldn't sell him more than my part of the time-share because I didn't own the other part. The fact is that, contrary to what I thought, and contrary to what I would have told Y, I never ceased being the owner of the time-share I thought I gave to X. Time shares not being on the menu of legitimate property rights, my efforts to transfer one to X were in vain. The entire land continued to be mine, and when I sell it to Y it becomes his.

Why should the law be so restrictive in the types of property it allows me to sell? Why should it be problematic to sell one kind of partial ownership (like the land minus the right to use its lumber) but not another kind?[7] That may sound like a less compelling question than why we don't allow prisoners to consent to torture or painters to consent to self-enslavement, but it turns out to be a question of surprising practical importance: it is something owners of commercial real estate would like to do all the time—and the law won't let them.

Why Don't We Let People Assume More Risks?

A man takes on a job that involves removing somewhat hazardous materials. The not insignificant health risks of doing this could be greatly reduced, if not eliminated, by a certain type of protective suit. The suit is expensive and the man tells his employer that he doesn't want one; he would rather get the money it would cost to buy one. The employer goes along with this. Later on the employee falls ill in just the way the suit was meant to prevent. He brings a case against the employer for negligence, and the employer, naturally, wants to say that the employee has nothing to complain about because he "assumed the risk," as the legal lingo has it. Should he be able to raise this "assumption of risk" defense?

Jurisdictions differ. The assumption of risk defense is considered problematic. Some jurisdictions recognize it; others once did but have abolished it; yet others abolished it and then reintroduced it. Why should this be so controversial? Why should there be any problem at all in letting the employer and the employee make a binding agreement that the employee will get extra compensation for not insisting on a protective suit and will not sue the employer if he gets sick down the road?[8]

Why Can Some Things Not Be Sold, Only Given Away?

Why can sex, for instance, not be sold? Even where prostitution is legal, it hardly bears the stamp of approval. Coercion, deception, or incompetence might be present in some cases of prostitution, but our aversion goes far beyond those cases. Paternalism, exploitation, and commodification have all been invoked by way of explanation, but as I already noted, I view those as explanations of last resort. Can one do better?

It is the same with body parts. You can donate your kidney or your cornea, and of course your blood, but selling them is frowned upon. Sometimes it is made illegal; sometimes the law just refuses to enforce such a contract. Sometimes, to be sure, it is allowed and enforced, and we generally don't frown upon it as much as we do upon prostitution. All the same, we heavily disfavor it. Why?

It is time that I explained how I propose to find an explanation of these and similar cases. I will begin the search for an answer with a little parable involving a doctor in an emergency room and a choice he has to make between three patients, each of whom would need his exclusive attention. Although highly artificial, this case has the virtue of bringing out with exceptional clarity features that are buried well beneath the surface of the more quintessentially legal cases, thus making it easier to figure out what is going on in those cases. Once we have found an explanation for this artificial case, we will then generalize that explanation to the more realistic cases—personal service contracts, tradable emission licenses, and so on.

CHAPTER TWO

A Parable

The Triage Cycle

Al and Chloe, husband and wife, have had a car accident. Al is badly injured and at risk of losing the use of both his legs—becoming a paraplegic. Chloe was lucky: the only injury she came away with was a broken index finger. There is exactly one physician on duty in the emergency room in which they end up, and he has to decide whom to treat first. What makes this a bit of a dilemma is that for both injuries, Al's as well as Chloe's, time is of the essence. Whoever gets treated second is at significant risk of having his injury become permanent: If treated second, Al is at high risk of becoming paraplegic. If Chloe is treated second, she is at high risk of losing significant dexterity in her index finger. (I trust the reader not to get distracted by the lack of medical realism here.) But although the choice the doctor has to make about whom to treat first is a distressing one, it is not in fact difficult: obviously Al has priority over Chloe.

But there is a complication. It is enormously important to Chloe not just that her index finger be restored, but that it be restored to its fullest use. Chloe is a pianist—not a professional pianist but a passionate amateur. Piano playing, she would say, is one of the deepest, most meaningful joys of her life. Impaired use of her index finger would have extremely unpleasant consequences for her psyche. That of course still does not mean that she would get treatment priority over Al. What creates a problem, however, is the position that Al takes in all of this. Al is deeply devoted to Chloe, some would say besotted, so much so that he insists that she be treated ahead of him. The doctor initially refuses, but when it becomes clear that Al simply will not let himself be treated before Chloe, he finally gives in. *Or is about to give in.* For just as he is about to begin treating

Chloe, another patient, Bea, appears. Bea has suffered an injury whose severity places her between Al and Chloe in the queue. She has, let us say, suffered an injury that would, if she does not receive immediate attention, deprive her of the use of *one* of her legs. That's not as bad as losing two legs (like Al) but worse than losing part of the full use of one's index finger (like Chloe). The doctor therefore decides that he cannot go on treating Chloe; he has to treat Bea, unless perhaps Al decides he wants to be treated after all.

On seeing what the doctor is about to do, Al and Chloe protest. Al tries to argue with the doctor as follows: "We happen to know that Bea is a perennially depressed poet. Whether her life is going well or poorly, she is depressed. If she loses her leg, she will be miserable. But she would be miserable anyway. Indeed one of these days we're convinced she will commit suicide. To Chloe, however, the ability to play the piano makes all the difference in the world. If she loses even an iota of her manual dexterity and her piano playing deteriorates as a result, she too will be miserable. But she would not be otherwise! And then of course there is my own happiness, which would be greatly enhanced if you treated Chloe first rather than Bea. In short, you would do a lot more for human happiness by first attending to Chloe!" This argument, I take it, would not persuade. But the fact that it would not persuade is worth noticing. It means that the doctor is not supposed to give priority to the happy pianist over the unhappy poet despite the fact that doing so would maximize overall contentment. The poet's claim to the doctor's services trumps the pianist's claim despite the fact that she stands to benefit far less by way of happiness than the pianist. We judge a claim for protection against the loss of a leg to be stronger than a claim for protection against the loss of some dexterity in one's index finger. And we don't think that the strength of such a claim depends on the amount of happiness produced by its fulfillment.

When the doctor shows himself unmoved by Al's plea, Al decides to play his trump card: "If you won't treat Chloe right now, then you better treat me. Obviously my injury is more severe than Bea's and I am entitled to priority." "Yes, of course," says the doctor as he sets out to treat Al. "Just a minute," says Al before the doctor can actually begin, "I wasn't insisting on my priority over Bea so as to really get treated. I only tried to draw your attention to the fact that whether you treat Chloe first or not, Bea is definitely not going to be treated first, because if you don't treat Chloe you will have to treat me. So you might as well treat Chloe first." The doctor reluctantly agrees and turns back to start treating Chloe. At this point, however, Bea chimes in: "This is outrageous! It's Al's wish plus Chloe's injury versus my leg! That is, you now have the choice between, on the one hand, helping Chloe and thereby honoring Al's wish and, on the other hand, saving my leg. Isn't it obvious which claim is stronger? What you are proposing to do surely is illegal. The law of negligence—not to mention common decency—requires that you carefully weigh the competing interests at stake here and choose to satisfy the more significant one. Is there any doubt that my interest in avoiding the loss of a leg is more significant than Chloe's interest in her index finger and Al's interest in having his wishes regarding Chloe honored? I demand that you treat me ahead of Chloe."

And so the doctor finds himself in a quandary or, rather, a cycle. The doctor has seemingly compelling grounds for giving Al's two-leg injury priority over Bea's one-leg injury. He also has seemingly compelling grounds for respecting Al's desire to have Chloe's index finger treated ahead of his legs. And he has seemingly compelling grounds for treating Bea's one-leg injury ahead of Chloe's index finger. This is what I will call the triage cycle, sometimes the original triage cycle, in contrast with some others constructed later on. This chapter is built around that cycle, or more concretely, around the question of how it is to be broken. Which of the three patients should the doctor treat first?

The Components of the Cycle Reconsidered

One of the steps in this cycle has to be rejected. At least one of the three priorities argued for has to yield: either the two-leg injury should not win out over the one-leg injury, or the index finger should not win out over the two-leg injury, or the one-leg injury should not win out over the index finger. But which of these three priorities is in fact the least compelling?

It will help to give each of the three steps in cycles of this sort a name. Let us call the first step, by which we grant Al's two-leg injury priority over Bea's one-leg injury, the basic priority argument. This is the step in the cycle that seems hardest to quarrel with. A two-leg injury is more serious and hence more deserving of treatment than a one-leg injury, and thus the priority of a two-leg injury over a one-leg injury seems like a very basic one indeed.[1]

Let us call the next step in the cycle the win-win argument. This is Al's argument that, since he prefers to have Chloe's finger treated rather than his own legs, and since Bea is in no way harmed thereby, the doctor should redirect his attention to the finger. In slightly more colloquial terms, Al is saying: "What is it to Bea whether I have my legs treated or Chloe has her finger treated instead? Bea is not going to get her leg treated either way. If I can't get Chloe's finger treated, all that will happen is that I will reclaim my own priority status. And what would Bea get out of that?" In the economist's more technical terms, he is arguing that treating Chloe's finger rather than his own two legs is the Pareto-optimal thing to do. Many people, probably most, will find the win-win argument irresistible. How could one possibly object to something that benefits some people and does no harm to the rest?

The final step in the cycle is the one by which Bea hopes to regain her priority. This is Bea's argument that it is outrageous for Chloe's finger to be treated ahead of her own leg. Let us call this the regained priority argument. The objection most people would raise to the regained priority argument would probably be something like this: "Al has a rightful claim to have his two-leg injury treated ahead of Bea's one-leg injury. He has chosen to give up that rightful claim for another claim, namely to have Chloe's finger treated instead. That surely is his prerogative. But then there is nothing really unfair about giving Chloe's finger priority over Bea's leg, even though looked at superficially it seems callous."

On reflection, however, this way of dismissing the regained priority argument starts to look less and less persuasive. Suppose we think of the claim she acquired as being exactly like a piece of property Al owns and can choose to give away to Chloe if he wants to, making her its new owner. In an emergency, property rights can usually be overridden for the sake of more important interests. Bea makes a convincing argument that her interest in her leg is just that, a more important interest. Therefore, she argues, Chloe's ownership of a claim to priority treatment can be set aside in Bea's favor. Put differently, suppose Chloe owned a piece of clothing, the use of which would allow the doctor to save Bea. There is no doubt the doctor would be permitted to simply help himself to that piece of clothing, whether Chloe agrees to it or not, in order to save Bea's leg. Bea's right in her leg is simply much more important than Chloe's property right in her clothing. In our case, the priority claim Al gave Chloe is like the piece of clothing.

There is another way of making this point that should help us appreciate its significance. It has to do with an often overlooked conceptual distinction that is both crucial and easily missed. The distinction is one that has only recently attracted the attention of moral philosophers and economists and whose full ramifications for a wide variety of issues are still being worked out. It is the distinction between claims and desires, or as it is sometimes put, between interests and preferences. Once that distinction is fully digested, it becomes much harder to reject Bea's regained priority argument. Let us see why.

Suppose a friend were to ask you for financial help with a dental treatment he cannot afford. You might be perfectly willing to help him out. But suppose that after you have given him this assurance, he tells you he would much rather use the money you offered him to do something else instead, which he thinks will make him happier—say, go on a cruise—and forget about the dental treatment. My guess is that you would balk and rescind your offer of help. But just exactly why are you balking? Is it because you think it frivolous to spend money on a cruise? That can't be the reason because you would balk similarly if he had asked to devote the money not to a cruise but to his church's charity. Perhaps you are balking because you think he will regret going on the cruise when he comes back and is still stuck with his bad teeth. That can't be the reason either, since you would balk similarly if he spent the money on something durable, like a gold watch, and never regretted the trade-off. Are you perhaps balking because you do not really believe that he will get more pleasure from a cruise than from improved teeth? No, you really do believe him; you recognize that letting him use the money on a cruise would be the win-win thing to do. And yet you balk. In all likelihood, you are balking quite simply because you feel morally somewhat obliged to help with dental treatment but much less so to help with a cruise. You feel that your friend has a strong moral claim on you with regard to dental treatment but a much weaker moral claim with regard to a cruise, despite the fact that his desire for dental treatment is much weaker than his desire for a cruise.[2] This illustrates an interesting property of claims and desires. The fact that your friend has a claim to something you could give him, on the one hand, and a strong desire for something else you could give him, on the other, does *not* give him a strong claim to that other thing as well. Shortly I will have a bit more to say about exactly why that is so , but *that* it is so should seem reasonably intuitive.

We are now able to see the real strength in Bea's argument that she regains her priority over Al when he redirects the doctor's attention from his own injury to that of Chloe. Bea is saying that even though Al's claim to getting his two-leg injury treated is stronger than Bea's to getting her one-leg

injury treated, and even though Al would much prefer to see Chloe's finger treated instead, it does not follow that his claim to getting Chloe's
finger treated is stronger than Bea's claim to getting her leg treated. Al's
claim to getting his two legs treated is like your friend's claim to getting his
dental problem treated. Just as your friend cannot transmute his claim for
help with dental treatment into a claim for help with a cruise, Al cannot
transmute his claim for help with his two-leg injury into a claim for help
for Chloe's finger.

If Bea is right, then the step in the cycle that ought to be rejected is the
second one—the win-win argument. Despite the fact that treating Chloe's
finger makes Al and Chloe better off, it seems the doctor ought not treat
Chloe's finger.[3]

More about Claims versus Desires

It will help in understanding the argument I have just made to have a
little more background on the distinction between claims and desires. In
a way, it is a perfectly commonplace phenomenon: it happens whenever
we strongly desire something to which we have little claim, or the reverse.
Whenever I want something another person owns, that would be such a
case: I strongly want it but have no proprietary claim to it. The reverse is
equally commonplace: anytime I don't much value what I own, my desire
is less than my claim to it. Despite, or perhaps because of, the common-
placeness of this distinction, it took two extremely astute philosophers,
Thomas Scanlon and Thomas Nagel, to pick up on its significance and
paradoxical character.

In a famous passage of his book *The View from Nowhere*,[4] Nagel cap-
tures that paradoxical character in a particularly memorable way. Suppose, he says, I have a headache. Then, he says, everyone has a reason to
want it to stop, and anyone who can easily do something to help me get
rid of it presumably ought to do it, or at least has a good reason to, even if
not, strictly speaking, an obligation. "The same," he writes "may be said of
other basic elements of human good or ill." However, he continues,

> many values are not like this. Though some human interests (and not only plea-
> sure and pain) give rise to [what Nagel calls] impersonal values, . . . not all of
> them do. . . . [I]f I badly want to climb to the top of Mount Kilimanjaro, not
> everyone has a reason to want me to succeed. I have a reason to try to get to the

top, and it may be much stronger than my reason for wanting a headache to go away, but other people have very little reason, if any, to care whether I climb the mountain or not.[5]

And then comes the clincher. He notes that this is true, strangely enough, *even if* "*as it happens [I] may be [quite willing] to put up with severe altitude headaches and nausea to get to the top of a mountain that high.*"[6]

You can see within Nagel's example the seeds of something like the original triage cycle, or even more straightforwardly, the seeds of my example with the dental treatment and the cruise. The situation Nagel pictures is one in which he has a strong claim to getting help from me with his headache, a claim that is stronger than my claim to remaining indolent. *My* claim to indolence, however, is stronger than *his* claim to getting my help with climbing Kilimanjaro. But he is willing to give up his claim to help with the headache in exchange for help with climbing Kilimanjaro. That would make it Pareto-optimal if, instead of helping him with his headache, I invest the same amount of help I would otherwise have devoted to the headache to helping him climb the mountain instead. And that gives us the familiar cycle. What neither Nagel nor Scanlon cared to spell out is what this means for consent and its power to cure and to bind. That is what I am undertaking here.[7]

The First Implications for Consent Made Explicit

What we have seen thus far is that in the context of the various triage cycles, we can most plausibly avoid a cycling problem by giving up on the win-win argument. The implications for consent are pretty clear: by rejecting the win-win argument—by not allowing Al to agree with Chloe to have her finger treated instead of his legs—we are invalidating an agreement under circumstances in which none of the usual reasons for doing so apply. There is no coercion or deception involved, there is nothing that impairs Al's or Chloe's ability to competently decide, there are no third-party effects, and so on. Nevertheless, we treat Al's right to have his legs treated as inalienable. The reason for this is not in any way obscure: if we do not, we will either get into a cycle or have to give up on principles that are at least as compelling as the win-win principle.

CHAPTER THREE

Lessons

The triage scenario is of course an elaborate contrivance. Its purpose is to highlight what more commonplace cases tend to hide. What I will now try to show you is that many of those commonplace cases in which consent seems problematic (even though they are not within any of the familiar exceptions: coercion, deception, etc.) resemble to a greater or lesser degree the triage scenario and that this resemblance explains why they are so problematic. To make the crucial similarities between the triage scenario and its various more realistic counterparts more transparent, it will be helpful to give each of the actors in the scenario a tag that will remind us of the role they play in my little parable. Let us therefore refer to Al as the Primary Claimholder (since he is the one with the primary claim to having his injury treated) and refer to Chloe as the Would-Be Substitute (since she is the one whose claim Al would like to substitute for his own) and to Bea as the Spoiler (since she is the one whose presence spoils the substitution of Chloe for Al).

I will begin by examining the problem of tradable emission rights—not because it is more important than the others, but because the triage scenario can be connected with it almost effortlessly. Nearly every aspect of emissions trading maps on fairly directly to an element of the triage scenario. With regard to the other categories of problematic consent, like assumption of risk, voluntary torture, prostitution, selling body parts, unorthodox property rights, and specific performance, a bit more work is required to establish the connection.

Tradable Emission Rights

A brief reminder of how the tradable emission system works: The government assigns to each enterprise an allotment of emission rights based on the amount of pollution the enterprise has been emitting under prudent management in the past. If sometime later the enterprise finds that it can do with fewer emissions, it will be allowed to sell its rights to someone who finds that he needs to be able to emit more. The economic advantages of such a system are generally acknowledged to be great: "From an economic point of view, the case . . . seems well-nigh indisputable. Environmental economists are therefore frankly dumbfounded when such 'unassailable' proposals nonetheless come under attack from environmentalists."[1]

The problem, as many of the critics of emissions trading see it, such as political scientist Michael Sandel, is that "turning pollution into a commodity to be bought and sold removes the moral stigma that is properly associated with it. If a company or country is fined for spewing excessive pollutants into the air, the community conveys its judgment that the polluter has done something wrong. A fee, on the other hand, makes pollution just another cost of doing business, like wages, benefits and rent."[2] Nonsense, writes a noted defender of emissions trading, law professor Cass Sunstein. The critics are just confused here, he says, by a mistaken analogy between pollution and ordinary crimes like assault, battery, robbery and rape: "The reason is that the appropriate level of these [latter] forms of wrongdoing is zero. But pollution is an altogether different matter. At least some level of pollution is a byproduct of desirable social activities and products, including automobiles and power plants."[3]

Now let us look at this problem through the lens of the triage scenario. To start with, let us imagine there is no regime of tradable emission rights. Imagine, further, that there are two manufacturers located next to a town—the Al Corporation and the Chloe Corporation. The Al Corporation produces something vital: a lifesaving medication of some sort. In so doing, it sprays the adjacent town with one hundred units of some pollutant. There is nothing illegal about what the Al Corporation is doing. Some harm, or risk of harm, to others is perfectly permissible, so long as it is "reasonable." Reasonableness depends, among other things, on the purpose for which the harm is imposed, in this case an eminently worthy one, the production of an important medicine. The Chloe Corporation, by contrast produces something far more frivolous, equipment for bungee jumping. At its current level of production, however, Chloe Corporation causes no significant pollution to the town. But Chloe Corporation would like to increase production, and if it did so, that would palpably increase its harmful emissions. Let us suppose that under existing tort law, such an increase in production would not be deemed "reasonable."

Next let us suppose that a regime of tradable emission rights is introduced. Every manufacturer is permitted to continue emitting the reasonable amount it has been emitting so far, but if it is able to decrease its emissions, it is allowed to sell its "right" to pollute, or any part thereof, to anyone who needs to increase his emissions. The overall amount of emissions will thus stay constant. Al Corporation has been considering reducing production of its lifesaving medication, and Chloe Corporation has been contemplating increasing production of its bungee-jumping equipment. They strike a deal whereby Al Corporation reduces its harmful emissions by forty units, and Chloe increases its own by the identical amount, the overall amount of pollution descending on the town thus remaining constant at one hundred units.

That arrangement is starting to look similar to the deal between Al and Chloe in the emergency room. Let us try to make the resemblance more precise. We can think of Al Corporation as being the Primary Claimholder here. But what exactly is the nature of its claim, and who does Al Corporation have primacy over? What is the counterpart here to Al's claim to get his legs treated?

What Al Corporation has a claim to is the production of medication and the attendant infliction of unwanted emissions onto the neighboring town. This is the counterpart to Al's claim to medical treatment. Chloe Corporation has no such claim—just like its namesake in the triage scenario.

But who in this context plays the role of the Spoiler, Bea? That role is played by the town's citizenry. There is a competition between the citizenry and the Primary Claimholder that is perfectly analogous to the situation in the emergency room. If the Primary Claimholder gets his way—gets his legs treated, or gets to emit pollutants—then the Spoiler's claim (Bea's, or the town's citizenry's) cannot be honored. In other words, just as Bea's claim to getting her leg treated has to yield to Al's claim to getting his two legs treated, so the town's claim to keeping its air pollution-free has to yield to Al Corporation's claim to producing medication and thereby inflicting such pollution.

The relationship between the town and the Chloe Corporation is correspondingly analogous to that between Bea and Chloe. The town has a claim to being free of pollution that is superior to Chloe Corporation's claim to increase its bungee production and thereby inflict additional pollution on the town.

When Al Corporation sells some of its emission rights (forty out of one hundred) to Chloe Corporation, it is transferring some of the priority it had over the town to Chloe Corporation.

What we now have is just about identical to the triage cycle and raises the identical difficulties. As in the triage cycle, we are able to make the basic priority argument that the Primary Claimholder (Al Corporation) should be allowed to burden the town with one hundred units of the pollutant for the sake of producing a lifesaving medication. We are also able to make the win-win argument that a deal between the Primary Claimholder and the Would-Be Substitute (the Chloe Corporation) is unobjectionable because it benefits both of them without adversely affecting the Spoiler (the town). Finally, we are able to make the regained priority argument that it is not reasonable for the Would-Be Substitute to impose forty units of pollution on the Spoiler for the sake of producing more bungee-jumping equipment. (That's why they were not allowed to do so prior to the creation of the tradable emissions regime.) If we are troubled by tradable emission rights, the root of the problem is thus the same as in our triage case: there is a cycle, and arguably the weakest link in the cycle is the win-win argument. The law making emissions tradable, however, treats the regained priority argument as the weakest link: it effectively rejects the town's argument that it is not reasonable for Chloe Corporation to impose forty units of pollution to produce bungee-jumping equipment.

There is a more compact way of bringing out the analogy between the original triage scenario and tradable emissions. One might summarize what is going on in the triage scenario by saying: "Al, having acquired priority over Bea for the sake of saving his two legs, is now trying to alienate that priority to someone who will merely use it to save her finger. What a waste of Bea's sacrifice!" Analogously, one might summarize what is going on in the trade emissions transaction by saying: "Al Corporation, having acquired priority over Bea Town citizens for the sake of producing lifesaving medication, is now trying to alienate it to someone who will merely use it to produce bungee-jumping equipment. What a waste of the town's sacrifice!"

Now, what exactly does all of this prove with regard to emissions trading? Does it show that the system is immoral and ought to be gotten rid of? Well, no, not exactly, or at least not necessarily. My aim has been to solve a puzzle—to explain the root of the widespread discomfort that such a system inspires by showing it to be in tension with some very fundamental, deeply entrenched, hard-to-contest justice-related intuitions. That tension is most acute, and its source is most evident, in situations like my triage scenario. But it is also at work, albeit less aggressively and less transparently, in situations that bear some resemblance to the triage scenario, like emissions trading. It is a tension we might well choose to live with and, somewhat paradoxically, might actually have an easier time living with once we understand its exact roots—not because the intuitions that generate that tension don't matter, but because it is often easier to live with a problem once we have taken its full measure.

Assumption of Risk

Let us now consider the innumerable ways in which the law restricts our ability to assume certain risks. Recall, for instance, the case of the employer who acceded to his employee's request not to buy him a protective suit but to pay him a higher wage instead. If the employee is injured and proceeds to sue the employer for negligence, many jurisdictions will hold the employer liable for negligence. The employee's eager assumption of the risk of injury is simply disregarded. With regard to other kinds of risky activities, we have seen that the law is even more intrusive: it criminalizes drug use, Russian roulette, drag racing, and so on. Not always and not everywhere, but often enough. How might one use the triage scenario to understand what is going on here?

Let us begin by modifying the triage scenario slightly. Let us take Chloe out of the picture, and let us suppose instead that Al suffered not only the two-leg injury but also the injury to his finger that we previously attributed to Chloe and that this time it is Al who is the passionate amateur pianist who cannot bear to see his manual dexterity diminished even slightly. Bea continues to be present and to compete for the physician's attention with her one-leg injury.

As the physician is about to start treating Al's two-leg injury, Al asks that he treat his finger instead, because, he explains, an injury to his finger is much more serious for him than an injury to his legs. He is fully prepared to sacrifice the use of his two legs to the preservation of his finger's full dexterity. The doctor is about to acquiesce, but then Bea launches her familiar line of protest: "How can you give priority to his finger over my leg? I can understand that his two legs have priority over my one leg, but his finger does not. The fact that he also has a two-leg injury that trumps my one-leg injury seems irrelevant as long as he is not having it treated." To underscore her point, Bea offers this analogy: "Suppose that what Al really wanted was to have neither his legs nor his finger treated but just to play a game of checkers with you—that's right, a game of checkers, with you, the only doctor on duty—from which treating my leg injury would take you away. He says to you that if you don't play checkers with him, he is going to insist on your treating his legs, but one way or another, you are not going to get to treat my leg. Would that lead you to play checkers with him and thus not treat anyone at all? Isn't the finger in this case pretty much the equivalent of a game of checkers?"

We now get a cycle that is not too different from the one we had before, except that it involves only two people, Bea and Al. Bea still plays the role of the Spoiler. But Al now plays the roles of both the Primary Claimholder and the Would-Be Substitute: by virtue of his leg injuries he qualifies as the Primary Claimholder and by reason of his finger injury he qualifies as the Would-be Substitute. The basic priority argument then suggests, as it did before, that Al has priority over Bea because a two-leg injury is more serious than a one-leg injury. The win-win argument suggests that since he prefers having his finger treated instead—and since Bea would not be treated in any event because if Al can't have his finger treated, he would have his legs treated instead—he should be able to do so. The regained priority argument suggests that Bea's one-leg injury should not lose out to Al's finger injury, just as it would not lose out to Al's desire to play a game of checkers with the physician. Arguably, then, the most plausible way to break the cycle is to deny Al the right to have his finger treated in lieu of his legs.

What does all of this have to do with the assumption of risk? In asking to have his finger treated rather than his legs, Al would assume a risk, the risk of great harm to his legs, but we will not let him. The reason for not letting him has nothing to do with coercion, deception, incompetence, paternalism, exploitation, or commodification. It simply arises from the need to avoid cycling, which can only be accomplished by restricting his ability to assume the risk or by rejecting other, even more compelling principles, like the basic priority argument and the regained priority argument.

We can think of all the other assumption of risk cases we have considered as disguised versions of this. People who assume the risk of serious bodily harm in some quid pro quo—like getting paid more or experiencing the thrills of Russian roulette or drag racing—are trying to exchange that claim for a Would-Be Substitute. This is the equivalent of Al's trying to get his finger treated instead of his legs. For this analogy to really work, there has to be someone to play the part of the Spoiler, someone like Bea. Such a person isn't hard to find: it is the public at large—the people who are required by the law of negligence to subordinate their own interests to those of the Primary Claimholder, that is, the people who must incur substantial burdens so as to avoid injuring the Primary Claimholder, Al. In effect, negligence law functions as a priority rule analogous to that giving Al's two-leg injury priority over Bea's one-leg injury and giving Bea's one-leg injury priority over Al's finger. Fundamentally, then, the problem with letting people assume any risk they want to is that they are simultaneously imposing hefty burdens on others. Those others are then in a position to say: "How can I be expected to work so hard to avoid injuring you when you squander the fruits of my efforts in a game of Russian roulette?" They are able to say this even though what the risk-assuming actor does has no harmful impact on them.

I won't pretend that this is totally compelling. Many people will not be convinced that Al cannot insist on having his finger treated, despite Bea's objections, and will correspondingly not want to deny others the right to take what risks they want so long as no one else is harmed. But that is all right. I am not seeking to give a knockdown defense of our restrictions on risk taking but merely to explain what makes them tempting. Sometimes we yield to that temptation and outlaw a risk; sometimes we resist it and let the risk taker take his chances.

Sex, Blood, and Body Parts

Sex, blood, and body parts we already noted are things that can be given away but not sold. Let's start with prostitution and see if the triage scenario can explain why the law steps between the prostitute and her customer—or, to be precise, why it steps between them when there is no coercion, deception, etc., involved.

Actually, all we would need to do in order to apply our previous analysis is to think of the prostitute as taking the place of Al and the public at large the place of Bea. In other words, the prostitute would become both the Primary Claimholder and the Would-Be Substitute, and the public at large would once again become the Spoiler. The prostitute's primary claim is to sexual integrity. It is a claim the public at large is expected to make significant sacrifices to respect (by trying to catch and punish sex offenders, for instance). She would like to give up this primary claim for a substituted claim to the money the customer would pay her in exchange for giving up her primary claim. It is the presence of the Spoiler, the public at large, that makes this problematic. The Spoiler is in effect saying, "You expect the rest of the world to treat as sacrosanct your claim to sexual integrity, and then you yourself give it away for a few dollars, a simple material asset to which you don't have nearly the same sacrosanct claim—because, after all, it is just a simple material asset."

There is a slight difficulty with taking this view of prostitution, however. The triage analogy might seem to prove a little too much here, because it looks as though someone might make the same kind of argument against ever allowing a woman to consent to sex—not just for money, but for free. In other words, what if someone were to say: "You expect the rest of the world to treat as sacrosanct your claim to sexual integrity, and then you yourself give it away for free?" Suddenly it seems as though the triage analogy leads us to ban not just prostitution but lovemaking. But we really only run into this problem if we think of lovemaking and prostitution as being at bottom the same kind of thing: sex for a benefit of some kind, the benefit being money in the case of prostitution and love, or at least the pleasure of sex, being the relevant benefit of ordinary lovemaking. Most of us, however, don't really think of them as being as alike as that way of putting it suggests. Instead we think of them as being about as alike as surgery and professional boxing. To be sure, both surgery and professional boxing involve some not-so-pleasant invasions of the body for the sake of some ultimate benefit (a medical benefit in the former case and some money and a trophy in the latter), but that still doesn't lead us to consider them as basically the same sort of thing. If we were to decide to ban professional boxing, that wouldn't lead us to think that, as a matter of logic, we really ought to ban surgery as well.

Voluntary Torture

What now of the problem of the prisoner who volunteers for torture? How might the triage scenario be adapted to explain our refusal to let him volunteer?

Let us once again picture the triage scenario without Chloe. Bea is still present, with her one-leg injury. Al is also present, with his two-leg injury but no finger-injury. The important new twist is this: let us suppose that

Al is a prisoner to whom the state offers the option of escaping his life sentence if he agrees to have his two legs chopped off without anesthesia. This is something he can only do if he still has two legs to sacrifice. You can see the difficulty: Bea will immediately protest, "How can I be expected to sacrifice my leg to enable this criminal to slightly improve his position, even if that means that the state gets to save the cost of housing him?" If we are going to accede to that protest, we will need to ban the proposed bargain.

That explains the problem with voluntary torture in this particular setting. But can we generalize from this setting? The ordinary prisoner does not find himself in an emergency room with someone like Bea hovering in the background. In what sense, then, can he be thought to find himself in an analogous situation? It is the public at large that plays the role of the Spoiler here. The prisoner plays both the role of the Primary Claimholder and that of the Would-Be Substitute. His primary claim is to not being tortured. What that means, practically speaking, is that we make it a crime to intentionally inflict pain on someone, and we pay law enforcement authorities to back that prohibition up with force. In addition, we make it a tort to engage in conduct that only *risks* inflicting pain (to be sure, not all such risky conduct—it has to be negligent), and we back that prohibition up by requiring perpetrators to pay damages to victims. What the prisoner would like to do is to exchange this primary claim against being tortured for something else: a shortened prison sentence. In other words, his situation is like that of Al in the variation on the triage scenario I presented in the previous section. In that variation I imagined Al as having suffered both a two-leg injury and a finger injury and as wanting to exchange his priority claim with regard to the two-leg injury for a priority claim with regard to his finger. The shortened prison sentence the prisoner wants to get in return for giving up his claim to not being tortured is the counterpart to the finger injury. It plays the part of the Would-Be Substitute. The reason we do not let the prisoner engage in this substitution is that that would, arguably, violate the interests of the Spoiler, the public at large—much as it would violate the interests of Bea if we allow the doctor to treat Al's finger ahead of Bea's leg. If we allow the prisoner to substitute one claim for another in this way, the Spoiler (the public) will once again be able to protest that he has been called upon by the law, both criminal and tort law, to make sacrifices so as not to impose undue risks of pain on the Primary Claimholder, and by allowing this substitution of claims, all these sacrifices are suddenly for naught: they will have been made not to protect the

Primary Claimholder against torture but to enable him to get his prison
sentence shortened.

Unorthodox Property Rights

The law, we noted, does not allow me to sell just any part of a piece of
physical property I own. Let's see more precisely what that means and how
the triage cycle can help us understand why the law is designed so oddly.

Let's remind ourselves of some basic facts of ownership I alluded to
earlier. For the most part, if I want to sell someone a piece of something
I own, I am free to do so. In fact the law takes a very sophisticated view
of what such a piece might look like. It need not just be a territorial slice
out of my holdings; it might be a "temporal slice," like the right to use
the land for a specified period of time: I might for instance give someone
a so-called life estate, whereby he gets to own the land until his death, at
which point it reverts back to me (or, if I am no longer around, my heirs).
More sophisticated yet, I might give someone all rights in the land *minus*
one: I might for instance let him have it on condition that he not use it for
pig farming, or on condition that he allow me continued use of it as access
route to my own land, or on condition that I get exclusive use of its lumber.
The law will treat these restrictions on someone's use of the land I sell him
just like the physical boundaries that circumscribe it.

The significance of treating such restrictions exactly like physical
boundaries only becomes clear once we think about what happens when
the person to whom I give the land then proceeds to sell it to someone
else. Do those restrictions apply to this new person as well? Is he too
barred from pig farming? Is he too required to let me use it as an access
route? And if ownership of the land was limited by some date (e.g., the
time of death of X, the person to whom I originally gave the life estate)
and X then sells it before his death to Y, does Y's ownership end when X
dies? The answer to all these questions is yes. The person to whom I sold
the property to begin with gets what I gave him and nothing more—that
means that the restrictions I put on him have to carry over to everyone
else to whom he sells it. Otherwise he would be able to sell more than he
owned himself, which makes no sense.

There is something at least mildly surprising in the law's treatment of
ownership as I have just described it. It is worth trying to put our finger
on exactly what makes it somewhat surprising. When I sell my land to X

on condition that it not be used for pig farming, there are really two possible views one might take of this transaction. First, one might say that I have entered into a contract with him that he not use the land in that way. Suppose we were in fact to take that view of the matter. Now imagine once again what would happen if X were to sell the land to Y. If X and I simply had a contract as far as the pig farming was concerned, then Y would not really be affected by the restriction. It would be a promise for X to keep (and if he does not keep it, to pay me damages on account of his breach)—unless he in turn had bothered to enter into a separate contract with Y requiring him to abstain from pig farming as well. But if X did not do that, then X's contract is X's business, and Y can engage in as much pig farming as he likes. Things are different, however, if we view the transaction not as a contract but as a transfer of ownership (i.e., as a transfer of property rights). We would then say that what I gave X was not simply some land but *land subject to the obligation not to use it as a pig farm.* If the matter is looked at in this way, X has really only received a certain subset of the bundle of rights that I, the original owner, held. The bundle included among other things the right to use the property as a pig farm, but I never gave him that particular right. As a result neither X nor Y, to whom he sold it, can use it that way.

So how does the law decide which way to treat this transaction between me and X—as a contract or as a transfer of ownership? Basically it is up to us, X and myself, to decide what kind of arrangement we would like to have. To be sure, if we aren't sufficiently clear about it, then the matter might end up having to be litigated, and a court is going to have to do some guesswork about what we really intended and resolve the case accordingly.

The ramifications of this are larger than one might think at first. Imagine I have sold this *land subject to some condition* to X and that X goes heavily into debt, so much so that he does not have the assets to pay off his debts. X's creditors thereupon try to take possession of whatever assets he has—including that piece of land. If my sale to X were conceived of as a simple contract not to use the land for pig farming, the creditors would probably be free to do with it what they want. The fact that X had a contract with me that he will no longer be keeping is of little consequence. X is in financial distress, and under those circumstances the law is prepared to cancel many of his contractual obligations. It has no choice: there are simply too many creditors with contract claims to satisfy them all. Whichever of his many creditors ends up with the land will thus be free to use it for pig farming if he wants to. On the other hand, if the transaction were conceived of as a sale of property, a transfer of ownership, consisting of *land subject to a condition*, the restriction on pig farming would continue to apply to that creditor: the pig-farming restriction is a right that I, the original owner, retained and am entitled to insist upon, and whatever financial difficulties X subsequently gets into will not entitle any of his creditors to take away something that belongs to me so as to pay for debts that X incurred.

There is, however, a big exception to all of this, which I illustrated earlier with the example of time-sharing. Time-shares aren't allowed. And while the condition regarding pig farming would be allowed, as would the condition regarding the access route or the condition regarding lumber use, other conditions that might not sound so different are not allowed. Suppose for instance a condition that required owners to give 5 percent of their annual income to charity or that prohibited them from living with someone of the opposite sex without being married and provided that if these conditions are violated the land go back to the original owner (me). As I noted, there is a fixed menu of things that are permitted to count as property. That menu does not include time-shares. It does not contain unusual conditions that do not, as the legal lingo has it, "touch and concern the land." Pig farming, access routes, and lumber use would all be considered to "touch and concern" the land, but the condition regarding 5 percent of my income and the condition regarding cohabitation are not. The question then is, why this fixed menu? Why this restriction to conditions that "touch and concern the land"? Why not leave it to the parties themselves to decide what exactly they want to transfer ownership in?

Why, in other words, will the law only let us treat certain restrictions on the use of property as being like physical boundaries and insist on treating others like contractual commitments and therefore not binding upon subsequent recipients of the property being transferred? Why does the law interfere with freedom of contract in this peculiar way? Why are only certain things eligible for being treated as property and others not?

One explanation that has been offered is that the law does this to keep things simple and manageable. If property rights could be designed in any which way, then—according to this explanation—it would simply become too hard for people to keep track of who owns what. More precisely, the argument goes, although it might seem that when one person sells an unorthodox property right to another it only affects those two people, that in fact is not so. There is what the economists call an externality—an effect on others that the two parties are not taking into account. "Suppose a hundred people own watches," write Thomas Merrill and Henry Smith, the two property scholars who have put forward this explanation, and suppose one of these people wants to sell some kind of unusual property right in the watch, say, a "time-share," the right to use the watch on Mondays. It is supposed to go back to the seller the rest of the week. In the aftermath of such a deal, "word spreads that someone has sold a Monday right in a watch, but not which of the one hundred owners did so." Now imagine one of the other watch owners wants to sell his as well—the entire watch, not just a time share. The buyer now has to worry whether the purported owner really owns the entire watch or only a Tuesday-to-Sunday time share in it. This is not something he would have to worry about if watches could only be sold in their entirety. "Thus by allowing even one person to create an idiosyncratic property right," Merrill and Smith point out, "the information processing costs of all persons who have existing or potential interests in this type of property go up."[4]

A similar problem arises, they suggest, if we allow people to sell land subject to weird conditions that have nothing to do with the land—like a condition that requires all future owners to give 5 percent of their annual income to charity or that prohibits them from living with someone of the opposite sex without being married. How would someone buying the land, they ask, ever know that he is only getting it subject to such a condition? The seller may not mention it to the buyer, and the prior owner who imposed it may not be around to tell him. Then once they have acquired the asset, that prior owner (or his heirs) may suddenly pop up out of nowhere and insist on enforcing this restriction the new owner knows nothing about. It is different, say Merrill and Smith, with conditions that actually have something to do with the land, like the conditions about pig farming, access routes, or lumber use. Those are conditions an inspection of the land would often reveal.

Let's now look at the problem of unorthodox property rights through the lens of the Triage Cycle, because that suggests a very different perspective than the one offered by Merrill and Smith. To connect the property rights problem with the triage scenario, it will be useful to think of property rights as being a certain kind of priority right, analogous to those treatment-priority rights involved in the triage cycle. Let's go back to the two different ways in which one might think about a sale of land that is subject to a condition like the one on lumber use—the contract view and the property view. We can think of each of these as giving rise to a different set of priority rights. If we think of the condition concerning lumber use as a contract right, we see that Y, who buys the land from X, to whom I sold it, is perfectly free to use the lumber, even though my contract with X said that only I could use the lumber. Another way to say this is that as far as the decision on lumber use is concerned, Y now has priority over me. If, on the other hand, we think of the lumber-use condition as a property right, my wishes rather than Y's continue to control lumber use. In other words, I now have priority over Y, rather than the other way around. Put differently, to have a property right, as opposed to a contract right, is to have an especially high kind of priority when disputes arise.

There is a wide range of somewhat subtler priority rights that go with having a property right. These are priority rights that are often overlooked but that will prove very useful in explaining the prohibition on unorthodox property rights. Here is one. The law allows us to take a variety of measures to protect our property rights against infringements—measures we are not allowed to resort to for the protection of less serious rights. If someone wrongfully enters my land, I can forcibly eject him, or I can seek the assistance of the police in doing so. But if someone wrongfully interferes with some promise someone made me—say, by getting the owner to sell him something he previously promised to me—there is really nothing I am allowed to do about that, other than sue the promisor for breach of contract. I can't usually go after the intermeddler. In other words, if a property right is involved, I acquire a kind of priority over an intermeddler that I do not get otherwise.[5]

Here is another, trickier priority right that also comes with having a property right. Take the case of a careless driver who causes an accident. Suppose that as a result he damages some of my property—let's say my car. Obviously he has to pay for that. But suppose instead that the accident does not actually damage anyone's property except his own. It does, however, cause a big traffic jam, and as a result a caterer who is supposed to come to my house at a certain time for an important event does not get there in time. Here too the careless drive has caused me some harm, by inadvertently interfering with my contract rights: he made it impossible for the caterer to keep his contract with me. That is *not* something the careless driver has to pay for. Why? Because interfering with a contract right is not of the same order as interfering with a property right. My right to claim damages from the careless driver can be thought of as another kind of priority right, one that goes with being injured in my property rights but not in being injured in my contract rights.[6]

Let's return to the triage scenario. Suppose that when the accident that brought Al and Chloe to the ER first occurred, before the ambulance even reached the accident site, Chloe was at much greater risk than Al. If he had not intervened courageously to help her, her injuries would have been much worse, whereas his would have been much slighter. In that case of course Chloe would have had priority over Al. By helping her, Al has in effect deprived her of that priority. Al is unhappy about that and would like Chloe to continue to retain that priority, even though, as a result of Al's actions, the basis for that priority has shifted from Chloe to Al. If my analysis of the triage scenario is right, that is not something he can do. The only way to shift a treatment priority from one person to another is to shift the basis for that priority. *But that is exactly the sort of thing the seller of the land is trying to do.*

When someone sells land to X and retains the right to use its lumber, what he is retaining is a piece of property, and with it, the priorities that come with owning a piece of property. But suppose that the condition he is imposing is that all owners of the land contribute 5 percent of their income to charity. Now he is not retaining anything that in any way resembles a physical asset. What he is retaining is something much more ethereal. Nevertheless he is trying to claim for it all the priorities that usually come with owning a physical piece of property: the priority over subsequent purchasers, the priority over X's creditors, the priority over intermeddlers, and so on. But something has to be substantial enough to count as the sort of thing that can generate such priorities. If what the original owner retains is too insubstantial, then if we allow him to tie to it just any priority he wants, that would be like Chloe "passing" her injury to Al (as a result of his courageous intervention) but nonetheless retaining her treatment priority over him (the treatment priority that comes with having a more severe injury).

That raises the interesting question of why some things are deemed substantial enough and others not and why the "touch and concern" requirement is used, among other things, to test for such substantiality. Physicality—thinghood in the narrow, old-fashioned, childlike, literal sense of something that can be physically handled—seems to be the basic criterion for such substantiality. The more thinglike something is, the more it will seem like property. Exclusive use of the lumber on some land seems like a claim to something pretty thinglike. The ability to require future landowners to contribute 5 percent to charity or not to cohabit without marriage does not seem like that kind of claim.

But whether or not thinghood is the right way to express the kind of substantiality involved is not so important; the really important question would seem to be why there should be that kind of requirement at all. Why can the priority rights associated with property only be conferred on something that meets some elusive substantiality criterion like thinghood? The best way to understand that is to focus on a specific example of such a priority right that goes with an asset that has the status of property, for instance the right to use physical force to defend against intrusions upon the asset. Purely economic rights (like the right to have a contract honored) will often be far more valuable to us than property rights, yet only property rights can be defended with physical force. We saw earlier that this is just part of a more general pattern. We have claims of varying strength to the integrity of our bodies, our property, our reputation, etc., which will often diverge greatly from our actual desire for those things. Any requirement that distinguishes between these various claims, or interests, is going to have a peculiar air of irrelevance about it for that very reason. It will involve some strange-sounding criterion, like thinghood, that seems to have no bearing on what we really care about, because by assumption, what we really care about is not determinative of the strength of our claims.

We are thus back to a question we have dodged before (in the section on claims versus desires): why we have moral claims to specific things (now understood loosely) like our bodies or our property or our reputations rather than to the utility, the happiness, that we hope to achieve with those things. It is a question to which I don't know the answer. Why is it that I envy someone his talents or his possessions but not his happiness? Presumably I want those talents and those possessions so as to achieve greater happiness. It seems absurd that I should envy him the means to that end but not the end itself. But we are now getting into deeper waters than I am able to navigate.

Specific Performance, Self-Enslavement, Organ Lotteries, and Draconian Penalties

Let us now see how this analysis sheds light on the vexing, long-standing issue of why the law does not grant specific performance of personal service contracts. One textbook answer is that personal service contracts are very hard to specifically enforce: we can force the opera singer to sing, but we cannot force her to sing *well*. Another textbook answer is that forcing someone to render a personal service is akin to slavery. Neither of these two answers seems very satisfactory. Each really only explains why parties might not want to enter into a specifically enforceable personal service contract in the first place. The impresario has to worry that no court could ever force the singer he hired to do a good job; the singer will worry about having made herself a temporary slave. Suppose, however, that the parties are willing to set aside these worries. They really would like to commit to a specifically enforceable personal service contract. Why does the law not let them?

The beginnings of an answer, strangely enough, can be found in the law regarding rape. For intercourse to count as consensual, the kind of consent that makes a commercial bargain consensual will not suffice. Commercial bargains simply require advance consent. Consensual intercourse requires contemporaneous consent. But while the requirement of contemporaneity is most conspicuous in the context of intercourse, it is by no means peculiar to it. It would seem that consent to any kind of bodily invasion has to be contemporaneous: sports, massage, surgery, not to mention voluntary euthanasia (in jurisdictions that permit it) all require not just consent but contemporaneous consent. The ban on specific performance of personal service contracts thus seems like just another manifestation of the same phenomenon.

But in a way, this simply broadens the mystery. Why does consent to bodily invasions have to be contemporaneous when it does not have to be with regard to other kinds of transactions? Why treat voluntary *ex ante* commitments concerning our bodies so very differently from similar commitments with regard to other assets?

Our analysis of the triage cycle serves to demystify what is going on here. As we just saw in our discussion of unorthodox property rights, it is not generally possible for someone to transfer his priority rights to someone else without also transferring the underlying basis for those priority rights. If Al wants to pass his priority to Chloe, he can only do so by also arranging for her to have a more severe injury than he. We saw that permitting someone to create an unorthodox property right amounts to letting him transfer a priority without also transferring its underlying basis. He would be trying to endow an asset that is not substantial enough (not thinglike enough) with priorities it does not merit—like the right to defend it with physical force. *But note that exactly the same would be true if we permitted someone to make a contract for personal services specifically enforceable.* To specifically enforce a contract amounts to using physical force, or the threat of it, to vindicate one's interests. If I give someone the right to use physical force to compel me to follow through on a promise,

I have essentially given him the right to defend his promissory interest against me with measures appropriate only to defending a *thing*, not a mere *promissory interest*. I have tried to pass to him a priority without the underlying basis for that priority, just like Al and Chloe. If I give the kidney club the right to force me to give up one of my kidneys—to proceed without my contemporaneous consent, solely on the basis of my advance consent—I am trying to let the club's enforcers act as though they were defending an asset already in their possession rather than vindicating a promissory claim to an asset still in *my* possession.

Here then we have the answer to the much-debated question of why one cannot sell oneself into slavery: to do so would be to make a specifically enforceable promise of personal services. We also have here the answer to a related question that has sometimes been raised concerning the use of very severe punishments to deter crime. People have asked what exactly would be unfair about draconian criminal penalties so long as they are announced well in advance.[7] Since the recipients of such punishment know in advance what they are risking, what is wrong with making them pay the price? In fact let us suppose that the draconian punishment was actually approved in a referendum in which the defendant himself voted in favor of it. How can he possibly protest its application? He can protest because advance consent to physical punishment is no different than advance consent to the removal of a kidney.[8] That does not mean he cannot be punished at all. Proportionate punishment does not require his consent; only disproportionate punishment does. But if the consent is not contemporaneous, it is like selling yourself into slavery.

What If Bea Were to Consent?

When we think about the triage cycle, one question that very naturally suggests itself is whether Al's and Chloe's problems would be solved if Bea were persuaded to consent (perhaps for money) to Al's bestowal of his priority claim on Chloe. There are of course analogous questions one could ask about the various real-life counterparts of the triage scenario: (1) Would it make a difference if the potential victims of industrial emissions consented to the tradable emissions program? (2) Would it make a difference if everyone who might interact with the person assuming the risk consented to his doing so? (3) Would it make a difference if society as a whole had more or less unanimously approved voluntary torture, organ sales, the specific enforcement of personal service contracts, and so on?

As it turns out, surprisingly strong arguments exist on both sides of this issue. It is helpful to present these arguments in the form of a dialogue between two interlocutors, debating the relevance of Bea's consent in the original triage scenario. On one side, we will suppose, there is Al, who thinks that consent cures all and that as long as Bea consents, no conceivable reason remains for not letting her alienate her priority to Chloe. On the other side, there is the doctor, who has to decide whom to treat first, and who thinks Bea's consent should not make much of a difference to his decision.

AL: May I remind you that before Bea showed up, you were perfectly willing to acquiesce in my request that you first treat Chloe rather than me. And why not, since there is no one around who could complain? You only changed your mind when Bea appeared. Now, you reasoned, there is someone with an injury more serious than Chloe's who could complain if you treated Chloe first. But if Bea consents to have you treat Chloe first, then once again everyone who could conceivably complain has given his OK. All reasons for not treating Chloe would then obviously have vanished.

DOCTOR: Well, it's not that simple. The problem with making Bea's consent relevant here is that she does not really have a stake in what you and Chloe are doing with each other. Whether you give your priority right to Chloe or not, Bea is not going to be treated. She therefore does not really care what you and Chloe arrange between yourselves. If you ask her whether it is all right with her that you give away your priority, she is virtually certain to say yes, especially if you were to offer her some token compensation for doing so. Come to think of it, I don't see why offering her a dollar wouldn't be enough to get her to say yes, once she understands that whether she says yes or no she is not going to get treated. What that tells me is that her consent really has no bearing on the matter one way or the other.

AL: Well, if, as you say, Bea has no stake, then that by itself seems like a compelling reason to do what Chloe and I want, since we are obviously the only ones who really have a stake in this. What Bea wants should simply be irrelevant.

DOCTOR: But we've been through that already. You are surely not going to argue that you and Chloe should be free to decide which of you two I treat first. That's what our earlier discussion of the triage cycle was all about. We decided that you are not free to alienate your treatment priority to Chloe, despite the fact that Bea will not be affected by your doing so.

AL: You're right. I forgot about that. I shouldn't have said what I said. What I should have said is that Bea really *does* have a stake in what Chloe and I are doing—provided we require her consent before we can go ahead. Because then we will need to buy her off and she might be able to hold out for a good deal of money. So since she has a stake, her consent should count, and we should be free to proceed once she has said it's OK with her.

DOCTOR: That is not what I mean by having a stake. What you are proposing would not make her different from anyone else in the world to whom we could give a veto right over what you and Chloe are doing. Any one of them would then acquire a stake in that sense, but that kind of stake is surely not a basis for giving anyone a veto right. What I mean is that Bea does not have the kind stake in the transaction that would lead us to give her such a veto right in the first place.

AL: Now you are losing me. Why do you say that Bea does not have the kind of stake in what is going on that should lead us to recognize her as having a veto right over whether I get to pass my treatment priority to Chloe or not? If she weren't around, I would get to pass my priority to Chloe. If she is present, I no longer get to do so, because if I did, she would then be entitled to complain about someone with a frivolous injury like Chloe getting treated ahead of her. That sounds to me like she has a stake.

DOCTOR: Let me make my point in a slightly roundabout way. I can't think of a way of making it more directly.

Suppose someone were to engage in some kind of activity that has the potential of preventing me from treating either you or Bea and that somehow leads to my treating Chloe instead, which is of course what you want to happen anyway. Do I need to be specific? Well, perhaps. So suppose someone is performing construction work in the hospital that has the potential of disabling some equipment that would be crucial for treating Bea's particular injury. (It wouldn't be needed for treating either you or Chloe.) Must that person make costly efforts to ensure that such a contingency will not occur, that the machine will not be disabled at the time that Bea might need to be treated? That seems ridiculous, since you actually prefer for Chloe to be treated and Bea would not have been treated anyway.

Is Bea entitled to compensation if the construction firm does not make enough of an effort to prevent this contingency so that I then end up treating Chloe instead of you or Bea? Again, that seems ridiculous, since you are actually pleased with the outcome and Bea is not denied any treatment she would otherwise have gotten.

Or suppose that Bea resorts to some kind of self-help to make sure that I treat you instead of Chloe—say, by disabling some crucial equipment I might need to treat Chloe? Is she entitled to impose significant risks on others for the sake of accomplishing that goal? Is she entitled to break laws to make sure this happens?

These questions are indirect ways of assessing the extent of her true stake in what you and Chloe are doing. And since the answer in each case would appear to be no , I conclude that her consent has no role to play in evaluating the arrangement between you and Chloe.

AL: Well, perhaps you are right in saying she does not really have a stake. But I will challenge your premise that because she does not have a stake, her consent is irrelevant. Consider the example of the person who is asked by his friend whether he will help her finance her dental treatment. He feels morally impelled to do so. Then she uses the money to finance a cruise instead. Her using the money for a cruise instead of dental treatment certainly does not affect him financially and perhaps not even psychologically. Nevertheless there is no denying that what she did is objectionable without his consent and unobjectionable with it. Stake just doesn't matter.

DOCTOR: I am not so sure consent works in the dental treatment case. Suppose he is asked whether she can use the money for a cruise instead and he says yes. After she comes back from the cruise, she complains once again about her tooth pain, expresses regret over spending the money on the cruise, and asks him for more money to pay for the dental treatment. Has her claim on him vanished because she misspent the money? It has perhaps diminished a little but not vanished. That shows that his consent is not really effective. He is not able to exchange, as it were, the obligation he has to help her with medical problems for an obligation to help her with a vacation instead.

AL: Now, let's be practical here. You say Bea's consent is irrelevant. But suppose that Chloe and I manage to persuade Bea to simply refuse to be treated, or even to leave the ER. Then aren't you free to heed my wishes and treat Chloe first?

DOCTOR: Yes, that would work. But now Bea isn't merely consenting to Chloe's treatment. She is making herself unavailable for treatment.

AL: So?

DOCTOR: Well, suppose that in our dental treatment example the potential benefactor, after having given his friend the money she first wanted for dental treatment and consenting that she use it for a cruise instead, just makes himself unavailable for future requests. He simply becomes unreachable. That might well work and successfully protect him from any reproach for refusing to help her further. But that does not mean that his original consent to what she was doing was effective. It simply means that he found a roundabout way, a functional equivalent, for making it effective.

AL: But refusing treatment is hardly roundabout.

DOCTOR: Roundabout or not, it still is not the same as consent.

AL: What a fine and pointless distinction to draw. Is formality what this is all about?

DOCTOR: Formalities can be very important. Even if we know that X would like to sell something to Y for a given price, we would not approve of Y's just taking X's property and leaving the money he knows would suffice without X's actual consent.

If, as I am inclined to think, the doctor has the better in this argument, we have arrived at the somewhat startling conclusion that arrangements that are unanimously desired by everyone in a given society might nonetheless be problematic. Even if in a plebiscite everyone votes to adopt a tradable emissions regime, it seems that might not be grounds enough for putting it in place. How strange, and yet it seems supported by some rather strong arguments.

Cycles without the Win-Win Argument

It is often thought that cycling in law is a rare thing. Law students encounter it only in a very select number of places. A cycling problem is known to exist in the rules governing the recording of land deeds and in some related contexts (having to do with property that serves as collateral for a loan). But that seems like a pretty narrow corner of the law. Cycling does not therefore seem very important. Looking at the triage cycle and its myriad reincarnations throughout the law should have convinced you that cycling problems are actually commonplace once one knows what to look for.

But one might come away from this chapter with the impression that most cycling problems arise out the havoc wrought by the win-win principle. That is not true. The win-win principle is of interest because of its connection with consent. But it would not be hard to construct cycles that do not involve the win-win principle at all. Here is a very simple way in which we might modify the triage scenario to generate a cycle that does not make use of the win-win principle.

Imagine that Al suffered his injury not in a car accident but because he attacked Chloe and she defended herself, resulting in her injuring her finger and his injuring his legs. When they both reach the ER, we might well be inclined to give Chloe priority over Al, given the way the injuries arose. But now suppose that Bea is in the picture as well, with her one-leg injury.

Now we get a cycle, but not one that depends on the win-win principle: Bea has priority over Chloe because a leg is more important than a finger. Al has priority over Bea because two legs are more important than one leg. Finally, Chloe has priority over Al because her injury is the product of his attack. I have little doubt that there are many actual cases that have this general structure.

Taking Stock

Sometimes, for no obvious reason, the law does not allow someone to agree to something, not because his agreement was coerced or because he was being deceived or because he is too incompetent to know what he is doing or even for more controversial reasons having to do with paternalism, exploitation, or commodification. Why?

We began by considering one such situation, a stylized triage scenario, in which it was much easier to understand than in the more realistic cases why consent might be a problem despite the absence of coercion, deception, etc. The more realistic cases—like personal service contracts—in which the courts refuse to recognize consent without quite knowing why, turned out, from an abstract point of view, to be equivalent to the triage scenario.

The justification for disregarding consent in all these cases, we saw, ultimately derives from a surprisingly innocuous-looking and hard-to-dispute premise: the idea that merely because X desires something more intensely than Y does, he does not as a result have a stronger legal or moral claim to it than Y. This is just another way of saying that there is a difference between claims and desires, or interests and preferences.

How is it that recognizing the existence of claims and the fact that they are distinct from desires leads to the disregard of consent? Put very generally, what is going on is this: when the law recognizes a claim, it implicitly puts a value, or price, on something. When the law declares that people may impose a risk of a certain size on others for the sake of object X but not for the sake of object Y, or when it declares that people are required to take precautions of a certain amount to avoid inadvertently damaging object X but not object Y, or when it declares that people may use lethal force to protect X but not Y, or when it declares that people may commit a crime to avert harm to X but not to Y, it is implicitly putting values on X and Y, a high one on X, and a lower one on Y. When the owner of X or Y

agrees to exchange them for something else, he too is putting values on X
and on Y, values that will often be different from the ones the law puts on
them. But it is hard to have something exchanged at one price in one context and at another price in another context. The coexistence of two such
prices is apt to give rise to a tension that on occasion results in cycling.

CHAPTER FOUR

The Social Choice Connection

The Root Cause of the Problem: Sen's Paradox

Every perversity in this book, I declared in the introduction, reflects some important paradoxical result in the theory of collective decision making (or, as it is more often called, social choice theory—the branch of economics that grew up around the study of elections and voting). The most fundamental of those results—Condorcet's voting paradox and Arrow's theorem—will prove to lie at the heart of certain legal perversities we will take up later. Only slightly less fundamental is a paradox discovered by the economist Amartya Sen, and it is this paradox that is most closely connected with the problem we have been considering so far: the issue of consent.

Sen's paradox emerges when one tries to extend social choice theory beyond regular elections. Sen suggested we think of all processes by which a decision somehow emerges from the interactions of a group of people as elections of sorts. Even if the process by which such a decision comes about is quite messy—nothing that could be summarized by a succinct phrase like "majority voting," or even by the more elaborate, multistage protocol by which an American president is elected—it still is amenable to being understood along the same lines as a more ordinary election. At least that was Sen's suspicion, and it proved to be a fruitful one.[1]

To think of all social processes as a kind of election is quite a dramatic step. Consider just a few things it will entail: When I decide to skip breakfast, or to listen to German military marches, or to read erotica, and I manage to do so without anyone stopping me, then those decisions are now considered part of a society-wide "election," albeit one in which my vote is capable of outweighing everyone else's. Why is my vote, in this weird type of "election," capable of outweighing everyone else's? Presumably because ours is a society in which everyone is entitled to do at least a few things (like skipping breakfast, listening to German marches, reading erotica) regardless of how the rest of society feels about it. Sen calls this kind of entitlement—to do something regardless of how others feel about it—a right. Indeed, he notes, this is almost surely what we generally mean when speak of someone's having a right: something we think someone should be able to do even if everyone else is supremely annoyed by his doing it. Sen adds that for a society to count as being even minimally protective of our liberties—"minimally liberal" he calls it; "minimally tolerant" is what I prefer to call it—people have to have at least a few such rights.

The next step in Sen's analysis is to imagine a slightly unusual situation. Let us continue to suppose that reading erotica is in fact one of those things we feel each of us should be able to decide for himself, regardless of how others feel. (Nothing in what I am about to say hinges on this specific example, but it happens to be the one that Sen used to explain himself.) Suppose further that our society divides itself into two kinds of people, whom we will call the Lewds and the Prudes. The Lewds, as their name implies, greatly enjoy reading erotica, and the Prudes do not. But it isn't just that the Lewds like it and the Prudes hate it. Each of them, we will suppose, is very passionate about his feelings. The Prudes aren't merely bothered if they themselves are confronted by erotica; they are offended by the very idea of others having access to it. In fact the Prudes' level of offense at having the Lewds gorge themselves on this kind of thing is so great that it outstrips even the nausea and disgust they feel when they are forced to look at such stuff with their own eyes. (That's because they think themselves to be far more immune to the erotica's pernicious influence than they believe the Lewds to be.)

The Lewds' feelings are symmetrical. Not only do they enjoy erotica, but they have a proselytizer's zeal to try to "loosen up" the Prudes by getting them to read some of it. And so great is their zeal that the indirect pleasure they would get from knowing the Prudes are being made to read erotica would be greater even than the direct pleasure they would get from reading the stuff themselves.

Now comes the paradox. It would seem that if the Lewds like to read erotica, then in a minimally tolerant society, they will get to do so, regardless of what the Prudes think. Conversely, if the Prudes hate erotica, then in a minimally tolerant society, they will get to avoid it regardless of what the Lewds think. The problem is that both the Lewds and the

Prudes would be happier if things were the other way around—that is, if the Lewds were to be denied access to erotica and the Prudes had it forced upon them. In other words, if we grant each group the right to read or not to read, then we will end up with a situation that violates the win-win principle: everyone would be happier if the Lewds and the Prudes did not have such a right. Therein lies the paradox: granting people rights seems not to mix with the win-win principle. Indeed it doesn't just seem that way; it really is that way. A society that respects individual rights cannot also respect the win-win principle. That is the gist of Sen's insight.

It's worth lingering over this a little to get its full paradoxical flavor. It will help if we put the problem into a very narrowly focused context. Imagine—as Sen asks us to do in one of his examples—that there is exactly one copy of *Lady Chatterley's Lover* around, and there are exactly two potential readers, Mr. Lewd and Mr. Prude. And suppose you are the person who has to decide what should happen to that copy of the book. You could give it to Mr. Lewd, to do with as he likes; or you could give it to Mr. Prude, to do with as he likes; or, finally, you could give it to Mr. Prude, but only on condition that he actually read it. Those are your three choices. Let's consider them in pairs.

Suppose you start out thinking that you like the win-win solution: give the book to Mr. Prude on condition that he actually *read* it, because that way Mr. Lewd won't mind that *he* doesn't get to read it, and Prude will be pleased to keep it out of Lewd's hands. Having provisionally decided that that is what you are going to do, you then start to imagine having a conversation with Prude in which he says to you, after you have already handed him the book: "I really don't want to read this stuff. It makes me gag. I know you gave it to me on condition that I read it. But would you really mind if I didn't? I know of course that that will make old Lewd very unhappy. But, really now, why do you care? If I suffer in the process of having to read it, that's something that ought to matter to you. As for Lewd, that nosy fellow's displeasure at not getting to control what I do in the privacy of my home surely shouldn't weigh with you too much."

Suppose then you find yourself moved by this argument and provisionally decide to cast aside the win-win solution and let Prude do with the book what he wants. But then you think some more about what you are on the verge of doing, and you imagine being approached by Lewd, who says: "Why would you give the book to someone who won't even look at it, when I would really enjoy reading it? I realize that if you were to give it to me instead of letting him just squirrel it away, that would make him very

unhappy. But why do you care? That nosy fellow's displeasure at not getting to control what I do in the privacy of my home surely shouldn't weigh
with you too much." Suppose you find yourself moved by this argument, in
turn, and provisionally decide to not give the book to Prude but to Lewd.
Then you think some more about this alternative, and you imagine being
told by Lewd: "You know, I would like it much better if instead of reading
this book I could persuade you to suggest to Prude that he read it. That
would make both him and me happier than if I were to just go ahead and
read it myself." If this last argument too moves you, you have now come
full circle back to the win-win solution. Putting together rights and the
win-win principle lands us in a cycle—that's Sen's paradoxical claim.

There have been objections to Sen's argument, and I will take those
up in a moment. But I want to postpone doing so until we have made out
the connection between Sen's paradox and the triage cycle and its various
real-world manifestations. The objections will then, as we shall see, almost
take care of themselves.

When we look at the triage cycle with Sen's paradox in mind, it will
become apparent that we are simply dealing with a special case of the
paradox. The triage cycle arose out of a combination of three different
arguments: There was the basic priority argument, by which Al claimed
priority for his two-leg injury over Bea's one-leg injury. There was the win-
win argument, by which Chloe, with Al's blessing, claimed priority over
Al. And there was the regained priority argument, by which Bea claimed
priority over Chloe. The basic priority argument and the regained priority argument are of course simply assertions of a right. The assertion of
those two rights then leads to a conflict with the win-win principle—just
exactly the kind of phenomenon that, according to Sen's paradox, is bound
to occur where rights of any kind are recognized. And the various more
realistic incarnations of the triage cycle we have considered are more of
the same. In sum, the law's problems with consent are simply instances of
Sen's paradox.

Why Sen's Critics Are Wrong

As I said, a great number of scholars have taken enormous umbrage at
Sen's suggestion that granting people rights and respecting the win-win
principle don't mix. That's understandable. In a way, it is a totally outrageous claim. People who believe in respecting others' rights generally
think that one of the most crucial of those rights is to strike whatever

bargains they please, provided they don't harm anyone else, because such bargains represent win-win arrangements. In other words, strong supporters of rights are generally also strong supporters of the win-win principle. Sen is claiming that their position contains a logical contradiction, that the various rights they simultaneously support do not coherently fit together.

Sen's critics have taken particular issue with Sen's analysis of the case of Lewd and Prude. As they see it, if the Lewds and the Prudes would both be happier if the Prudes read the erotica and the Lewds did not, then we should simply let them make a suitable arrangement with each other to such effect. And if they freely came to such an arrangement, then Sen cannot really say that any rights are being violated, even though it is true that *in a sense* they don't get to decide for themselves whether to read or not, having waived that right in return for something else they wanted: The Lewds waive their right to read in return for the Prudes waiving their right *not* to read. It is generally part of a right that the right holder is able to exchange it for something else he values, which is what the Lewds and Prudes would be doing. In this way, say Sen's critics, we are able to respect both the win-win principle and a person's right to decide for himself certain highly personal matters. Sen's paradox seems to have disappeared. In fact, they say, it only came about because Sen started out with a strange view of a right as something that cannot be given up.[2]

The triage cycle allows us to see what is wrong with this criticism. It allows us to see this in both an abstract and a very concrete way. Let's start with the abstract perspective. The suggestion that the conflict between the win-win principle and rights can always be bridged by a suitable bargain clearly won't work for the triage cycle or for its various real-life cousins. We just spent several chapters exploring the reasons for that. In the triage cycle, the win-win principle and the various rights claims stand in an irreconcilable conflict.

Now let's make the same point in a more concrete way by taking a closer look at the case of the Lewds and the Prudes, bearing the lessons of the triage cycle in mind. The critics are saying that if we simply allow the Lewds and the Prudes to enter into a bargain with each other whereby each voluntarily waives his right to decide for himself whether to read erotica or not, we get to respect the Win-Win principle without running afoul of anyone's rights. But let's consider this bargain up close. We are supposing that under this bargain the Prudes commit themselves to reading and the Lewds commit themselves to *not* reading erotica. Now let us scrutinize with the utmost care exactly how their legal and moral relationship is being changed by this bargain. *More specifically, let us ask what would have happened, before they struck their bargain, if the Lewds had tried to interfere with the Prudes' right regarding erotica and the Prudes had tried to interfere with the Lewds' rights.* If the Lewds had interfered with the Prudes, the Prudes would have been able to call on the police or to protect their right to do as they wish on their own. And if the Prudes had interfered with the Lewds, the same would have been true for the Lewds.

Let's next consider what things are like after the bargain. Something very crucial has changed now: for the Prudes to interfere with the Lewds' rights and vice versa means something entirely different than before. Whereas before, the Prudes would be interfering with the Lewds' rights if they interrupted their reading of erotica, now the Prudes would be interfering if they failed to follow through on their promise—their promise to subject themselves to erotica. Conversely, whereas before the Lewds would be interfering with the Prudes' rights if they shoved erotica in front of their eyes, now they would be interfering if they failed to follow through on *their* promise—the promise to avoid erotica. *If, therefore, the bargain between the two groups had in fact succeeded in accomplishing what it was intended to, namely to transfer the Lewds' rights to the Prudes and vice versa, then it should now be the case that the Lewds can summon the police to force the Prudes to read erotica, and the Prudes can summon the police to tear any erotica the Lewds are reading out of their hands.* Nor do they need to depend on the police. If the bargain between the two groups had successfully transferred all of the Lewds' rights to the Prudes and vice versa, then each group should now be entitled to use modest physical force to get its promises enforced. But that is pretty clearly not true. The bargain is not going to have any such effect, and from our examination of the triage cycle we know why: because a contractual right constitutes a much weaker kind of claim than a property right. (Remember, that's why there is no specific enforcement of contract rights.) It is thus not possible to bargain one's way out of Sen's paradox. The paradox is here to stay.

Further Connections with Social Choice Theory: The Antifairness Theorem of Kaplow and Shavell

Sen's paradox and the triage cycle thus turn out to be mutually illuminating. But Sen's paradox is not the only result in social choice theory that connects with the triage cycle in such a fruitful way. Another result of more recent vintage is an insight by legal scholars Lewis Kaplow and

Steve Shavell (who also happen to be economists). It is an insight they claim should dramatically change the way we think about the law. More specifically, they say, it should radically change the way in which we assess the merits of a particular legal rule, which is of course the most basic task legislators, judges, and legal scholar have to engage in. It means answering questions such as, Should we have a no-fault divorce system? Should negligent drivers have to compensate their victims? How severely should we punish drunk driving? And so on.[3]

Traditionally, arguments about the merits of a legal rule have almost always been of one of two kinds. They either address themselves to the usefulness (or uselessness) of a law or to its fairness (or unfairness), though that is not necessarily the language used. Instead of usefulness, one often speaks of welfare or efficiency or practical consequences. Instead of fairness, one often speaks of equity, respect for rights, deontological justice, or just plain justice. Usefulness and fairness will often be at loggerheads, and everybody understands that. What's fair need not be useful and vice versa. Think about the suggestion that we should punish drunk driving by imposing a life sentence on anyone caught doing it—whether or not he actually caused harm. From the point of view of fairness, that seems outrageously disproportionate punishment. But it might well be efficient: the deterrent effect would be so great that at the cost of ruining the lives of a few drunk drivers, we would have prevented a large number of deaths. Another example: justice might seem to suggest that in a divorce proceeding a judge should carefully consider the fault each party bears in the breakup of the marriage and then divide the assets accordingly. Efficiency directs our attention to the incredible cost of trying to figure out fault in this kind of context as well as the unfortunate incentives doing so creates, as each side tries to deviously manipulate the other into looking like the one who is really at fault in breaking up the marriage.

In formulating a legal rule, we will thus often have to strike a balance, accept a little bit less fairness in return for some practical benefit and vice versa. To the question of exactly how the balance between justice and efficiency should be struck, there is, naturally, no definitive, universally accepted answer. It is thus hard to argue, rather than merely disagree with, either those who tilt in the direction of fairness or those who tilt the other way. This too everybody understands.

Well, not quite everybody. For into this blithe consensus barged Kaplow and Shavell with their claim—set out at length in their book *Fairness versus Welfare*—that there is one and only one way to strike the balance between fairness and usefulness: *ignore fairness and focus exclusively on usefulness*. A law is desirable, they insist, only to the extent that it increases welfare. They begin by noting that there is one principle on which both the advocates of fairness and the advocates of usefulness (or welfare, or efficiency, etc.) would agree, and that is the win-win principle. Everyone agrees (Kaplow and Shavell say), whatever else they differ on, that if a legal rule can produce a state of affairs that is better for literally every member of society, then it should be adopted, both as a matter efficiency *and* as a matter of fairness. This is where the theory of social choice comes in.

Suppose, they say, we asked people to rank all possible states of affairs that might come about as a result of adopting one or another legal policy. Suppose we then aggregate these individual rankings in some fashion into a master ranking. Suppose further that we insist that that ranking respect the win-win principle: if there is unanimity that a particular alternative is better than some other alternative, then it must be ranked that way. Suppose, finally, that in ranking them we pay attention not only to people's preferences but to one or another of the fairness principles legal scholars have endorsed (e.g., "No disproportionate punishment" or "The spouse at fault should pay extra" or "All victims of negligence deserve to be compensated by the negligent actor"). Kaplow and Shavell claim to have proved that if we tried to do this, we would inevitably end up in a cycle. Put differently, if our ranking system respects any of those fairness principles, it will inevitably violate the win-win principle. The only way to avoid violating the win-win principle is to ignore fairness and concentrate on welfare instead. You can see why I call this the antifairness theorem.[4]

Here is a highly simplified version of the argument they offer. Like Sen's paradox, it is best grasped in the context of a specific example. Kaplow and Shavell ask us to consider the law of traffic accidents. Justice here seems to require, many people would argue, that negligent drivers compensate their victims. Now let's just see, say Kaplow and Shavell, where this kind of principle might end up leading us. Let us imagine, they say, that over the course of a lifetime every citizen will wind up being the victim of exactly one negligence-caused traffic accident. And for simplicity's sake, let's assume the severity of the injury is always the same. Finally, let us imagine that just as everyone ends up being a victim on exactly one occasion, they also end up being perpetrators (i.e., negligent drivers) on exactly one occasion. In other words, everyone imposes as much risky and injurious conduct on others as he is subjected to by them.

What an exclusively welfare-oriented economist would say about such a world is that there should probably not be any compensation for accidents because over the long run everyone will be paying out as much as he will be taking in, and since the process of litigating such cases and enforcing the resulting verdicts will cost money, everyone would be better off if all injuries were simply allowed to lie where they fall. The upshot is that we should, under such circumstances, abolish the tort system as we know it.

Someone who believes that fairness requires that all victims deserve to be compensated by the negligent actors who caused their injury, and no one else, would *not* be willing to sign off on that. As he sees it, everyone deserves to be compensated by the negligent actor who injured him, when and if an accident has occurred. Whether or not the victim has perpetrated an equivalent wrong against some other person has no bearing on which claim he has against the person who has just now injured him. Saying this, however, puts one squarely into conflict with the win-win principle, since everyone would be better off if no compensation were paid.

To be sure, the example is highly unrealistic, but that is really irrelevant. Kaplow and Shavell are making an analytical point. If the principle about compensating victims of negligence leads to unacceptable results in some admittedly contrived circumstances, that allows us to conclude that it cannot be trusted even in cases where the result does not seem so manifestly unacceptable. An analogy will help make this point clearer. Suppose a critic of the deterrence theory of punishment points out to one of its supporters that deterrence theory might under certain, admittedly contrived, circumstances call for the execution of a person we know to be innocent. It wouldn't do to say, "Well, this is unlikely to ever happen. So let's not worry about it." Any theory of punishment that allows for the execution of a person one knows to be innocent cannot be trusted even in those cases that are likely to arise.

Debating the Implications of the Antifairness Theorem

Although many profess to be completely persuaded by Kaplow and Shavell's arguments, there has been no dearth of criticism. More specifically, what critics have tried to do is to confront Kaplow and Shavell with counterexamples to their theorem—namely, fairness-based principles that would not seem to conflict with the win-win principle. The counterexamples are all cooked from the same recipe. Let's see how they work.

Let's return to a principle we already know to conflict with the win-win principle: "All victims of negligence should be compensated by the negligent actor." Suppose now we amend that principle to read: "All victims of negligence should be compensated by the negligent actor *unless everyone would be better off if they were not*."[5] This looks like a fairness-based principle that, almost by definition, could not conflict with the win-win principle, because whenever such a conflict arises, the fairness part of the principle simply yields.

By way of response, Kaplow and Shavell ask us to consider the possibility that abolishing liability for traffic accidents would not make literally everyone better off, but *nearly* everyone: there would be a few persons who would be made worse off by a smidgeon, whereas most everyone else would benefit a lot. If we evaluate this policy under the critics' proposed principle ("All victims of negligence should be compensated by the negligent actor unless everyone would be better off if they were not"), then by that criterion, say Kaplow and Shavell, such an "almost-win-win" situation would not pass muster. And isn't that pretty absurd?

But there is a better criticism that we can make of Kaplow and Shavell, based on our analysis of the triage cycle. In a way, the triage cycle is a perfect illustration of Kaplow and Shavell's claim that fairness and the win-win principle don't mix. They certainly don't mix here. They cause us to get into a cycle. But the triage cycle also illustrates something else—that Kaplow and Shavell are wrong in thinking that fairness should always obviously lose out to the win-win principle. In the context of the triage cycle and its real-world counterparts, we concluded quite the opposite, that the win-win principle would have to lose out to fairness. In other words, the triage cycle undercuts the lesson Kaplow and Shavell would draw from their antifairness theorem. The triage cycle exemplifies a case in which the win-win principle very plausibly fails. In other words, the triage cycle is a case in which we found it more plausible to preserve priority rights at the expense of the win-win principle rather than the other way around.

But there are some unorthodox aspects to this conclusion. First, it involves endorsing the idea most people will find to be anathema, namely that fairness wins out even when *everyone* is made worse off as a result. Everyone! There is no denying that this is a very unpleasant thing to have to do, bordering on the absurd. Restricting one's freedom of contract under circumstances where everybody would be better off if we did not seems an extremely costly way of satisfying whatever our other ethical commitments may be. But as I am about to show you, it is not nearly as costly as it appears at first.

Most of the time there are ways of circumventing restrictions on freedom of contract. We saw for instance that it is possible to get around the restriction of giving away one's priority claim in the ER by finding a way of shifting the basis for that priority—by finding a way of diminishing one's own injury in such a way that it results in a corresponding increase in the injury of the person to whom one wants to pass the priority. It might also be possible to get around it by paying Bea to leave the ER or to refuse treatment. Prohibitions on the outright sale of certain things—organs, sex, etc.—can often be circumvented by not making the money a direct quid pro quo. Prohibitions on the assumption of risk can be circumvented by attenuating the relationship the benefited party has to the risk: an employer simply farms out a task that requires the incurring of risk and then leaves it to the employee how to accomplish it. (The prohibition of unorthodox property rights can be gotten around in innumerable other ways, one of the most common being the use of a lease into which all sorts of conditions may be incorporated even if they do not "touch and concern" the property.)

Indeed it can be argued that this is the sort of thing lawyers are in the business of doing when they find suitable ways of structuring transactions. But is it not ridiculous to have a prohibition only to then have lawyers find clever ways around it? What is the point? Kaplow and Shavell realize this and think it is a devastating point against fairness theories that they should result in such maneuvers. They single out as particularly silly in this regard the fairness-based distinction between killing someone and letting him die. The law rigidly distinguishes between two ways of causing harm, bringing it about or just letting it happen—killing or letting die. We are liable for the former, but not generally for the latter, except in special circumstances—if the victims of our inaction are our children or others toward whom we have some special duty. In this, the law of course merely follows commonsense morality. To distinguish between action and inaction in this way, Kaplow and Shavell note, will lead to violations of the win-win principle. We might all be better off if the distinction were abolished and our rules simply focused on whether what we are doing or not doing were bringing about a good or a bad result. But that is not their main point about the distinction between killing and letting someone die. Their main point is that the distinction is often very easy to circumvent through maneuvers that do not seem to have any moral significance—and what is the point of taking a legal or moral rule so seriously when it can so readily be gotten around by doing some morally irrelevant things?

Suppose we are building a hospital, they say, and in the course of construction it is inevitable that at least one worker will die in an accident.

Believers in the killing/letting die distinction will have no problem with building the hospital. "Suppose, however," Kaplow and Shavell write, "that the leader of the polity had available a button and that just before the worker was about to die, time stood still for a moment; if the button was pushed, the worker would die and the project would proceed to completion, but if it was not pushed, the work done to date would disintegrate, and construction would have to begin anew." Now we would be actively killing the worker rather than just letting him die, and so we can't go forward. Thus they conclude: "It would seem that the only . . . lesson to draw from such examples is that changes in the technology of such things as push-buttons or in other factors that one would have thought to be entirely arbitrary as a matter of morality are in fact of potentially crucial moral significance," a "result that would seem to require some defense."[6]

Indeed. It does seem strange that these factors that appear entirely morally arbitrary are in fact of crucial moral significance. But this is a larger issue. It turns out that it is impossible to design a plausible legal system that does not have this feature. Even the kind of system Kaplow and Shavell envision is vulnerable to this. The challenge therefore is not a challenge at all, since all legal regimes are open to it. This will be taken up in part II, in the context of our exploration of loopholes.

Last Thoughts on Win-Win Transactions

Many of the failures of consent encountered and explained in the first two chapters can be seen as special cases of two theorems in the theory of social choice, Sen's liberal paradox and Kaplow and Shavell's antifairness theorem. Thinking about such cases—especially the triage scenario—serves to cast an interesting new light on those theorems. They serve to disarm Sen's critics by showing that any plausible conception of a right really does have an aspect of inalienability to it. In addition, they serve to undercut the lessons that many people, especially Kaplow and Shavell, would draw from the antifairness theorem—namely, that there is no room in the evaluation of a law for fairness, since fairness means violating the win-win principle—because these cases show us why sometimes the win-win principle is worth violating.

PART II

Why Is the Law So Full of Loopholes?

CHAPTER FIVE

The Irresistible Wrong Answer

Frontsies and Backsies

Some of the best legal scholarship I know comes in the form of cartoons. The cartoons I have in mind are the work of the Harvard-trained lawyer and cartoonist Ruben Bolling and concern a wacky character named Harvey Richard, Lawyer for Children, who specializes in advising and representing children in their playground disputes. Proceeding from this screwball premise, Bolling offers striking and illuminating analogies for some of the profoundest problems of legal theory. A particularly inspired example involves little Suzie, who very much wants to cut into a long line of children queuing up in front of the ticket window of a movie theater. She asks one of her friends to let her go in front of her, but her friend is only willing to let her go in behind her, to which the person already behind her successfully objects. So Suzie consults Harvey Richard: is there anything she can do to avoid having to go to the back of the queue? Richard explains to Suzie that what she has run into is the *frontsies-are-fine-but-backsies-are-not* doctrine. He then suggests a lawyerly solution to her problem: just ask your friend to grant you a *frontsie* first, so that you can enter the queue in front of her, but promise that you will then grant her a *frontsie* in turn, by trading places with her, so that when all is said and done, you will have taken the queue spot right behind her but without violating the rule against *backsies*; you did it all by a sequence of *frontsies*. He has been writing, he adds, a law review article on just this problem, called "Double Frontsies as a Solution to the No Backsies Rule."

What Suzie has done here, with the help of her lawyer, is to find a loophole in the *no-backsies* rule, allowing her to effectively nullify it. The cartoon brilliantly illustrates the kind of activity that lies at the heart of legal

FIGURE I.

practice. The exploitation of loopholes is in fact the lawyer's daily bread, which makes it all the more strange that both lawyers and nonlawyers profess such outrage about it. Actually, the point should probably be put the other way around: what is strange is that, given the contempt in which loophole exploitation is held, it is nevertheless central to legal practice. What can a profession whose main preoccupation consists of this kind of activity say for itself? This is the issue the next several chapters take up. Specifically, I intend to answer three questions about loopholes: First, why is the law so riddled with them? Second, why, once detected, do they usually go uncorrected? And finally, should lawyers be reluctant to exploit them, or should they feel free to?

Some Typical Loopholes: A Menu of Test Cases

Notice that *what* constitutes a loophole is not among the questions I seek to answer. That is because when I speak of loopholes I mean pretty much what everybody else means—seeming glitches in the formulation of a law (it could be either statutory or case law) that allow clever lawyers to help their clients do things that appear to subvert its purpose. But although we don't need a precise definition of loopholes before we can try to explain them, we do need some good examples, both to clarify what we are talking about and to serve as test cases against which to evaluate different explanations of the loophole phenomenon. Here, then, are some typical instances of loophole exploitation.

Forum Shopping

A couple wants to get divorced more quickly, or easily, than they are allowed to by the state in which they happen to live. So they relocate to a more hospitable forum, only temporarily of course, to get the quick and easy divorce they are looking for. This kind of thing is probably the most rudimentary instance of "forum-shopping" there is. It is also often mentioned as the most quintessential form of loophole exploitation there is, although many profess to being puzzled by whether what is being exploited is a loophole in the divorce law of the state whose law the couple is trying to escape or in the divorce law of the state they are trying to come within or in the conflict-of-laws rule that says that where you live determines what divorce law should be applied to you. No matter—one of these, or perhaps all of these, appear to be circumvented when the couple temporarily relocates.

Asset Protection

What goes by the name of "asset protection" are the various stratagems by which one can try to put one's assets beyond the reach of actual or potential creditors. The most mundane of these is incorporation. By turning his business into a corporation of which he is the sole shareholder, the owner can ensure that in the event of bankruptcy, creditors can only deprive him of the business's assets. His personal assets are beyond their reach. Among the most notorious of the asset protection strategies is the kind of case I mentioned in the introduction—the doctor who has made unfortunate investments in some real estate partnerships and anticipates soon having to declare bankruptcy and to turn over all of his assets to his creditors. Just before that moment arrives, he buys an expensive house in Florida and invests the remainder of his funds in some special pensions and insurance. Creditors won't be able to touch the house, the pension, or the insurance, because they are considered "exempt" assets, so basic to one's survival that no one can ever insist that they be used to repay outstanding debts.[1] Also notorious is the not uncommon practice of deliberate self-impoverishment by the elderly: someone might decide to give all his assets to his adult children to avoid having to use them up to pay for his care. Instead, having turned himself into a person without assets, he can now ask the government to look after him. This is but a small but quite representative sample of the strategies by which debtors exploit loopholes in their obligation to pay their debts.

Tax Shelters

Here let me give just one example of a tax-lawyerly subterfuge that I hope can serve as an adequate stand-in for all the other stratagems tax lawyers have invented. It involves the reassignment of one's income to one's children. Consider the case of a father who makes a cash gift to his son every year in the amount of $10,000. Giving away a part of his income to his son will not affect either the father's or the son's tax liability. The $10,000 was part of the father's income, on which he was taxed, but is a mere gift to his son, on which no one is taxed. The father, however, would prefer to have the $10,000 attributed to his son rather than himself so that his son, who is in a lower tax bracket, will be the one paying taxes on it. The most straightforward way of accomplishing this is to give the son an asset that generates an income stream of $10,000. And so they proceed in the following way: one year, the father gives his son a somewhat larger cash gift than usual—$100,000. Immediately thereafter he asks his son for a loan of $100,000, on which he promises to pay 10 percent interest (the going interest rate, let us assume). The son then hands back to the father the $100,000 he has just received from him and in return receives $10,000 from him for the indefinite future.[2]

Now, what exactly is the point of this weird rigmarole? Haven't we ended up exactly where we started—the father paying $10,000 every year to his son? Well, we haven't ended up precisely where we started because the tax situation of the father and the son is rather different now. Let us assume that the purpose of the $100,000 loan is to help the father operate his business. The father may then say that the $10,000 annual interest payment is a business expense, to be deducted from his annual income. The son, of course, must now report the $10,000 as income on which he will now be taxed (which he would not be if it were a mere gift). Still, the son will be taxed at a much lower rate than the well-to-do father would have been.

Thus when all is said and done, the father is giving his son $10,000 every year, just as he did before, but that amount is now taxable to the son rather than to the father, and the IRS ends up with less revenue, since the son's tax rate is lower than the father's. In other words, through what looks like sheer magic—not magic, just a loophole most people would say—they have managed to accomplish indirectly what the law did not allow them to accomplish directly.

Litigation-Proofing

A firm has put a new product on the market that looks like a great money-maker, but there are hints in some of the product-testing data of possible hazards. Long before anything untoward happens to anyone, and long before a lawsuit in which it might be asked to turn over these data, the firm makes sure to destroy all documents older than a fixed number of months, thereby disposing of all potentially incriminating documents. Obviously, if the firm had done this after a suit was brought against it, it could be charged with obstruction of justice. But if the firm is following a program of routine file-disposal that eliminates the documents well in advance of litigation, it is safe.

The loophole the firm is exploiting here arises as part of the law forbidding obstruction of justice. Since an action can only count as obstructive if it takes place once a suit is about to materialize, any obstructive action taken ahead of time is thus beyond the law's reach.

Contrived Defenses

Consider the defendant who provokes his intended victim into an ill-considered attack on him, to which he responds by killing him in "self-defense"—as happens for instance in the *Death Wish* movies of the 1970s. Charles Bronson plays a law-abiding New Yorker who turns vigilante when his family falls victim to a brutal crime. He takes on the criminal element by seeking out the most dangerous spots in Central Park at the most dangerous times of night, affecting the appearance of a vulnerable, befuddled tourist, money all but spilling out of his back pocket, and when inevitably he is accosted by a vicious mugger, he has a gun at his ready and mows him down. Criminal law has great trouble figuring out how to deal with such cases of contrived self-defense, which to some look like a loophole in the law of homicide. The problem is a serious one because it goes well beyond the law of self-defense. It also arises in the case of the defendant who renders himself non compos mentis so he can commit his crime in a state of insanity, or the defendant who remains willfully blind to certain otherwise incriminating aspects of what he is doing so that he can claim ignorance as a defense, or the defendant who creates some kind of emergency so that he can commit his crime under cover of necessity or duress. In all of these cases the defendant has contrived to "create the conditions of his own defense."[3] Technically the defendant obviously qualifies for a defense, but does he really remain entitled to it when he manufactured the circumstances on which it is based? This is sometimes referred to as the problem of the *actio libera in causa* and is considered one of the most vexing problems in all of criminal law.[4] We seem to have here a whole cluster of loopholes that has the potential of undermining virtually every criminal prohibition.

Political Asylum by Bootstrapping

A would-be immigrant to the United States might try to bypass the usual waiting lines for an immigrant visa by turning himself into a political refugee. Having arrived in the United States on a visiting visa, he disseminates some statements that make him a candidate for immediate imprisonment if he returns to his home country. Then he claims political asylum. This looks like a loophole in our immigration laws.[5]

The lawyers among my readers will have no trouble extending this list, but these six should prove sufficient for our purposes. There is nothing especially exotic about them, and they affect vast stretches of law. Indeed one legal scholar, Lynn LoPucki, has argued in a brilliant essay called "The Death of Liability" that the loophole represented by the asset protection strategies has the potential of swallowing up all of legal liability.[6]

About each of these arguable loopholes one might then ask the three questions with which I began: Why are they there? Given how much offense they give, why have they not been eradicated? And finally, what about the lawyers who exploit them—are they doing something dishonorable, unethical, or illegal?

An Atypical Loophole: The Intentional Foul as a Legal Phenomenon

What we have seen so far are the most typical kinds of loopholes, the kinds most people are likely to associate with that label. But there is another, somewhat special, often overlooked kind of loophole. It does not really have a name; at least not in the legal context. It does have a name in the other context in which arises, which is sports. There it is referred to as the "intentional foul," or, less often, the "professional foul." Take the case of a basketball player like Shaquille O'Neal, who is known to be an extremely formidable player in all but one aspect of the sport, free throws, which he is comparatively mediocre at. Opponents would frequently take advantage of this by committing an intentional foul to prevent him from scoring. The penalty for such a foul is two free throws, which O'Neill often muffs. Something similar happens in soccer. As a player is about to score, the goalie might stop him with an illegal tackle—an intentional foul—thereby incurring a penalty kick, which with some luck he might actually deflect. An intentional foul, as should now be clear, is not merely conduct intentionally violating a rule of the game but conduct for which the offender fully expects to be punished but that he finds strategically useful to commit anyway. Many more fanciful versions of this could be imagined (and have occurred) than these two simple cases, but there is no need to spell them out, since I don't particularly want to take up, let alone explain, the ethics of intentional fouls as they occur in sports.

What I do want to take up is the parallel phenomenon in law. Here is a simple example of an intentional foul in law. For the sake of simplicity, I will resort to our familiar triage scenario. The doctor has to choose among several patients needing a certain organ transplant. He makes a mistake. As a result the patient whose life depends on getting the organ right now does not get it, and a patient who could afford to wait longer and whose life does not really depend on getting an organ at all (though it could be significantly improved thereby) gets it instead. Let's suppose the mistake arises in a truly egregious manner, enough so that the doctor would be liable for some kind of homicide—manslaughter or maybe even murder. Now suppose the opportunity still exists for the doctor to change course: it would be possible, it turns out, for the doctor to remove the already implanted organ from the less deserving recipient and transplant it into the more deserving patient. Should he do so? Most people's intuition would say no. This is very much like those infamous hypothetical cases in which a surgeon saves the lives of five persons needing a heart, two kidneys, and two lungs by killing an innocent bystander and redistributing his organs to the five.

Now suppose the doctor does it anyway. That is, despite the fact that we judge it to be immoral and illegal for him to forcibly extract the organ from one patient and transplant it into another, and despite the fact that the authorities, as well as the victim, would be entitled to forcibly stop him if they could, he proceeds to do just that. What is his liability going to be now? He would no longer be guilty of a homicide, since no one has died. He would presumably be guilty of an aggravated assault against the patient whose organ he removed. Overall, however, his legal position is much improved—*even though he did the manifestly wrong thing!*

The intentional foul—more precisely, the legal counterpart to the intentional foul—also seems like a sort of loophole. It is not, as we shall see later, particularly rare. And we can ask about it the same questions we asked about the more ordinary kinds of loopholes: why does it arise, why does it persist, and is it legitimate for lawyers to take advantage of it?

What the Courts Have Done about Loopholes—and Why It Has Not Worked Very Well

Courts have taken three approaches to these kinds of cases, to which one might give the following labels: the form-versus-substance approach, the intent-to-evade approach, and the spirit-versus-letter approach. Let's see exactly how they work and how well, or rather how poorly, they work.

The Form-versus-Substance Approach

In the form-versus-substance approach is how a court would typically deal with an employee who seeks to reduce his taxes by receiving most of his income in kind—the company car, the company apartment, and so forth. The court would say that although in form what he is getting is not income (he is not getting money), in substance it is. It is also the approach a court would use to deal with certain imperfectly executed versions of the aforementioned loophole-exploiting maneuvers. Consider the couple that seeks to avoid the family law of state X by establishing domicile in state Y but in fact makes only desultory efforts to establish the new domicile, never doing quite everything that we associate with a properly established domicile (e.g., by continuing to spend most of their time in state X). Here too courts would presumably say that they are domiciled in Y only in form, whereas they are still domiciled in X in substance. Indeed the approach would presumably be used for all versions of forum shopping, asset protection, tax shelters, bootstrapping, contrived defenses, or litigation-proofing in which the actor only pretends to satisfy the prerequisites for a certain legal benefit but fails to do so in actuality.

Herein, however, lies the true limitation of the form-versus-substance approach: it only works well in cases in which the legal actors are pretending to be doing something other than what they are actually doing. But most instances of loophole exploitation involve people who are actually doing what they claim to be doing. If courts are to strike down these other transactions as well, they need to resort to something other than the form-versus-substance approach—such as one of the two following approaches.[7]

The Intent-to-Evade Approach

In the intent-to-evade approach a court will overrule all maneuvers that the defendant would not have engaged in but for the law whose effect he is trying to avoid. Some versions of the tax law's so-called economic substance doctrine essentially come down to this: as long as the defendant structures his transaction in a way he would never have chosen but for the tax law, it will be judged to lack economic substance and struck down as impermissible tax evasion.

This approach would lead a court to strike down wholesale all the stratagems I have described so far. In all of them, the defendant proceeded as he did only because he thought this might allow him to avoid an unwelcome rule of either divorce law, debtor-creditor law, income tax law, criminal law, or immigration law. And therein lies the problem with this approach. It really makes far too clean a sweep of things. Think of how it would work if we took it to its logical conclusion in criminal law. It implies that since in all cases in which a defendant is deterred from a crime merely by the prospect of punishment (that is, he is doing what he is doing primarily on account of the law), he could be held liable as though he had actually committed the crime—obviously an intolerable outcome. (There are some fixes for this problem that have been tried, but none of them work very well.)

The Letter-versus-Spirit Approach

A court using the letter-versus-spirit approach asks whether a given stratagem subverts the spirit, purpose, or rationale of the law, and if it does it will be struck down. The first worry most people have about it is that it seems to get us too far away from the literal wording of a statute, something that always makes lawyers uneasy. But the problems with this approach go much deeper. Let's see what happens when we actually try to apply it. Take the couple that relocates for an easier divorce. Is it against the spirit of the abandoned state's divorce law to let them get an easy divorce by moving out? In a way it is: the law was surely not meant to encourage people to emigrate to obtain a divorce. On the other hand, the state has no desire to regulate the divorces of people other than its citizens or residents. If the emigrating couple, then, has really stopped being either citizens or residents, would it really be consistent with the spirit of the law to continue to try to control what they do? The spirit-versus-letter approach is starting to look rather unhelpful. We run into the same sort of questions with every one of the stratagems on our menu of test cases.

Given such difficulties, why have these three approaches held such sway since time immemorial? The answer is that they are based on an extremely persuasive underlying theory of loopholes, which I will spell out in the next section, and the deeper difficulties of which I hope to lay bare.

The Deeper Logic behind What the Courts Have Done: The Mismatch Theory

The best way to get at the theory implicit in the courts' approach to these cases is to ask how judges would be inclined to answer the three questions with which I began: Why is the law riddled with loopholes? Why do they persist even after they have been identified? And what should lawyers do about them—ignore them, exploit them, or something else?

The deeper logic behind the courts' position is basically an appeal to the unavoidable imperfection of all human creations. Legal rules, whether created by legislation or common law, are doomed to be over- and under-inclusive with respect to their true rationales. Type 1 and type 2 errors are what two commentators have aptly called these two kinds of mismatches between a rule and its underlying purpose, borrowing a leaf from statistics.[8] If they were asked to name the reasons for this mismatch, they would probably name two: limited foresight and limited hindsight. Limited foresight means that it is impossible for the rule maker to anticipate all situations in which the rule might have to be applied in the future. Limited hindsight means that, even where one is able to anticipate such situations in theory, it might be hard to determine when one is actually encountering them in practice. Consider the asylum seeker. Even if the drafters of our asylum law correctly anticipated the possibility of a strategic dissident who only speaks as he does in hopes of winning quick and permanent residence in this country and tried to exclude him, it would be extremely hard to determine whether that is who we are dealing with in any given case. In short, the answer provided by this mismatch theory of loopholes to my first two questions is this: loopholes both arise and persist because of the rule makers' unavoidably limited foresight and hindsight.

How do I know that this is the theory implicit in what the courts are doing? Because the methods they have designed to cope with them are most easily explained by presupposing it. Each of the three approaches that courts have relied on seems designed to frustrate those who look as though they are trying to take advantage of the inherent imperfections of rule creation. Start with the person who engages in transactions that look like one thing but really are another. He seems to be taking advantage of the rule's inadequate specification of the essential attributes of the thing being regulated. The form-versus-substance approach seems designed to catch that kind of actor. Then there is the person who is trying to take advantage of the fact that the law has failed to block off some particularly circuitous access route to his forbidden desired end. The intent-to-evade approach seems designed to catch this kind of actor. Finally, there is the person who is not pretending to be doing anything other than what he is doing and who is not obviously doing what he is doing only on account of the law but who nevertheless seems to be attaining an end the law meant to frustrate. The spirit-versus-letter approach seems designed to catch this last kind of actor.

This brings us to the third of my questions about loopholes: how, according to this traditional view of loopholes, should lawyers behave with regard to them? Fundamentally, on this conception of loopholes, the lawyer's strategic use of them is to be frowned upon. As the tax scholar David Weisbach puts it, referring specifically to tax shelters: "There is no social benefit in tax planning. . . . [T]ax planning, all tax planning, not just planning associated with traditional notions of shelter, produces nothing of value. . . . No new medicines are found, computer chips designed, or homeless housed through tax planning." Weisbach then adds an important twist to this traditional line of argument. Tax planning, he says, is not merely of no social benefit, it is "worse than worthless." Consider, he says, "a silly but instructive example. Suppose a clever lawyer invents a new shelter called the back-flip shelter. Under this shelter, if you successfully perform a back-flip, you get 10 percent off your taxes. (A back-flip is pretty straightforward compared to many shelters.) For each individual, attempting the back-flip is a good idea—the cost of the back-flip is well less than the taxes saved. But even though each individual may have a strong incentive to do gymnastics, society is worse off. If everyone manages the back-flip," and manages to get 10 percent off his taxes, the government will then have to raise the tax rate to make up for the 10 percent of its revenue it has lost. As a result, when all is said and done, "everyone's taxes are exactly the same with and without the back-flip shelter, except that with the back-flip, normal taxes are higher and are then reduced by the tax gymnastics." But although everyone is back to paying the same taxes as before, they are nevertheless worse off *because now they have to perform a back-flip in addition to paying those taxes.*[9]

But there are different schools of thought about what exactly this means for how the law should treat, and how morality should assess, the loophole-exploiting lawyers, even if they are universally frowned upon. Some view it as exclusively the province of the legislature to minimize loopholes (by drafting laws more carefully, or by adding an antievasion rule that codifies the "intent-to-evade" test mentioned earlier). Thus they consider it a legitimate exercise of the lawyer's craft to try to squeeze through those loopholes until the legislature has succeeded in eliminating them.

This makes little sense to others. We are all interested in the creation of a well-functioning system of fair rules, they say. Loophole exploitation frustrates that effort. So why hesitate to discourage lawyers from engaging in it? Do not be taken in, they add, by an unconscious but completely inapt analogy to a conventional free market in which we can expect an invisible hand to channel all selfish activities into an optimal outcome. If we are concerned about loopholes, then in addition to trying to close them as best we can, we should discourage lawyers from making use of them.

The Root Causes of the Mismatch

So what, if anything, is wrong with the mismatch theory? I do, after all, call this chapter "The Irresistible Wrong Answer." I will get to that in the next chapter. But before doing so, let me point out what is right about it. What is right about it is that rules really do tend to be over- and underinclusive, either overshooting or undershooting the goal they were meant to reach. What is also right about it is that the gap between the goal and the rule at times creates opportunities for clever lawyers and their clients to get away with things the law would rather they did not. I have no doubt that some loophole-exploiting behavior is really of this kind. One question this naturally raises is why there has to be such a gap. To be sure, when a law is first written, it is easy to understand how limited foresight might give rise to it: it's hard to guess in advance all that might go wrong with the rule. But then why wouldn't improvements over time shrink or eliminate the gap? Things aren't that different with what I called the problem of limited hindsight—the difficulty of distinguishing the sincere from the "strategic" political refugee, for instance—because here too it seems as though with time and experience we would get better at alleviating, perhaps even eliminating, the gap that limited hindsight creates.

Only recently has the near-tragic inevitability of the gap between rules and their underlying goals been properly understood, largely as a result of the deeply insightful work of three legal scholars, Fred Schauer, Larry Alexander, and Emily Sherwin (much of it contained in two ingenious books, *Playing by the Rules* by Schauer and *The Rule of Rules* by Alexander and Sherwin).[10] A simple, if contrived, example will work best to convey the gist of their insight. Suppose a friend of mine has been accused of murder. The evidence against him is overwhelming. I have little doubt that he will be convicted as things now stand. However, I have known the defendant since childhood. I have no doubt whatsoever that he is innocent and the victim of either bad luck or a frame-up but that in any event he could not possibly have committed what he is charged with. How do I know that? Just because I know his personality and background, not because I have access to some tangible piece of evidence that contradicts the mountain of evidence the prosecution has assembled against him. You may wonder how I can be so sure, given that mountain of evidence. Let's say we take it as a given. Just imagine a case (surely such a case is not logically impossible) in which it is reasonable for me to be so sure. Anyone in my position, let us stipulate, would feel the same way. If I could testify in his behalf and convince the jury that any reasonable person with my knowledge of his character would believe him innocent, he would be exonerated. But it is in the nature of the situation that I am unable to do that. Whatever I say will be largely disregarded because I am known to be this close friend and because all I can offer is my general familiarity with his character. There are no concrete things about him that I can lay out for the jury so as to convince them of what I, however reasonably, am convinced of.

My friend will be convicted and probably executed, given the look of things. And so I decide to do something drastic—to perjure myself in his behalf. I invent a persuasive alibi and manage to testify about it so compellingly that the jury acquits him. So far, so good. After he has been acquitted, more evidence comes to light. It demonstrates that he is indeed innocent, but it also reveals the alibi I testified about to be the complete fabrication it was. The authorities do not take kindly to this discovery, and in due course I am prosecuted for perjury. I plead the defense of necessity: it is true, I admit, that I lied, but the lie was for a larger purpose. I needed to save an innocent person's life. A lie for a life—is that not exactly what the defense of necessity was intended for?[11]

Should I be convicted? To see the problem with letting me go, let us generalize the approach I am advocating somewhat. That is, let us suppose that we adopt a general policy that whenever someone reasonably thinks that by perjuring himself he will promote rather than hinder the cause of justice, he is entitled to do so and may then invoke the necessity defense. If we allow this to become the general practice, judges and juries listening to testimony will have additional reasons, beyond those they already have, for distrusting *all* testimony: they will have to take into account the possibility that even someone whom they would ordinarily find trustworthy might well be testifying as he is only because under the circumstances as they (reasonably) appear to him, he is promoting rather than hindering the cause of justice. The result will be less accurate fact-finding and more erroneous verdicts: more erroneous acquittals and more erroneous convictions.

What we have here is a genuinely tragic situation. Surely I am doing the right thing trying to save my friend by lying in his behalf. Surely too the legislature is doing the right thing by making perjury punishable, necessity or no necessity, because that maximizes the accuracy of verdicts and in the long run minimizes the number of erroneous convictions and executions, as well as erroneous acquittals. This awkward relationship between the rule and the situation to which it is being applied is an unavoidable result of trying to bring about the best outcome in most cases.

The larger difficulty here is stated by Larry Alexander thus: *"There is an always-possible gap between what we have reason to do, all things considered . . . and what we have reason to have our rules (and the officials who promulgate and enforce them) require us to do."*[12] We have good reason to adopt an unyielding, exceptionless rule against perjury. But we also have good reason, when the occasion arises, to try to commit perjury anyway. Such a gap can be found with absolutely every rule.[13]

It will not be immediately evident how the theory of the gap relates to loopholes. But the connection will quickly become apparent once we think about something like consumer protection legislation. More specifically, consider the case of the door-to-door salesman. Consumer protection law has put in place a variety of devices by which to insulate customers against undue pressure from door-to-door salespeople. The idea, of course, is to ensure meaningful consent. To that end, door-to-door sales are typically deemed revocable for three days. The salesman is required to give each customer a stack of documents containing elaborate disclosures, warnings, and statements and restatements of the customer's rights, all printed in specifically prescribed print sizes, and dozens of other precautions of this sort. Now consider a customer who is neither pressured nor deceived, who consents, and who does not use his three-day rescission period to revoke. Later on he tries to wriggle out of the deal by pointing out that the disclosure forms he was given employed a somewhat smaller print size than required. The law frequently provides that this kind of defect is actually grounds for invalidating the deal, at the discretion of the consumer. This is a kind of loophole. The law was meant to protect unsophisticated consumers. It does not make an exception for sophisticated consumers because case-by-case adjudication is likely to get this wrong more often than right. The salesman here is in the position of the witness who perjures himself. The law punishes him (by invalidating the transaction) unjustly in the interest of minimizing more frequent injustices against future customers, and future salesmen, down the road.

In sum, if we were to rewrite the answers the mismatch theory gives to the loophole problem in light of the argument about the inevitable gap between a rule and its underlying purpose, they would go as follows:

(1) Why are there loopholes? Because "there is an always-possible gap between what we have reason to do, all things considered . . . , and what we have reason to have our rules (and the officials who promulgate and enforce them) require us to do." As applied to loopholes, this means we have reason to allow categorically and in advance, when the law is passed, something we have far less or no reason to allow at the moment at which someone is about to take advantage of it. We have reason to pass a law that risks letting sophisticated consumers take advantage of consumer protection laws to get out of promises they should keep. But we have less reason to let a consumer take advantage of that law in a specific case.

(2) Why, once detected, do loopholes go uncorrected? Since we have little reason to let a sophisticated consumer take advantage of consumer protection law in a given case, his doing so constitutes loophole exploitation. But since at the same time we have ample reason to pass a law that risks creating situations in which this might happen, we feel that we cannot do anything to correct the loophole.

(3) And how, under the circumstances, should we feel about the lawyerly exploitation of loopholes? Under this approach, the lawyer's use of loopholes is somewhat akin to the diplomat using diplomatic immunity to get away with parking violations or even more serious infractions and is thus to be deplored, but nothing more than moral disapproval, and maybe sporadic case-by-case intervention of the courts in the most extreme instances, is probably appropriate, for the same reasons that caused the loophole to be created in the first place.

Taking Stock

There is no doubt that rules are over- and underinclusive, and only with the benefit of the work of Alexander, Schauer, and Sherwin can we clearly see why that is inevitably so. That in and of itself is an important fact worth noting about rules. But are we allowed to take the next step and conclude that what we have here is a theory of loopholes, that this inevitable gap is what lawyers exploit when they engage in loophole-exploiting behavior. It seems terribly tempting (though not, interestingly, a step that Schauer, Alexander, and Sherwin urge us to take), and no doubt it accounts for some loopholes. It is hard to see how it could *not* to be true. And yet, as we are about to see, it really isn't.

CHAPTER SIX

What Is Wrong with the Irresistible Answer?

There are four basic problems with the mismatch theory. In this chapter we will encounter three of those. The fourth and most fundamental one I postpone till the next chapter—because it is more than a problem. It will actually point us toward what I believe to be the real solution to the loophole conundrum. The four problems I am about to lay out have the same general character: they are in the nature of counterexamples to the mismatch theory. They are phenomena that one should expect the mismatch theory to be able to explain if it really worked but that, as we shall quickly see, it manifestly can't explain.

The First Counterexample: Evading God

Perhaps the most immediately compelling counterexample to the mismatch theory is the way the devout treat religious commandments. They circumvent them with a brazenness that would put the most aggressively loophole-exploiting lawyer to shame. Indeed Jesuitic and Talmudic reasoning are famous for the ways in which they seem to offer legalistic-looking shortcuts for complying with divine commandments with a minimum of inconvenience and sacrifice. To circumvent God's prohibition on the lending of money, the Jesuits recommend something called a "Mohatra contract," under which the would-be lender buys something from the would-be borrower and sells it back after a predetermined time for a predetermined price somewhat in excess of the one at which he bought it. The "profit" in this transaction is of course the functional equivalent of the interest rate, and the "something" that the lender temporarily buys is the functional equivalent of collateral. To circumvent the prohibition against dueling, the Jesuits recommend contriving to create a situation of self-defense: let your opponent know that you will be taking a stroll to a certain location at a certain hour. When you then encounter him there at the appointed time and you see him take position for the planned fight, your participation in the duel has become nothing more than self-defense. Talmudic scholars recommend that to circumvent God's prohibition on operating a business or even performing such a minimal task as turning on a light on Shabbat, Jews hire a gentile (the "Shabbes goy") to perform that task for them. The literature setting out and elaborating on such recommendations is no small part of a theological library.[1]

The mismatch theory cannot make sense of these religious ruses. If the mismatch theory is right, what devout believers are doing involves nothing less than taking advantage of God's failure to give a sufficiently airtight statement of his commandments. But that is clearly not what the devout see themselves as doing. Now, you might say that the mismatch theory never claimed to explain anything other than the law. But therein lies its problem. If one sees a phenomenon that resembles something that goes on in the law to a T, then it seems plausible to think that it is the same sort of phenomenon and that any explanation for that phenomenon within the law should also apply outside of law. And that is quite clearly not true of the mismatch theory.

The Second Counterexample: Evading Tyranny

Loophole exploitation also flourishes in another unexpected realm—dictatorial regimes. Subverting the ruler's orders by seemingly obeying them but actually undermining them in subtle ways, though often in plain sight, is one the oldest forms of successful risk-minimizing resistance. All this is beautifully illustrated in two books by the anthropologist James C. Scott, *Weapons of the Weak* and *Domination and the Arts of Resistance*.[2] One of his more striking examples involves a protest action by the Polish antigovernment union Solidarnosc:

> In 1983, following General Wojciech Jaruzelski's declaration of martial law aimed at suppressing the independent trade union Solidarnosc, supporters of the union in the city of Lodz developed a unique form of cautious protest.

They decided that in order to demonstrate their disdain for the lies propagated by the official government television news, they would all take a daily promenade timed to coincide exactly with the broadcast, wearing their hats backwards. Soon, much of the town had joined them. Officials of the regime knew, of course, the purpose of this mass promenade, which had become a powerful and heartening symbol for regime opponents. It was not illegal, however, to take a walk at this time of day even if huge numbers did it with an obvious political purpose in mind. By manipulating a realm of ordinary activity that was open to them and coding it with political meaning, the supporters of Solidarity "demonstrated" against the regime in a fashion that was awkward for the regime to suppress.[3]

In a similar vein, there is a story about the former East Germany (not recounted by Scott). In 1988 a group of East German high school students tried to find a way of protesting against East German militarism without incurring the usual penalties associated with such gestures. After a careful search through East Germany's official army newspaper they found an embarrassingly bad poem titled "Love Song to My Kalashnikov Machine Gun" and posted it on the school's bulletin board, adding the coy caption "A poem which has impressed us deeply and given us much food for thought."[4]

These episodes make no sense under the mismatch theory. Since a dictatorship is not bound by the rule of law—since it does not matter that the rule drafted technically does not encompass the conduct the defendant engaged in—why should it be possible to get around the commandment in this way? And yet it is. Something else must be going on. To be sure, one might argue that the dissenting behavior was just too ambiguous to safely distinguish supporters from opponents or that it was not clear whether it is worth the effort required to suppress it. But that seems not quite satisfactory. If the mismatch theory were right, one would expect to see much less circumvention of law under a dictatorship than one does.

The Third Counterexample: Evading the Guilty Conscience

Like everyone else, when I want to deceive someone, I find it much easier to mislead than to lie. I have of course done both, but given the choice, I prefer indirection to outright mendacity. It's not that I fear legal liability and think that this is a good way to avoid it—unlike the defendant in a famous perjury case, who, when asked whether he had a bank account in Switzerland, said "My company does," thus leading opposing counsel to erroneously infer that he did not have one, when really he did. In this way, he in fact successfully avoided being convicted of perjury, but the situations in which I try deceive people carry no risk of legal liability. It is just that I am much less likely to get a bad conscience from being misleading than from telling lies.[5]

The reason this humdrum fact about deception seems worth contemplating is that it poses a further challenge for the mismatch theory of loopholes. When I mislead, rather than lie, I am engaged in a legalistic-looking stratagem, but there is no law that I am anxiously trying to circumvent. There is no legislature that somehow drafted the rule against deception in an underinclusive way, allowing me to take advantage of the gap between the letter and the spirit of the rule. I do what I do because it eases my conscience. In other words, I am once again engaged in something that resembles loophole exploitation to a T, but it couldn't possibly be explained by the mismatch theory.

Lying by indirection is of course just one example of what looks like loophole exploitation in everyday life. I might prefer to break up with my lover by provoking a quarrel that causes her to do the breaking up, even though it is perfectly transparent what I am doing. Or I might willfully shut my eyes to a needy bystander who is suffering some kind of emergency rather than openly decline to help, even though it may be quite obvious to both of us what I am doing. In none of these situations am I trying to get around a rule that someone wrote in an underinclusive way. I do what I do because it eases my conscience. This too is not something the mismatch theory can make sense of.

That is not to say that what is going on here is inexplicable. What explains it is something that has nothing to do with the mismatch theory— namely the nonconsequentialist character of everyday morality. To see what I mean will require a brief explanation—for many readers just a reminder—of what I mean when I call everyday morality nonconsequentialist. There are two fundamentally different views of morality prevalent among moral philosophers, legal theorists, and others who have occasion to think about these matters: the consequentialist (basically utilitarian) view and the nonconsequentialist (often called nonutilitarian, or deontological, or rights-based, or fairness-based) view. The consequentialist view holds that we ought generally to do what will bring about the best consequences. (Sophisticated, contemporary forms of consequentialism are actually worlds apart from traditional nineteenth-century utilitarianism because the kinds of consequences that are to be maximized do not merely consist in the maximization of overall utility. Whatever it is that we think is important might count as a desirable consequence.) What has always troubled critics of consequentialism is the possibility that under such a view we might be called upon to do unspeakable things to a few people because that would bring about wonderful benefits to many more people in the long run. It is the kind of worry familiarly illustrated by cases in which we could, by torturing a terrorist's child, force him to reveal where he hid a bomb that might blow up a building full of people, or in which we could, by killing an innocent prisoner, prevent a lynch mob from killing many more people in the course of a riot, or in which we could, by killing an uninvolved bystander, provide many more people with necessary life-saving organ transplants. This criticism is often expressed with the slogan about the ends not justifying the means.

Everyday morality appears decidedly nonconsequentialist. Rightly or wrongly, most people are viscerally outraged by, or at least cannot contemplate engaging in, these kinds of trade-offs. They really do not believe that sufficiently important ends can justify the use of any given means. There is a kind of corollary to this slogan about means and ends that most of us generally don't reflect on, though it follows pretty directly. To say that the ends don't justify the means is of course just another way of saying that means matter greatly, not just ends. We judge conduct both by the means used and the ends attained. But that implies that sometimes the same end if attained by one set of means might be permissible and if attained by another end might not. In other words, if we find we can't achieve a certain end by one means, without being very immoral, we might well be able to do so by another means. Let's make this more concrete. While a friend of mine is standing in line to buy a movie ticket, I suddenly see someone from across the street aim a heavy rock at him. I quickly try to think of a way to save him. It occurs to me that I could drag the person standing in front of him into the path of the rock, thus saving my friend, though probably killing that innocent bystander. It next occurs to me that if I did that I would be guilty of murdering the bystander. Finally, however, it also occurs to me that there is a much simpler way of protecting my friend that will not get me into trouble: simply pull him out of the way. The person in front of him would still be hit, and presumably killed, by the rock, I realize, but I surely could not be blamed for *that*. Here we have a case in which the end of saving my friend seemed at first morally off limits, but a change of means—from what is sometimes called a "shielding" maneuver to a "ducking" maneuver—rendered it morally acceptable.[6]

Although the possibility of this kind of maneuver is really an inevitable logical corollary of the means-ends slogan, it is not something people feel comfortable endorsing, and they will often reject it if asked about it. There is nothing terribly surprising about people rejecting the logical consequences of something they profess to believe in. Logical inconsistency in our beliefs is, if anything, less remarkable than consistency. What is remarkable, however, is that although most of us would reject the corollary, we in fact act perfectly consistently with it. In other words, our behavior is more logically consistent than our stated beliefs, which is somewhat atypical. Usually it is the other way around. The kind of maneuver I just described, exploiting the means-ends slogan by altering the means to get to seemingly forbidden ends, is something we routinely do in everyday life: the stratagems I described involving lying by indirection, precipitating a breakup rather than breaking up outright, or willfully blinding oneself to another person's emergency are all examples of this sort. Recognizing that something can't be done in one way, we find another way, and our conscience is eased.

It is this corollary of the means-ends slogan that lies behind the kind of everyday behavior that resembles loophole exploitation in the law. The corollary evidently has nothing remotely to do with the mismatch theory. And that surely counts as a further significant strike against that theory.[7]

Taking Stock

We have encountered three formidable counterexamples to the mismatch theory—three types of phenomena outside the law that closely resemble loophole exploitation, which one would expect to be accounted for by whatever theory explains loophole exploitation within the law, but which the mismatch theory is at a loss to explain: evasion of religious rules, evasion of law in totalitarian regimes, and evasion of the principles of everyday morality. So we must look for a better answer to the loophole problem. My fourth and final counterexample to the mismatch theory—yet another type of loophole exploitation that it cannot explain—will actually point us in the direction of such an answer.

CHAPTER SEVEN

The Voting Analogy

Majority Rule and the Killer Amendment

The most potent class of counterexamples to the mismatch theory involves the exploitation of apparent loopholes in one particular subset of rules—the rules of voting. Here is an example.

Some time ago a certain law school was facing a problem with professors who kept missing the deadline for turning in their graded exams. When this problem had reached crisis proportions, someone made a dramatic proposal for dealing with it—a $100-a-day late fee. The proposal had to be approved by a majority of the faculty. There was little doubt that it would be approved, since a straw poll had shown that two-thirds of all faculty members supported it. There was, however, a small but determined opposition. K., who was part of this group, thought of a way to derail the majority's plan. To this purpose, he put forth what will seem to those not already familiar with this sort of thing a somewhat odd amendment to the proposal. He suggested that the proposed penalty be increased from $100 to $1,000. The amendment was put to a vote and it passed: the amended proposal now put a $1,000-per-day penalty on late graders. But when the amended proposal was then put to a final vote, it was rejected, and not just by a slim margin. Almost two-thirds of the faculty voted against it. What had happened? (For those not familiar with parliamentary procedure, I should point out that when someone proposes an amendment to an existing proposal, and that amendment is then voted on favorably, that does not mean that the amended proposal has now been adopted. It means that the amended proposal rather than the original one, will be put up for a final vote. In other words, the faculty was going to vote on the $100 penalty to begin with. K. then suggested substituting his own proposal for a $1,000 penalty in its stead. That suggestion was put up for a vote, and when a majority supported it, that meant that the $1,000 proposal, instead of the original $100 proposal, would now be put before the faculty to vote for or against.)

Conversations with his colleagues prior to the vote had convinced K. that the faculty fell into three roughly equally large groups. First, there was a group he thought of as the Radicals. They desperately wanted action to be taken on this matter, the more drastic the better. They approved of the $100 penalty but would have been even more enthusiastic about a $1,000 penalty. Then there was another group, the Moderates. The Moderates liked the $100 penalty but would never support something as severe as a $1,000 penalty. Finally, there were the Conservatives, who would most have liked to preserve the status quo. But in conversation with the Conservatives, K. discovered that they had a certain radical streak: if action were taken, they all felt, it should be very decisive action. If a penalty were imposed, it would be better for it to be $1,000 rather than $100. Among other things, they thought, that would mean that the penalty would not constantly have to be changed as rising salaries and inflation eroded its severity. K.'s list of the preferences of the various groups is shown in the table below.

	1st preference	2d preference	3d preference
Radicals	$1,000/day	$100/day	status quo
Moderates	$100/day	status quo	$1,000/day
Conservatives	status quo	$1,000/day	$100/day

When K. proposed to amend the $100/day proposal and change it to $1,000/day, he was therefore supported by the Radicals and by the Conservatives, and the amendment passed. Then the amended proposal was put up for a vote, and the joint opposition of the Moderates and the Conservatives killed it, which is what K. had been scheming to achieve.

What K. did here is a perfectly commonplace maneuver in parliamentary settings. It happens all the time when a bill is proposed that a majority supports but a determined opponent manages to kill with a killer amendment: an amendment that will garner enough support to be attached to the bill but will result in depriving the bill of its majority support.

The proposal of a killer amendment looks like the exploitation of a loophole. The law faculty started out with a rather clear indication of its wishes—two-thirds favored the $100 penalty proposal—but by some trickery K. managed to prevent the group from getting its wish. That at least is one way of looking at the matter (not the only one, but we will get to that).

Closing the Loopholes in Voting Rules: The Discoveries of Borda, Condorcet, and Arrow

Can such loopholes be closed? That requires us to first be clear about what gives rise to them. I mentioned in the introduction the so-called voting paradox discovered by the eighteenth-century French mathematician Jean de Borda, namely the possibility that in an election a majority might support candidate Bertrand over candidate Cecil, and Candidate Alain over Candidate Bertrand, and yet a majority would also support, not as one would hope, Alain over Cecil, but Cecil over Alain. The situation exploited by K. is perfectly analogous. A majority prefers the $1,000 penalty to the $100 penalty (which is why the amendment passed), and a majority prefers the status quo to the $1,000 penalty (which is why the amended proposal failed), yet a majority would prefer the $100 penalty over the status quo, which is of course what makes things so perverse. This intransitivity allows one to achieve whatever one wants, as long as one can influence the order in which the votes are taken. In other words, by making sure that the undesired possibilities ($100 and $1,000) are first matched against each other and that the winner is then matched against the desired outcome and no further votes are taken, you can guarantee that your choice prevails. This is what K. managed to do. The quick answer to the question of whether this kind of loophole can be closed is thus that it can't be done as long as we stick with majority voting. Given the intransitivity of majority voting, a clever parliamentarian will—under the right circumstances—be able to get his way by stirring something like a killer amendment into the mix and making sure that the alternatives under discussion are voted on in the requisite order.

But can the loophole be closed by switching to a different system? When Borda first noticed that majority voting could be become intransitive, he proposed what he thought was a perfect solution. His system required each voter to rank all available alternatives; those rankings would then be averaged and a final ranking obtained. In other words, if voter 1 ranks candidate A first, voter 2 ranks him second, and voter 3 ranks him third, then the average ranking of candidate A would be 2. This method does not suffer from the intransitivity problem, and the trick that K. played on his faculty would therefore not be possible.

Unfortunately, as was soon recognized, Borda's method is vulnerable to a stratagem not all that different from the killer amendment. Again, suppose the electorate has three candidates to choose from: Alain, Bertrand, and Cecil. Out of one hundred voters, let us suppose that forty would rank Cecil first, Bertrand second, and Alain last. Another thirty would rank Alain first, Cecil second, and Bertrand last. The remaining thirty would rank Bertrand first, Alain second, and Cecil last. Do the math, and you will find that that gives the highest average rank to Cecil (with an average rank of 1.9), the second highest to Bertrand (with an average rank of 2), and the third highest to Alain (with an average rank of 2.1).[1] So far, so good. Where things get interesting is if we ask what would happen if the academy suddenly learned that they made a mistake about Bertrand: the work he is most renowned for, is in fact mistakenly attributed to him. Let us suppose that as a result of this news, every voter would now put Bertrand at the bottom of his list. Not surprisingly, that will mean that Bertrand will now end up with the worst possible ranking. What is surprising, however, is what all of this does to the relative ranking of Cecil and Alain. If we redo our calculations, in light of the voters' changed preferences, we suddenly find that Alain has the highest ranking and Cecil second highest. Somehow Bertrand's worse showing has served to confer an advantage on Alain. How utterly bizarre: why should the relative fortunes of Alain and Cecil be affected by new information having to do only with Bertrand?

This sort of thing turns out not merely to be a problem with Borda's method, but to afflict innumerable other, seemingly reasonable voting methods. Donald Saari, a prominent mathematician and social choice theorist, offers a striking illustration of how this problem keeps turning up in the most unexpected places—in this case the world figure-skating championship in Birmingham, England. Figure skating is judged by a panel of judges, whose ratings of the skaters in several different categories are combined by a complicated scoring system into an overall ranking. After all but one skater had had their turns, the American Nicole Bobek was ranked second and seemed virtually assured of a silver medal. In third place was a French skater, Surya Bonaly. The last skater to perform was the American Michelle Kwan. Kwan's performance, stronger than anyone had expected, put her in fourth place. Nothing strange about any of that. But Kwan's performance had a further effect as well. Under the scoring system being used, the rankings of Bobek and Bonaly suddenly, and to everyone's consternation, ended up being reversed. Bonaly was now in second place and Bobek in third. None of the judges had changed his votes. It was just an odd and unanticipated outcome of the way in which votes were combined that somehow, in the aftermath of Kwan's unexpectedly strong showing, Bonaly ended up being ranked ahead of Bobek. How completely bizarre. As Saari puts it, "Although delightful, what did Michelle Kwan have to do with the relative merits of Nicole Bobek and Surya Bonaly? Both had skated earlier than Kwan, and the judges had publicly expressed their evaluations of the two skaters' relative merits with irrevocable scores that were immediately flashed on TV sets across the world. What did Kwan's performance have to do with Bobek's and Bonaly's?"[2]

In the introduction to this book I told a joke used by voting theorists to drive home just how strange the kind of thing that happened in Birmingham really is. It's the joke about the man who goes into a restaurant and decides to order the chicken dish rather than the fish or the steak that are also offered. As he is about to order, the waitress mentions to him that the fish that day would not be such a good choice, not being all that fresh, whereupon he changes his mind and orders the steak instead. What happened in Birmingham comes pretty close to this: Having seen Bobek and Bonaly, the judges ranked the former ahead of the latter, while holding their judgment about Kwan in abeyance, pending her performance. Next, having seen Kwan perform, and having decided that she was neither as good as Bobek nor as good as Bonaly, they nevertheless changed their minds about the relative merits of Bobek and Bonaly. Well, of course they didn't really change their minds. The voting system they used only made it look as though they had changed their minds. But a voting system that creates such an appearance is pretty hard to accept. Most of all it is hard to accept the strategic implication this has: inasmuch as the collectivity's selection between chicken and steak is influenced by what they are told about fish, they can be maneuvered away from chicken and toward steak by introducing totally irrelevant information about fish. It means that someone who wants to derail the candidacy of Cecil, in favor of Alain, can do so by introducing seemingly irrelevant information about Bertrand. In other words, something very much like the killer amendment loophole is still with us.

Can one do better? That is the question a budding economist named Kenneth Arrow put to himself in the late 1940s. To put the matter slightly more precisely, he asked himself whether it is possible to come up with a halfway decent voting system that does not have this chicken-steak-and-fish problem. Of course he gave it a more dignified name. What he was looking for, he said, was a system in which the final outcome was "independent of irrelevant alternatives." By a halfway decent system he simply meant one that did not have the transitivity problem of majority voting and respected the unanimous wishes of the electorate, by which he meant that if every voter ranks alternative A ahead of alternative B, then the voting system as a whole should do the same. It is hard to see how a halfway decent voting system could possibly fail to do this. (Note that majority voting flunks both these conditions: it isn't transitive and, as we already saw, it will sometimes allow A to win out over B even if every single voter prefers B to A.) There is one more condition that a halfway decent voting system should meet, and it almost goes without saying: we want this to be a *collective* voting system—it can't be a dictatorship. Indeed it seems strange to even think of a dictatorship as a voting system, although in a technical sense it is, albeit one where the outcome simply reflects the wishes of one voter, the dictator.

This, then, was the objective: find a voting system that is transitive, respects unanimity, is no mere dictatorship, and is independent of irrelevant alternatives. That's a pretty modest set of demands to make on a voting system. Ideally one would want a lot more, but this is the rock-bottom minimum. The startling answer Arrow found was that this objective simply can't be achieved.

It will be worth our while to acquaint ourselves with the gist of Arrow's argument, because it can cast enormous light on the problem of legal loopholes. Understanding it will help us first to see why voting rules are subject to intractable loopholes and later on why other legal rules are as well. Arrow's argument has the reputation of being technical and inaccessible. But it is not actually technical in the way that most great quasi-mathematical insights are: no higher mathematics is required, only a willingness to think through an intricate, counterintuitive, and ingenious argument. Moreover, the essential core of the argument can in fact be made perfectly accessible by focusing on a radically simplified version of the problem. Still, readers who do not have the patience for the mildly off-putting intricacies that follow can skip ahead, since I will restate what I say here in several different forms later. It will help in understanding Arrow's argument if we transplant it into a very concrete setting—the choice the figure-skating judges have to make among the three contenders, Bobek, Bonaly, and Kwan.

To drastically simplify things, assume we have just two judges and three skaters and some system for combining their rankings that does not suffer from the inconsistencies of majority voting and that faithfully reflects the judges' unanimous choices (whenever they happen to be unanimous). Implicit in each ranking of the three skaters are three comparative judgments: Who is better between Bonaly and Bobek? Who is better between Bobek and Kwan? And who is better between Bonaly and Kwan? If both judges are to have some say in this (otherwise we have a dictatorship) then there must be at least some situations in which each judge gets his way over the disagreement of the other. This is crucial.

Let's begin by supposing that Judge A ranks Bonaly ahead of Kwan, whereas Judge B does the opposite. Let's suppose further that our voting system lets A have his way in this rather than B. What we have then are the following rankings:

Judge A: Bonaly, Kwan

Judge B: Kwan, Bonaly

Overall ranking: Bonaly, Kwan

Let's further suppose that Judge A ranks Bonaly ahead of Bobek, whereas Judge B does the reverse, ranking Bobek ahead of Bonaly. If each judge is to have some say in the overall outcome, then presumably we would like this time around to let Judge B have his way, so that we get the following set of rankings regarding Bonaly and Bobek:

Judge A: Bonaly, Bobek

Judge B: Bobek, Bonaly

Overall ranking: Bobek, Bonaly

If we then combine these two overall rankings, we get

Bobek, Bonaly, Kwan

So far, so good. But there is a problem lurking. I have not yet said anything about how A and B feel about Bobek compared with Kwan. Let's suppose they both agree that Kwan is better than Bobek. (In other words, Judge A ranks the three skaters Bonaly, Kwan, Bobek, and Judge B ranks them Kwan, Bobek, Bonaly.) If they both agree that Kwan is better than Bobek, how can we have an overall ranking that does the reverse? In other words, as it stands, the voting system has the unacceptable feature of sometimes contradicting the unanimous wishes of the judges.

Suppose then we tried to remedy things by adding a provision to the voting rule that says that whenever an outcome flies in the face of a unanimous preference of all voters, it is to be changed in accordance with those wishes. In other words, if both judges agree that Kwan is better than Bobek, then that has to be incorporated into the overall ranking. If we do just that and nothing else, however, we end up in a massive inconsistency: we will have said that Bobek is better than Bonaly (to accommodate Judge B's judgment) and that Bonaly is better than Kwan (to accommodate Judge A's judgment) and that Kwan is better than Bobek (to accommodate their unanimous judgments). But that's no ranking; that's a cycle.

Of course we don't necessarily run into such a cycle just because we are trying to accommodate the preferences of both A and B. We only got into the cycle because of the particular way in which A and B happened to rank the skaters. But that immediately suggests a way out of our predicament. Let A and B give their input just as they did before (A deciding between Bonaly and Kwan and B deciding between Bonaly and Bobek), but if their particular rankings happen to generate a cycle, then override the wishes of one of them to the extent necessary to restore consistency.

In other words, when we get into a cycle as we just did, we will disregard one of the three conflicting judgments to get out of the cycle. We will either disregard A's preference regarding Bonaly and Kwan or B's preference regarding Bonaly and Bobek. We only do this, however, if those preferences get us into trouble, not otherwise.

Which of the two skaters is ultimately affected will depend of course on whether we restore consistency by deleting one of A's judgments or one of B's judgments. To keep things simple and concrete, let's assume that we decide to reestablish consistency by disregarding B's preference of Bobek over Bonaly. The ultimate ranking will then be Bonaly, Kwan, Bobek.

Now notice that we only had to disregard B's preferences between Bonaly and Bobek because of the way B felt about Kwan relative to Bobek. If for instance he had thought Bobek better than Kwan, rather than the other way around, we would never have gotten into a cycle and we could have left both A's preference regarding Bonaly and Kwan and B's preference regarding Bobek and Kwan intact. It is only because of the way the two judges feel about Kwan that Bonaly ends up ahead of Bobek in the final outcome. If at least one of them had felt differently about Kwan, then Bobek would have ended up ahead of Bonaly.

In other words, we cannot help letting the two judges' feelings about Kwan influence the relative position of Bobek and Bonaly in the final outcome— which is just another way of saying that the relative ranking of Bobek and Bolany will depend on the (seemingly) irrelevant alternative called Kwan.

Even if one has followed along the argument step-by-step, it is still likely to seem puzzling. Let's put aside the figure-skating example and ask in a more general way, how it is that the final ranking of two alternatives, *a* and *b*, might end up being affected by the voters' feelings about a third alternative, c? Is there some more compact and intuitive way of capturing what is going on here? Let me try.

One way to think about a voting system is as a highly formalized compromise device: a way of achieving an accommodation between the divergent wishes of a group of voters, in this particular case just two. Now suppose that there are only two alternatives at issue, a and b, and the only thing required of the voting system is to rank either a ahead of b or b ahead of a. If we have only two alternatives and only two voters and one of them puts a ahead of b and the other does the reverse, then there isn't really much any voting rule can do except to opt for the wishes of one of the two voters. One of them necessarily has to end up being something of a dictator. Compromise under these kinds of circumstances just isn't to be had.

Next, let us add a further alternative, c, to the set of options. Now there are opportunities to be more equitable: one can let one voter have his way with regard to the relative ranking of a and b and make it up to the other voter by letting him have his way with regard to the relative ranking between c and one of the other alternatives. What kind of compromise makes the most sense will partly depend on exactly how the two voters feel about c relative to a and b. But *one can easily imagine the possibility that the kind of compromise that will make the most sense is to no longer let the voter who previously got his way with regard to* a *and* b *(when* c *was not around) continue to do so but make it up to him by letting him get more of his way with regard to the relative ranking of* c. *In this way, then,* c's *entering into the picture might well lead us to revise our original ranking of* a *and* b. Looked at in this way, the so-called irrelevant alternative makes a difference to the relative ranking of a and b because it actually *is* relevant. It just doesn't *look* relevant. Arrow's theorem can be interpreted as revealing that seemingly irrelevant alternatives really *are* relevant and that independence of them is neither to be had nor to be desired.

Arrow's theorem is not, in the first place, about the strategic exploitation of voting rules. The most important thing about it is obviously the surprising thing it tells us about collective decision making: that such decision making cannot satisfy the most rudimentary requirements of fairness and rationality that we might impose on it. But the most relevant thing for us are the implications it was soon discovered to have for what came to be called "voting manipulation": virtually all voting regimes are rife with possibilities of strategic exploitation. The fact that no reasonable voting regime satisfies the independence of irrelevant alternatives already goes some way toward showing this, since it establishes the universal possibility of influencing an election outcome by strategically introducing information about an irrelevant alternative and thereby influencing the relative ranking of other alternatives. But there was much more to come — a series of results that are often collectively referred to as the "Arrow impossibility theorems" (even though most of them were discovered by others inspired by Arrow's original contribution). The killer amendment is really only the beginning. The gamut of strategic opportunities is wide and afflicts nearly all voting methods.

Consider for instance a strange property of the Borda method of voting that I haven't touched on so far. Suppose we divide the electorate into two groups. All members of the first group make their rankings. We total them up by the Borda method, calculate the average rank of each candidate, and discover X to be the winner. We do the same thing for the second group and find that once again X is the winner. Now suppose we had not divided them up but instead simply taken the group as a whole, calculated each candidate's average rank, and then chosen the winner on that basis. *We might well find that the winner is someone other than X.* This sort of thing is not unique to the Borda method but common to many extremely appealing voting rules. The strategic implications are clear: you look at the outcome we would get if we divided the decision-making group into many subgroups, compare the outcome with the what we get if we do not, and then try to set things up to suit your preferences. In the political context, this is what's known as "gerrymandering."

Or consider a more general sort of finding about the possibilities of voting manipulation. Suppose we have an election among five candidates, whom the various members of the electorate rank in vastly different ways. Suppose we try to select the winner by a plurality vote and find it to be Candidate A. Next we try to select the winner by the Borda method and find it to be Candidate B. Next we try to select the winner by a plurality vote followed by a runoff among the two top vote getters and find the winner to be C. We try two other fairly appealing-looking methods and find the winner to be D with the first and E with the second. In other words, it is generally possible, for any given set of candidates and any fixed set of preferences, to find a method that generates whatever ranking we want. The actual outcome of the election is as much a function of the method used to count votes as of the preferences of the voters. By strategically choosing the right voting method, we can thus generate whatever outcome we want.[3]

The relevant upshot of this extended excursion into voting theory is short and simple: any voting regime that is even remotely appealing—in the sense of satisfying some very basic requirements of fairness and rationality—is vulnerable to manipulation. Manipulation of this sort seems to be yet another special instance of loophole exploitation.

How Voting Manipulation Further Undermines the Mismatch Theory

If we consider voting manipulation to be a form of loophole exploitation, it will represents a further challenge, and a particularly formidable one, to the mismatch theory, because the loopholes being exploited here have nothing to do with over- or underinclusiveness of voting rules. To see this more clearly, let us ask what would happen if we tried, for example, to apply the spirit-versus-letter test to a specific instance of voting manipulation. That is, what if one asked whether a particular instance of voting manipulation agrees with the letter but not the spirit of the voting rules that it tries to exploit? We would then in effect be asking whether voting manipulation frustrates the real wishes of the collectivity, as they would have been expressed by an *un*manipulated voting process, and whether it puts in its place something other than the collectivity's real wishes. Well, does it?

Consider again the killer amendment by which the proposed lateness penalty was derailed. Did the killer amendment prevent the collectivity's "real" wishes from being expressed? What were the collectivity's real wishes? Two-thirds of the faculty would have preferred the $100/day outcome over the status quo. That certainly makes it look as though it was being manipulated into sticking with the status quo when it did not really want it. On the other hand, if the $100/day alternative had in fact been chosen, two-thirds of the faculty would have preferred the $1,000/day outcome. And two-thirds preferred the actual outcome, the status quo, to the $1,000/day outcome. In other words, with regard to each outcome there is an alternative that a vast majority would prefer. K. had not brought about an outcome that was less representative of the wishes of the faculty than any other that might have prevailed. Each proposal therefore had as much or as little a claim to being considered the "real" wish of the collectivity as any other. In other words, K.'s behavior here, though clearly manipulative and of a loophole-exploiting sort—cannot really be described as somehow taking advantage of a divergence between the letter and the spirit of the voting rules.

What makes voting manipulation an especially potent counterexample to the mismatch theory is that this is a context that (a) involves legal rules (unlike my other counterexamples, which do not); (b) cannot possibly be made to fit with the mismatch theory, however much one is willing to stretch or bend it; and (c) can be persuasively explained by an alternative theory, the theory of social choice (i.e., Arrow's impossibility theorems and related results). In this specific context, we are actually able to answer completely the three questions with which I began part II:

1. Why does these kinds of loopholes arise? Because the Arrow impossibility theorems prove that all plausible voting rules are doomed to have them.
2. Why do these loopholes, once discovered, not get filled? Because voting rules that avoid them—simple dictatorships, for instance—are unacceptable on other grounds.
3. Is it all right to exploit this kind of loophole? Sure, since we are not in any way undercutting the "real" wishes of the collectivity by doing so. Indeed the political scientist William Riker views this sort of thing as an important parliamentary skill, no less respectable than artful rhetoric, and equally worthy of study and diligent practice. He even has a special name for it: heresthetics, defined as "structuring the world so you can win."

Not so fast, some readers will now say. Aren't there in fact some legal limits on voting manipulation? Aren't "gerrymandering" and "voting dilution" constant subjects of judicial critique and intervention? What about that whole branch of law dedicated to regulating voting rights? Doesn't that show that in fact voting manipulation is not freely tolerated?

The significance of voting rights law is easily misunderstood. Courts have indeed taken issue with certain ways in which legislatures have changed the voting process, especially by creating "safe" districts for incumbents. They did so in a series of somewhat controversial decisions based on the disputed meaning of the Voting Rights Act and a number of basic constitutional provisions. For our purposes all that matters is that none of these judicial interventions invalidate voting manipulation. They might invalidate a particular instance of it because of the particular result it produced because it greatly diminished the influence of a specific constituency, for instance. And even if the courts wanted to eliminate voting manipulation, that would be a little like outlawing gravity.[4]

Taking Stock

What we have done so far is to find a particular type of loophole exploitation—the manipulation of voting rules—that can only be explained as an outgrowth of Arrow's theorem and not by the mismatch theory. But does this help with loophole exploitation outside the voting context? Can one persuasively generalize from voting manipulation to the strategic gaming of other kinds of laws? That's what I will try to do in the next chapter.

CHAPTER EIGHT

Turning the Analogy into an Identity

Loophole Exploitation as Voting Manipulation

I noted in the introduction that Arrow's theorem and social choice theory
are not just about voting. They have relevance to decision making more
generally. Specifically, whenever decision making is multicriterial—that is,
when it attempts to synthesize a variety of criteria into a final choice—it
is doing something closely analogous to synthesizing the preferences of a
variety of voters into a final ranking. The application of legal rules can be
thought of as an instance of multicriterial decision making. It should thus
be possible to interpret a great deal of loophole exploitation as a variation
on voting manipulation.

What exactly does it mean to construe Arrow's theorem as a theorem
about multicriterial decision making? Let me remind you of what I said
about that in the introduction. There the task was to rank several cars that
differed from each other along a variety of dimensions: price, safety, looks.
Each car is ranked initially by price, then by safety, then by looks. We will
thus end up with three separate rankings that will have to be consolidated
into a master ranking. Most of the traditional voting rules can be turned
into devices for doing so. For instance, we might use the Borda rule: average, for each car, the rank it has under each of the relevant criteria, and
then obtain an overall ranking of all cars based on that average. Or we
might use the plurality method: rank the cars according to how many of
the criteria put it in first place. Or we might use the plurality method with
a runoff between the two top contenders, and so on. Everything we know
about the paradoxical properties of these methods would thus seem to
carry over to multicriterial decision making, including the ubiquitous opportunities for loophole exploitation.[1]

It is important, however, not to overlook some crucial differences between voting and multicriterial decision making. While they are similar, they are most definitely not the same. Criteria are not voters, and I am not just being literal minded when I say that. Voters have preferences, which they can change. Criteria aren't like that. They are fixed. It wouldn't make sense to talk about a criterion having changed its mind. Why does that matter? It matters because Arrow's theorem and its progeny, as originally formulated, *really only apply to voters who are capable of changing their minds*. Let's go back to the requirement of independence of irrelevant alternatives that plays such a crucial role in Arrow's theorem. The requirement tells us how a sensible voting rule should handle the situation in which voters change their minds about the relative ranking of alternative c vis-à-vis the other alternatives, a and b, while not changing their minds about a and b. More precisely, it tells us that as long as the voters don't change their minds about the relative ranking of a and b, that relative ranking should stay intact, regardless of how their preferences regarding c have changed. (In other words, as long as voters don't change their preferences between steak and chicken, the relative ranking of steak and chicken should stay the same, however much voters change their minds about where fish should rank in that hierarchy.) Since criteria can't really be said to ever change their minds about anything, it would seem as though Arrow's theorem doesn't actually apply to them.

But even though the original Arrow theorem does not apply, close analogues of it do, and that is true across the board of most of the results of social choice theory. They require some adaptation, but their essential logic carries over. Arrow himself proved a direct analogue of his original theorem for the multicriterial setting. To see how it works, let's go back to the problem of choosing among cars, having ranked them each according to price, safety, and looks. A sensible multicriterial decision-making method, Arrow says, should meet the following minimal requirements. First, it should not be intransitive. In other words, it can't be the case that the method ranks car a ahead of car b, car b ahead of car c, and car c ahead of car a. So far things are no different than in the original Arrow theorem. Second, the method should respect unanimity: if according to price, safety, and looks car a is better than car b, then the method should rank car a ahead of car b. Once again, things are exactly the same as in the original theorem. Third, the method should be genuinely *multi*criterial. It should not simply go by price or safety or looks while ignoring the other criteria. This of course is the direct analogue of the requirement that the voting method not be a simple dictatorship. We still haven't strayed too far from the original theorem. The fourth and final requirement Arrow would impose is that in deciding how to rank car *a* relative to car *b*, it should not matter whether car *c* is also on offer. To return to the old joke, if someone has decided to have chicken rather than steak or fish, it would be absurd if on being told that the restaurant was out of fish he changed his mind to steak. This is closely analogous but not the same as the original requirement of independence of irrelevant alternatives. (In terms of our joke, the original independence of irrelevant alternatives condition addressed the situation in which, having chosen chicken, you learn that the fish, which you did not choose, *while certainly available, is worse than you thought*, whereupon you choose the steak instead.) It is similar enough, though, that Arrow retained the same name for it. This new multicriterial version of the Arrow theorem then states that there is no method of multicriterial decision making that meets these extremely modest-sounding basic requirements. The proof of this multicriterial version of Arrow's theorem is closely analogous to the original.[2]

An immediate implication of the analogue version of Arrow's theorem is that the strategy of the killer amendment is going to be even more relevant in the context of multicriterial decision making than in the original voting context. If someone is apt to change his mind between chicken and steak depending on whether fish is also on the menu, then we can influence his choice by putting it on the menu or taking it off depending on what we want him to do. Moreover we can in general expect everyone to behave in this absurd-looking way, provided everyone is trying to avoid behaving in even more absurd-looking ways, such as violating the other, even more basic requirements of sensible decision making: transitivity, unanimity, and not sticking to just one criterion to the exclusion of all others.

In some ways, the multicriterial version of Arrow's theorem is even more startling than the original version. After all, it is one thing for a *collectivity* to behave in a way that we *would* judge irrational if an individual behaved that way. It is another for an individual to behave that way. And yet it turns out that we are all pretty much doomed to behave this way, not because of any special cognitive failings, but because the logic of the situation precludes anything else.

How does all of this apply to law and legal loopholes? Let's return to our menu of test cases.

Contrived Defenses

Consider again the case of the devious defendant who contrives to create a situation in which he can kill someone in self-defense—for instance by making sure that he has no acceptable escape routes available. He does this both to tempt his enemy to act and to be able to respond with deadly force rather than being obliged to retreat. (This essentially describes the conduct of the Charles Bronson character in *Death Wish*—going into Central Park in the middle of the night, hoping to be attacked and to get the chance to respond in kind.)

In thinking about this kind of case, let's begin with the ordinary, *uncontrived* version of this situation, in other words a normal case of self-defense. The defendant has been attacked. He has two feasible options: he can kill the attacker and save his own life, or he can not kill him and be killed himself. If we were to rank these in terms of permissibility, we would rank them both as equally permissible. Now let's alter the situation slightly. Let's suppose that the defendant has three options, the third option being an opportunity for an easy and safe retreat. If, once again, we were to rank these three options in terms of permissibility, we would put into the top rank (consisting of all permissible options) the option to retreat and the option to be killed; we would put into the bottom rank (consisting of the impermissible options) the option to kill instead. If we put it this way, we can see that the addition of the retreat option has altered the ordering of the two previous options: the option of being killed has stayed at the top, but the option to kill has moved to the bottom. In other words, we have here two options whose relative ranking depends on the presence or absence of a third. When we encountered this phenomenon before, as part of our consideration of choice procedures more generally, this is what we considered a violation of the principle of independence of irrelevant alternatives (as formulated in the multicriterial version of Arrow's theorem)—the principle that says that a man choosing between chicken and steak should not be influenced by the presence or absence of fish.

This third alternative—the retreat option—can be exploited by being deliberately removed or added to the set of available options. If the defendant makes sure well in advance that he will not have a retreat opportunity once the attack occurs, he will have put among the top (i.e., legal) options the right to kill the attacker.

The logic of Arrow's argument allows us to see why this sort of thing is inevitable. The doctrine of self-defense seeks to accommodate two different, somewhat conflicting principles, by allowing each some influence over the outcome under certain circumstances. The first I will call the principle of no disproportionate punishment. It reflects the idea that just because someone attacks another person, even if he does so with deadly force, he does not deserve to receive the death penalty. We would not ordinarily give someone the death penalty if he were being prosecuted for such an act, so naturally we hesitate to let his victim do the equivalent in self-defense. This hesitation is reflected in the way in which the principle of no disproportionate punishment would rank the available options. If the defendant is able to make a safe retreat, then under this principle the category of permissible actions would contain two of the three options: making a retreat and allowing oneself to be injured (or killed). The category of impermissible actions would contain the option of killing the attacker. But as I said, there is a second principle that the doctrine of self-defense tries to accommodate. Let's call this the rights principle, the principle that says that you have a right to stand on your rights and do whatever is necessary to forestall someone's interference with them. Under this principle, all three options—retreat, allowing oneself to be injured, and killing the attacker—are all permissible. The problem is that the principles conflict. They each impose a certain ranking on the options, and those rankings partly agree and partly disagree—a typical multicriterial decision-making problem. We ran into this problem in the voting context, in my truncated version of Arrow's proof. There the question was how to accommodate the wishes of two different figure-skating judges regarding the ranking of three skaters. We discovered there that if we simply let one of them control the ranking between two of the skaters and we let another control the ranking of another two, we occasionally ended up with a cycle. The compromise we were then forced to accept was to give one of the judges quasi-dictatorial control over the rankings whenever anything else would produce a cycle. But in those cases in which respecting both judges' preferences did not produce a cycle, the previously excluded judge would finally get to have some influence. Alas, such a compromise, we saw, immediately leads to a violation of the requirement of independence of irrelevant alternatives.

In connection with multicriterial decision making we can't exactly do the same, since principles never change their preferences, but we can do something analogous: we can let each principle have its way depending on which of the options under consideration are in fact available. And this is exactly what the law does: the law follows the principle of no disproportionate punishment when all three possible options—retreating, allowing oneself to be injured, killing one's attackers—are available, and it follows the rights principle when only two of them—allowing oneself to be injured or killing one's attacker—are available. Once again, that entails a violation of the independence of irrelevant alternatives: how two things are ranked—namely the option to allow to oneself to be injured and the option of killing one's attacker—now necessarily depends on the presence or absence of a third "irrelevant" alternative, namely the option of retreat. This then produces a loophole in homicide law: the opportunity to "contrive" a defense by removing the retreat option.

Up to a point, what I am saying about self-defense is of course perfectly obvious and uncontroversial. There is nothing new in the observation that if someone eliminates his access to certain benefits, he might force us, as a matter of law and morality, to be more generous with him than we otherwise would feel compelled to be.[3] But what is not usually noticed is that this is but a special instance of a dependence on an irrelevant alternative, or that it arises out of the multicriterial character of the decision-making situation. Once we think of it that way, we are then bound to appreciate how impossible it will be to eliminate this loophole or to object to its exploitation.

It might be hard at first to accept that what we have here really is a proper analogue to the kind of voting manipulation in which an outcome is influenced by injecting an irrelevant alternative of the killer amendment variety. After all, the retreat option hardly looks like an irrelevant alternative. The availability of retreat seems highly relevant to the question of whether killing the attacker should be part of the victim's menu of permissible options. But it is important not to get hung up on the literal meaning of the term "irrelevant alternative." As I noted before, one way of putting Arrow's theorem is to say that it shows that seemingly irrelevant alternatives really are not—that in any even moderately rational multicriterial decision-making process seemingly irrelevant alternatives will prove to be extremely relevant. The same is true in the contrived self-defense scenario. The retreat option seems from a certain plausible-looking vantage point very irrelevant. If we are evaluating an actor who is determined to either kill or be killed but would not dream of retreating, then whether he has the retreat option available to him seems like a rather irrelevant factor in evaluating his decision. It seems even more irrelevant when we contemplate his foreclosing the retreat option solely to make the killing option a permissible one. From another vantage point of course the retreat option seems highly relevant, because it appears entirely reasonable to only let someone kill his attacker if he absolutely needs to, and if he has a retreat option open to him, then he really doesn't need to.

Another reason it may be hard to think of the retreat option as an irrelevant alternative is that we feel far more uneasy about lawyers exploiting such alternatives than about canny legislators who do the same in the voting context. And sometimes we feel uneasy in the extreme. Would we really allow someone to quite simply foreclose his own opportunity for retreat so that he may then go on to kill the attacker? That depends on exactly how he does it. It will not do for him to walk to the door through which he might have escaped, lock it, throw away the key and then kill his attacker. But the reason this maneuver does not work is because it comes too late. To be effective, the retreat option has to be foreclosed much earlier. Walking into a dangerous place, like Central Park in the middle of the night, and continuing to stroll until one is confronted by a knife-wielding mugger also forecloses retreat, but because the foreclosure occurs quite a while before the threat was encountered, we feel rather differently about it. Indeed the further in advance of the attack the defendant acted to foreclose retreat, the less uneasy we feel about it—however strategic his behavior. Someone who joins the police force hoping to encounter a suitable self-defense opportunity wouldn't even rate a minor scruple.

A final reason it might be hard to view contrived self-defense as agenda exploitation is that the law seems to treat it far more harshly than agenda manipulation in the legislative context. Many criminal codes explicitly try to make self-defense unavailable to someone who contrives to place himself in such a situation. But it quickly becomes clear that they don't really mean what they say. As long as the defendant makes his preparations sufficiently far in advance of the event (e.g., joins the police force to get his chance at a self-defense killing), he is beyond reproach. Not because it would be so hard to figure out what he is up to—let us assume he is entirely explicit about his designs—but because we actually don't feel we are entitled to object under such circumstances.

If, then, we are prepared to view the contrivance of a defense as being just an analogue of voting manipulation by injection of an irrelevant alternative, the answers to the three questions with which I began the exploration of the loophole problem would be as follows:

First question, why does this loophole arise? Answer: because we are trying to rank three alternatives in such as way as to at least partially accommodate two different principles.

Second question, why does this loophole persist? Answer: because we don't want to abandon those two principles.

Third question, what should lawyers do about this loophole? Answer: feel free to exploit it with all the verve of a skilled and determined parliamentarian.

Bootstrapping

Next let us revisit the case of the would-be immigrant to the United States who tries to bypass the usual waiting lines for an immigrant visa by turning himself into a political refugee: Having arrived in the United States on a visiting visa, he disseminates some statements that make him a candidate for immediate imprisonment if he returns to his home country. Then he claims political asylum.

The situation of the strategic immigrant is closely analogous to the contrived self-defense case. Indeed it is virtually identical. Before he makes his provocative pronouncement, we can think of him as having three options we must rank as to their permissibility: (1) staying in the United States (and speaking out or not speaking out against his home country's government); (2) going home and risking persecution by speaking out against the government; and (3) going home, keeping quiet, and living unmolested. At the outset, (2) and (3) will be ranked in the top category, the category of permissible conduct, and (1) will be ranked in the bottom category, impermissible conduct. By making his provocative statement while in the United States, the defendant has eliminated (3) from the choice set—he can't go home and live in peace. And now the relative order of (1) and (2) has been changed. Both are now in the top category, permissible conduct. Making the provocative statement thus becomes the equivalent of arranging for the presence or absence of a retreat option in the self-defense case.

As in the contrived self-defense case, the dependence on irrelevant alternatives arises from the need to rank three alternatives in such a way as to accommodate two different principles. The principles here are of course different from those in the self-defense case: our desire not to admit the entire world into our country and our desire not to deliver someone into the hands of a death squad or a concentration camp. We combine them by letting the first principle hold sway if all three options are available and letting the second hold sway if one of the three options—going back home and living in peace—becomes unavailable.

In answer to our three questions, we should therefore say: This loophole arises because there is multicriterial decision making going on. It persists because the principles being accommodated have persisted. And exploiting the loophole seems no different than exploiting the retreat option in the case of contrived self-defense.

Asset Protection

Consider again the practice of exemption planning. A debtor declares bankruptcy: this means he must give up all of his assets and distribute them to his creditors, however insufficient they are to repay his debts; in return he gets a fresh, debt-free start. There are, however, limits to this duty to give up all his assets—it does not extend to the shirt on his back or other equivalently basic necessities. Thus if the debtor's only assets are that proverbial shirt on his back and its functional equivalents, he is free to either use them or not use them to pay his creditors. In other words, the option to pay by giving up exempt assets and the option not to pay are both ranked in the top category, permissible conduct.

Now let us add some nonexempt assets, and the option to avoid paying drops to the bottom, impermissible conduct. The option to pay by giving up his exempt assets remains at the top, however. Again the relative ranking of the option to not pay or to pay by giving up exempt assets has been changed by the presence of a third alternative, the option to pay with nonexempt assets.

The two conflicting principles being accommodated in this case are, on the one hand, the desire to make people pay their debts and, on the other, the desire not to deprive them of basic necessities (home, old-age pensions) or essential parts of their person or personhood (gold teeth, musical instruments, in some states). The first principle prevails when the debtor faces a choice of three options: paying with exempt assets, paying with nonexempt assets, or not paying at all. The second principle prevails when he only has two options left: paying with exempt assets or not paying at all. By converting nonexempt into exempt assets, the debtor is thus able to avail himself of the legal relevance of "irrelevant" alternatives. The situation really is on all fours with the previous two cases: instead of depriving himself of a means of retreat, as in the self-defense case, or a means of safely returning to one's home country, as in the immigration case, here the legal actor deprives himself of the means of repayment. Equally on all fours is therefore the conclusion: as long as we remain committed to those two principles, this loophole will remain unclosable. And if we tried to close it by embracing another set of principles, a new loophole is likely to appear in a different place—just as long as that set contains more than one principle. That is the logic of multicriterial decision making.

Tax Shelters

The tax shelter case we considered involved a father who makes a cash gift to his son every year in the amount of $10,000. To make this money taxable to his son, who is in a lower tax bracket, he gives the son an asset that generates an income stream of $10,000, namely a cash gift of $100,000. Immediately thereafter he asks his son for a loan of $100,000, on which he promises to pay 10 percent interest per year. If we assume the loan involved money that he used in his business, it can be considered a business expense, which is deducted from his income. To be sure, the son must now report it not as a mere gift but as income on which he should be taxed. But this is exactly what they hoped to accomplish, since the son is in a much lower tax bracket than the father.

The father's options at the outset, before he engages in this maneuver, are two: to pay or not pay a certain amount of money to the IRS. The initial ordering of those options is clear: the option to pay is ranked at the top in terms of permissibility, and the option not to pay is ranked at the bottom—it is impermissible. But there is something that can reverse that ordering: the transfer of an income-generating asset (like a lump sum of cash). But what, practically speaking, does it mean to transfer an asset? It means that certain options available to the original owner have been removed from his option set; in turn, certain options previously not available to the recipient have been added to his. For instance, as long as the father has not transferred the lump sum, so that his annual $10,000 payment is regarded as a gift to his son rather than as interest payment on a loan, he might decide at any point that the tax he has to pay on that $10,000 should really be subtracted from the gift. And of course he retains the right, any time he feels like it, to discontinue the payments. All those options, and many others, disappear once he makes the lump sum transfer. To be sure, he has no interest in those options: he does not want to reduce or cancel the gift to his son. The option is in that sense completely irrelevant to him, as are the others that he gives up by transferring the asset. But it seems understandable that nevertheless it might be legally relevant. One of the ways in which it is legally relevant is that it changes the relative ordering of the payment options previously available to the father. No longer being the owner of the asset—and no longer having the options that go with being an owner—the father is no longer liable for income generated by it.

What we have here, then, is another instance of a relative ranking depending on an "irrelevant" alternative—in this case the various things one can do once one is the owner of the asset, which neither the son nor the father had any interest in taking advantage of.

To see more clearly how one can construe the tax shelter case as being analogous to voting manipulation, or more specifically the use of a killer amendment, it might help to make very explicit how it is parallel to the contrived self-defense case, where that connection is most transparent. Here is one way to put the matter. In the self-defense case, the defendant who has a retreat option is permitted either to retreat or to let himself be killed. What he is not permitted to do is to kill to save his life. Why? Because having to retreat isn't burdensome enough to warrant his taking a life, albeit the life of the attacker. Why is it not too burdensome? Because it forecloses too few options: he is giving up very little by having to retreat. Most of what he wants out of life he can still achieve even if he has to retreat. I put the matter in this stilted and artificial way to make the parallels to the tax case more salient. In the tax case, the taxpayer (the father) owes taxes on income he gets from an asset, even if he passes the income on to someone else to make use of. Although he has given away the income generated by the asset, he still has access to enough of the other ownership-based rights, or options, associated with the asset not to make it unfairly burdensome for him to have to pay taxes on the income. Once those ownership rights disappear altogether, because he has turned them over to his son, things change. Paying taxes on money when one neither gets to make use of the money nor enjoy the other opportunities that come with being an owner of the asset is just too much.

Let us sum the matter up by asking our three customary questions. What gives rise to the loophole here being exploited? The fact that the tax system appears to be trying to accommodate several different criteria, each imposing somewhat different rankings on the available options, one of which one might call the "earnings principle" and the other of which one might call the "use principle." From the point of view of the earnings principle, one might say that the taxpayer has three options: (1) make active use of his rights as an asset owner and pay taxes on the income from it, (2) make no active use of his rights and pay taxes on it nevertheless, and (3) make no active use of his rights and pay no taxes on it. The earnings principle would rank (1) and (2) as the only permissible options and (3) as impermissible. Taxes have to be paid on everything one earns, whether one then makes use of it or not. From the point of view of the use principle, all three options are permissible. The compromise chosen is to give weight to the earnings principle when all three options are available and to the use principle when option (1) has disappeared (i.e., the owner had given up his ownership rights). This is what renders irrelevant options so influential—the presence or absence of ownership rights by the father, even though he cares not one whit about exercising them.

The answers to the second and third questions—Why does this loophole persist? Should lawyers feel free to exploit it?—will now be self-evident. The tax shelter will survive, and lawyers should feel free to use it as long as we honor those principles.

A Contrary Intuition

I have I hope demonstrated that at least these fairly typical loopholes in law are the result of the fact that the legal doctrines they exploit are multi-criterial in nature, and as long as the law tries to accommodate these particular criteria, these particular loopholes will exist. But of course I am making a more general claim as well, which is that as long as the legal doctrines are multicriterial in character—which virtually all legal doctrines are—loopholes of this kind are bound to arise. If you change the doctrine to close a particular loophole, others will arise, because multicriterial decision making continues to be involved, and multicriterial decision making means dependence on irrelevant alternatives.

The idea that all multicriterial decision making should be dependent on irrelevant alternatives is bound to clash with the intuitive perception most people have of their own multicriterial decision making—which is after all the decision making they are engaged in most of the time. Let's try to sort out what is right and what is wrong about this intuition.

Consider a teacher grading student exams. Suppose the way he does it is to assign two provisional ratings to each exam, one for content and one for presentation (meaning style, organization, clarity, and so on). The ratings are on a scale of 0 to 4, in other words the familiar A through F scale. He then averages those numerical ratings for an overall rating, rank-orders the student exams by their overall rating, and assigns final grades, let's say by giving an A to the first 10 percent, an A-minus to the next 20 percent, and so on down to the Fs. This will not feel to him, nor does it look from the outside, as though it is in any way dependent on irrelevant alternatives. In other words, if all of a sudden, having graded a hundred exams, the teacher discovered there was one more exam than he had realized, it seems that could not possibly affect the relative ranking of the other students. To be sure, it might result in pushing a student who was at the outer bounds of the top 10 percent from the A category into the A-minus category, but that does not change his ranking relative to other students.

The teacher's intuitive sense that his relative ranking of the other students is not affected by whatever he thinks about the hundred-and-first exam is completely correct—*up to a point*. But if that is true, have we then come across a counterexample to Arrow's theorem? No, we haven't, but let's see exactly why. Suppose the teacher has awarded an exam a 4.0 rating for content, giving that student the highest rank on the content dimension. Suppose further that he awarded that same student a 3.6 rating for presentation, giving him the fourth-highest rank on the presentation dimension and an overall rating of 3.8. That turns out, let us suppose, to be the second-highest overall score. In other words, his overall ranking is 2.

Let's contrast this case with a slightly different one. Let's suppose that the student had received only a 3.9 for content rather than 4.0, but let's assume that that still makes his the top-ranked exam. Let's further suppose that he received a 3.5 for presentation rather than a 3.6, but that that still makes his the fourth-ranked exam, the same as before. In other words, the student continues to be ranked number 1 for content and number 4 for presentation, but his "raw" scores are slightly lower. What does that mean for his final overall rating? The "raw" figure is a simple average of 3.9 and 3.5, in other words 3.7. Does that "raw" score continue to translate into an overall ranking of 2? The answer is we don't know. We would have to know more about the other students' numerical scores before we could determine that. Now notice what that means for this particular ranking method: just because we know that a student ranked first on the content dimension and fourth on the style dimension does not mean we can determine what his final ranking will be. That's because the students' final rank is not determined exclusively by his relative ranking on the two dimensions but by his numerical score. Arrow's theorem, however, is concerned only with ranking methods in which the final ranking depends *exclusively* on the ranking achieved under the various criteria being considered. In other words, Arrow's theorem doesn't really apply to this kind of method. The fact that there is no dependence on irrelevant alternatives thus does not contradict the theorem.

Nevertheless, this example might make it appear as though Arrow's theorem is significantly less interesting or important than it appeared at first. After all, what the teacher is doing is probably a fairly common form of multicriterial decision making, and it would seem to follow that at least when engaged in this type of decision making we don't need to worry about the influence of irrelevant alternatives. Moreover, to the extent that legal rules mirror this type of procedure, it seems loopholes no longer are an issue.

But not so fast. Appearances here greatly deceive. Arrow's theorem turns out to be relevant even to this kind of decision making, because dependence on irrelevant alternatives is in fact still an issue: it has merely gone into hiding, while continuing to play a role. The best way to see this is with an analogy. Let's revisit my figure-skating example. Let us suppose that some of the judges are disturbed by the fact that the skaters' relative performance in a given year will depend so much on who happens to be skating in competition with them. In other words, they want to do something so that whatever someone like Kwan does cannot change the relative ranking of Bonaly and Bobek. As it happens, someone has what seems to him an inspired idea that looks as though it might achieve this. "Our problem," he explains, "is that we have been ranking skaters relative to each other rather than ranking them on an absolute scale." How does one come up with such a scale? What he suggests is that we form a fictitious lineup of a wide range of skaters who have participated in the Olympics over the last several years, including not only instances of phenomenal performances but also many that were mediocre or worse. These performances should be made available to the judges in some kind of video library. Judges should then be asked to judge each of the present skaters as though she were competing against that fictitious lineup. They should do this with every presently competing skater and then rank these skaters against each other according to how they would have done in their imaginary competition with the fictitious lineup. That will be their final rank, the one that determines who gets the gold, the silver, and so on. "By this system," our would-be reformer explains, "we have removed all worries about the possibility of changing relative rankings: a skater's position relative to another will no longer depend on what other skaters she happens to be competing with. Of course whether she gets the gold might still be affected by whether some skaters who are better than she happen to be out sick that day. Still, the relative rank of each skater is impervious to change." In other words, haven't we now achieved something pretty close to independence of irrelevant alternatives?

Or have we? Has the dependence on irrelevant alternatives *really* all but gone away? No, not really: each skater is ranked as she is because of the particular fictitious lineup we have them all compete in. Had we chosen a different lineup, the outcomes would have been very different. *In other words, the influence of irrelevant alternatives has simply receded to a different tier, the video library.* All that someone who wants to strategically influence an outcome therefore needs to do is to include the right kind of "irrelevant" alternative in that library.

Things are very similar with the exam-grading teacher. When assigning scores for content and presentation, the teacher surely has in the back of his mind exemplars of what kind of analysis merits a 4, what kind of organization merits a 2, and so on—in other words, he carries within his head the counterpart to that video library of skaters. *These exemplars are now the "irrelevant" alternatives.* If we could just get him to include among these exemplars some others he has not considered so far—note that we are not trying to change his mind about anything but only trying to get him to add a further exemplar to his mental video library—the rank of many of his students is apt to change.

Thus, even when we think we are engaged in a form of decision making that is impervious to irrelevant alternatives, we have probably only changed the location from which the irrelevant alternatives exert their influence.

Loopholes and Persuasion

The archetypical lawyer in most people's mind is the advocate, the professional persuader, whose job it is to is to put his client's view of the matter in the best possible light. There is something inherently manipulative about partisan rhetoric, and people sometimes feel uneasy about that, indeed sometimes even lump it with loophole exploitation as one of the many ways in which lawyers pervert justice (especially when it means discrediting a witness the lawyer actually thinks is truthful), but that is not the usual perception. The usual perception is that one-sided argumentation is perfectly legitimate. My analysis of loopholes has some bearing on the question of whether it is.

It will be helpful to have before us some good illustrations of advocacy. A fairly typical example would be the case of the doctor who decides to disconnect his terminally ill patient from life support. Did he merely let the victim die (no liability), or did he actually kill him (murder)? The prosecution, trying to characterize this as a killing, will emphasize all the physical activity that went into disconnecting the patient and how, without that physical activity, the victim would not have died. The defense, trying to characterize this as a letting-die, will emphasize how much physical activity would be required to keep the life-support system going, so that we should think of the doctor as merely withholding further treatment.[4]

Modern psychologists have a name for what the lawyer is doing in these cases. They call it "framing." The very same event will be judged radically differently depending on how it is framed, and what a good rhetorician does is to capitalize on that. What psychologists mean by *framing* is most readily illustrated by two famous examples constructed by the founders of this line of inquiry, Amos Tversky and Daniel Kahneman. The first example asks you to make a decision between two governmental health policies. More concretely, you are told that a disease will soon break out that will result in the death of six hundred people if nothing is done. If you pursue one of the two policies on the table, four hundred people will die. If you pursue the other, the outcome is iffier: everyone might die, but there is a one-in-three chance that no one will die. Most people will try to save everyone by opting for the riskier policy. The surprise comes when the same choice is described slightly differently. Suppose you are told: if you pursue the first policy, you will save two hundred people for sure; if you pursue the second policy, you might not save anyone (there is a two-thirds chance of that) or you might save everyone (a one-third chance of that). *Now* most people want to play it safe, the opposite of what they wanted to do before in the identical situation. Tversky and Kahneman constructed and tested countless such scenarios. Here is just one more. You are asked to imagine yourself taking the subway to the theater but discover on arriving that you lost your $50 ticket. Will you buy another? Many people are reluctant. But suppose instead you are told to imagine that you did not lose the ticket but still have to buy it at the ticket counter. You did, however, lose a $50 bill in the subway. Will you still buy the theater ticket? Most people say yes. Of course here too the two situations are at bottom the same. In both versions, you are deciding between going to the theater and being $100 poorer and not going to the theater and only being $50 poorer.[5]

As psychologists see it, these are examples of irrationality. Frame the issue one way and we give one kind of response; frame it another way and we give another. Psychologists presumably would say that what the lawyer is doing is trying to exploit this irrationality. Some psychologists might be willing to concede that this kind of thing is rendered less objectionable because each side gets to do it in turn. Others, however, would not make even this concession: after all, they might say, if what the lawyer did was to destroy evidence, we would not be comforted if we knew that both sides were doing it. The bottom line is that psychologists would take a very dim view of what the zealous advocate is doing. He is, by their lights, trying to confuse a judge or jury into rendering an irrational decision.

My analysis of loopholes suggests a rather different view of legal advocacy. It suggests that what the lawyer is really doing when he tries to characterize the facts in one way rather than another is to inject into the agenda an alternative that he hopes will lead us to take a different view of the alternatives previously considered. This is only slightly different from what he does when he engages in loophole exploitation. In loophole exploitation the alternative is actually created or removed (retreat in the case of self-defense for instance), but in persuasion it is only injected "for consideration." It is as though, rather than preparing the fish dish to get the customer to switch from steak to chicken, the restaurant had merely asked him to think about how he would feel about steak versus chicken if he also considered the possibility of having fish (even though that is not an option at present). Is the person who reacts to this by switching his choice being irrational? If he is a multicriterial decision maker, not really. This is bound to happen. It is, to be sure, a framing effect. The restaurant is trying to frame the issue with fish in it, rather than the other way around. But there is nothing irrational about this framing effect. And the lawyer who tries to capitalize on it is not therefore trying to take advantage of anyone's irrationality. In the end, then, loophole exploitation and skillful persuasion turn out to differ only by a hair, and inasmuch as we never felt too uneasy about the latter, we have one more reason not to feel too uneasy about the former.

This is not of course how people usually think about what is going on when a choice is reframed. It is not, they would say, that the choice set is being changed but that the available choices are being redescribed in ways that make them either more less attractive. My suggestion is, in effect, that what redescription often amounts to is the injection of hypothetical alternatives into the choice set, which, if they were actually present, would change the choice made.

Loopholes and Kaplow and Shavell's Antifairness Theorem

In part I of this book we looked at the proposal of legal economists Lewis Kaplow and Steven Shavell that legal doctrines should be designed solely with regard to their implications for welfare. We should certainly never adopt a law that has the potential of coming into conflict with the win-win principle. To shore up their claim that principles of fairness were surely never persuasive enough to trump the win-win principle, they drew attention to what struck them as a particularly absurd-looking aspect of most fairness-based principles. It had to do with a fairness idea they found particularly vexing, the distinction between killing someone and letting him die or, more generally, between actively harming someone and letting a harm befall him. They illustrated their point with an elaborate example involving the construction of a hospital that would necessarily entail the death of at least one of the workers involved in the project. Although believers in the act-omission distinction would not generally have a problem with such a project, despite its human cost, because they would not count this as a case of active killing, they might if the example were changed slightly if, for instance, there were a button that would have to be pushed so as to trigger the worker's death, but that, if not pushed, would undo all the work that had been accomplished.[6] If we push the button, we would be engaged in an active killing, which is off limits. But that has an absurd-looking implication, as Kaplow and Shavell see it: something so arbitrary as a push button shouldn't have such bearing on questions of morality. They might have added, though I think they would regard it as implicit in what they said, that one of the sillier implications of attaching moral significance to "the technology of such things as push-buttons" and the like is that it allows people to get around burdensome legal restrictions by resorting to technological tricks: by making sure, for instance, that the way in which lives are sacrificed in the course of a risky project never involves a specific moment in which the only way to continue the project is to inflict death on an identifiable individual.

When first discussing this example, I admitted that it does seem strange that these factors that appear entirely morally arbitrary are in fact of crucial moral significance. And I said that this was a larger issue. I claimed that we would in due course see that it is impossible to design a plausible legal system in which factors like this do not play a significant role. Even the kind of system Kaplow and Shavell envision is vulnerable to this. Their challenge, I said, is therefore not a challenge because it does not distinguish among legal systems.

We are now in a position to understand why that is. Any approach to legal decision making—including one that is concerned with welfare maximization—is bound to be multicriterial in nature, and multicriterial decision making we now know is vulnerable to maneuvers resembling the killer amendment. For the outcome of a decision to depend on the presence or absence of an irrelevant alternative will often seem as silly, and exploitable, as one based on the availability of a certain push-button technology.

It might not seem immediately evident that a method of decision making that maximizes welfare is in fact dependent on irrelevant alternatives. A social planner maximizing a welfare function is the direct analogue of a consumer maximizing utility subject to a budget constraint. And it is not immediately evident why such a consumer is bound to be influenced by irrelevant alternatives. But let's take a closer look at such a consumer who is choosing among different commodity bundles, trying to maximize his utility subject to a budget constraint. His ranking of commodity bundles is of course a multicriterial decision process in that the commodities he is considering, and the bundles of these commodities, have a variety of different attributes that he has to take into account. The results of this decision process are described by a utility function (depicted by the indifference curves familiar from introductory microeconomics courses). In making these rankings, the consumer is very much in the position of the judges ranking the skaters. How does he generate a ranking for each commodity? Apparently in a way that does not entail reranking two bundles with respect to each other once a third bundle has been added to the mix. *But that can only mean that he is doing something closely analogous to the fictitious lineup method I described in connection with my hypothetical figure-skating judges.* Whatever method he uses to derive the utility scores he assigns to each commodity bundle thus depends on the commodity bundles he has implicitly, rather than explicitly, included in the calculation by making them part of that lineup. He is therefore as vulnerable to having his choice altered by the introduction of "irrelevant" alternatives as the skating judges. And what goes for the ordinary consumer choosing among commodity bundles also goes for the social planner ranking not commodity bundles but various possible society wide outcomes—by which they mean the various possible levels of welfare for the members of that society—that different laws might bring about.[7]

Taking Stock

Where does all of this leave us with regard to the problem of loopholes? Legal doctrines can be thought of as multicriterial decision-making devices. That means they are structurally very similar to the voting rules that form the subject of the Arrow impossibility theorems. What these

theorems established is that all voting rules trying to synthesize the preferences of multiple voters into a final choice are bound to be subject to manipulation. Arrow's own multicriterial analogue to his theorem establishes
that any decision-making rule that synthesizes multiple criteria into a final
verdict is subject to something closely analogous to voting manipulation.
When such a decision-making rule happens to be a legal doctrine, these
analogues to voting manipulation are what we perceive as the exploitation
of loopholes.

We have only looked so far at a small subset of loophole-exploiting behavior, the subset that happens to be most closely analogous to the introduction of a killer amendment in the voting context. I suspect it would
prove surprising and illuminating to take all known types of voting manipulation and explore what their legal counterparts would look like. We
would get a much better sense than we have so far—than even lawyers
have so far—of just what it is that lawyers actually do for a living. I won't
try to do anything as grand as that in this book. Rather I will limit myself
to looking at one more type of loophole—the legal counterpart to the
intentional foul—and trying to understand its roots and its inevitability
with the help of the analogy between legal rules generally and voting rules
in particular.

CHAPTER NINE

Intentional Fouls

Intentional fouls, recall, are violations of rules in which the violator fully expects to incur the penalty but rightly calculates that he will come out ahead anyway—like the basketball player who intentionally fouls an opponent to prevent him from scoring, thus incurring free throws by way of penalty but still deeming himself and his team most likely better off as a result. It does not seem amiss to call an intentional foul a kind of loophole, in that the person engaged in it is doing something we don't really want him to do, but he gets away with it under the rules, at least in the sense that he comes out with a net advantage from having done so.

I said that there are many legal counterparts to intentional fouls but only offered one example. Let us now see why this is in fact an important and not uncommon kind of legal loophole, by examining three prominent instances of it in criminal law.

Varieties of Intentional Fouls in the Law

Crimes of Mitigation

Let us suppose that a defendant has poisoned several people. The toxin he uses ravages a particular bodily organ. So as not to be distracted by actual medical facts, let us think of a fictitious organ; I will call it the glichin. Having poisoned several people's glichins, let us imagine that the defendant suddenly comes to feel remorse and wants to do what he can to undo the harm he has wrought. As it stands, all of his victims will die unless provided with a glichin transplant. Actually no one needs an entire glichin to stay alive—part of one will do—though one's quality of life will not be as high as if one had an entire one. But there is no potential donor in sight.

The defendant then considers grabbing an innocent bystander, extracting the bulk of his glichin, and parceling it out among his victims. Should he do so?[1]

This question involves the kind of choice familiar from numerous utilitarian dilemmas. Is it permissible to carve up one person to use his organs—his two kidneys, his two lungs, and his heart—to save five? Is it permissible to kill an innocent prisoner to appease a dangerous lynch mob that will otherwise end up killing many more innocents? Is it permissible to acquiesce in the request of the guerrilla leader to shoot one of ten prisoners if he will otherwise kill all ten? The answer given by those who are not out-and-out consequentialists is no. And it would thus seem that the answer with respect to the glichin should be no as well—even if removing part of someone's glichin won't actually kill him.

Now let us closely compare what would happen if the defendant did what we think he should do and what would happen if he did not. If he does what we think he should do, he will let the five die and will in the end be guilty of five murders. Suppose instead that he disregards our advice, removes the bystander's glichin, slices it up, and transplants the various pieces into his various victims. He would then be guilty of several attempted murders and one assault—pretty clearly less than he would be guilty of if he had followed our advice. In other words, if he does the right thing he ends up more blameworthy than if he does the wrong thing.

One might think at first that this is not so very different from the run-of-the-mill case in which someone profits from a wrong—as when he robs a bank and never is caught or robs a bank, is caught and punished, but having managed to secrete the money, gets to enjoy it once he is released and therefore still comes out ahead.

To see just how different this case is from that more familiar instance of profiting from one's wrong, let's imagine that there are two people who have behaved identically so far and who both end up at the same decision node, where they need to choose whether or not to remove the glichin of an innocent to save their several victims. They both consult God, and he tells each of them just what we would expect: don't assault strangers to steal some of their glichin. One of them decides to follow God's advice and the other does not. Who ends up with the better moral ledger? Who is more likely to enter the pearly gates? Quite clearly the one who disregarded God's advice, since he will only end up guilty of several attempted murders and an assault, whereas the other will end up guilty of several murders. Of course, this sort of scenario could not be imagined with the more humdrum sort of profitable wrong. The bank robber, even if he gets to enjoy his loot, will not come out ahead of the law-abiding citizen on the day of Final Judgment. But the perpetrator of this kind of an intentional foul will.

It might be thought that all of this is the consequence of paying too much attention to consequences and too little to mental states. It might seem as though if we only judged someone who attempted murder to be as bad as someone who carried it out, then the whole paradox would disappear. To be sure, this specific paradox would disappear, but an analogous one would quickly take its place. Just imagine that the defendant is considering two courses of action. The first plan involves poisoning several people and subsequently rescuing them by assaulting and extracting the better part of an innocent bystander's glichin. The second plan involves poisoning the several but then *not* rescuing them. Under the first plan, the defendant will be judged less blameworthy than under the second plan, *even though the second plan emerged from the first plan simply by excising a certain morally objectionable feature from it*. Here now we have the same paradox, while making blameworthiness solely dependent on someone's state of mind.

How many situations are like this? Think about it this way. All we really need to do to construct such a situation is to take any one of the classical utilitarian dilemmas—like the lynch mob example—and to imagine someone who has wrongfully inflicted some kind of serious harm that he could mitigate if he engaged in one of these unpalatable utilitarian trade-offs. Sticking for the moment to the lynch mob example, imagine a ruler who first whips up the frenzy of the crowd but then wants to backtrack: he will still minimize his blameworthiness by killing the innocent prisoner rather than letting the lynch mob run amuck and kill many more innocents. Or take the case of the man who tortures the innocent child of a terrorist to get him to reveal the whereabouts of a bomb. If he himself caused the bomb to be hidden in the first place (without being told where it is) but then has remorse and wants to mitigate the consequences and can only find out where the bomb is hidden by such torture, then he too will minimize his blameworthiness by pursuing the immoral course of action. Or consider the old case about the shipwrecked sailors, one of whom, Dudley, carves up another, Parker, the cabin boy, for the rest to feed on. Suppose it had been Dudley himself who had intentionally caused the ship to founder in the first place; then he too will minimize his blameworthiness by carving up the cabin boy rather than having some greater number die on his account.

Other more distant instances of this situation exist. Consider the typical informer's dilemma: should you rat out your fellow criminals to the authorities to save yourself? It feels both right and wrong. We might try to explain the dilemma as involving a kind of intentional foul. Ratting on his confreres may be a villainous act, but it might nevertheless reduce not just one's liability but one's blameworthiness to do so.

Crimes of Self-Restraint

Douglas MacArthur loved to tell a story about his father, Arthur MacArthur, a stupendously successful military man in his own right, and a bribe he almost took. The older MacArthur was then an army captain stationed in New Orleans. A cotton broker approached him, desperately hoping to secure the temporary but illegal use of some army transport facilities. "The bribe was to be a large sum of cash, which was left in [MacArthur's] desk and a night with an exquisite Southern girl. Wiring Washington the details, MacArthur concluded: 'I am depositing the money with the Treasury of the United States and request immediate relief from this command. They are getting close to my price.'"[2] To see the interesting moral questions lurking in this example, let us imagine that MacArthur's superiors refuse his request for a transfer, and let us suppose further that he is dead serious in his fear of yielding to temptation. Suppose that in his desperate concern to forestall his own future wrongdoing, he deliberately commits some minor infraction that causes the army to punish him by transferring him to another, less temptation-fraught post. Given his reasons for committing the infraction, has he acted wrongly? In the alternative, suppose that MacArthur had decided to stay at his post—that is, not contrived to have himself transferred—despite his desperate and well-founded fear about his own ability to withstand temptation. To be sure, he keeps warning and imploring his superiors to move him, but he has no success. Suppose that eventually things come to pass just as he feared they would. He is tempted and he yields. Can he still be blamed, given how hard he tried to avert this contingency? If he can, we have here another instance of an intentional foul. For if MacArthur had done the wrong thing—had committed the infraction that would have resulted in his transfer—he would end up with a better moral record than if he had not.

Cases like this have been taken up repeatedly in the philosophical literature. In an article titled "Oughts, Options, and Actualism," Frank Jackson and Robert Pargetter pose the following hypothetical:

Professor Procrastinate receives an invitation to review a book. He is the best person to do the review, has the time, and so on. The best thing that can happen is that he says yes, and then writes the review when the book arrives. However, suppose it is further the case that were Procrastinate to say yes, he would not in fact get around to writing the review. Not because of incapacity or outside interference or anything like that, but because he would keep on putting the task off. (This has been known to happen.) Thus although the best that can happen is for Procrastinate to say yes and then write, and he can do exactly this, what would in fact happen were he to say yes is that he would not write the review. Moreover, we may suppose this latter is the worst that can happen. It would lead to the book not being reviewed at all, or at least to a review being seriously delayed. Does that mean he ought to decline the invitation to review it?[3]

In responding to hypotheticals like these, philosophers tend to split into two camps. The first, whom one might call the idealists, say that "the fact that Procrastinate would not write the review were he to say yes is irrelevant. What matters is simply that it is possible for Procrastinate to do so." The second group, whom one might call the realists, say that "the fact that Procrastinate would not actually write the review, were he to say yes, is crucial. It means that to say yes would be in fact to realize the worst. Therefore Procrastinate ought to say no." Interestingly, however, the only question that attracts philosophers' attention is the rightness or wrongness of turning down the review. What does not receive any attention is the intentional-foul aspect: if one sides with the idealists, it seems that doing the wrong thing would minimize blameworthiness.

Perhaps these examples are too frivolous to make my point. More serious ones certainly exist. Consider the debate about preventive detention and harsh punishment. Imagine a society plagued by rising crime rates. As crime rates go up, so does police brutality, vigilantism, and most alarming of all, the number of illiberal, draconian, immoral-seeming laws seeking to cope with the rising tide of crime. Astute observers looking ahead just a few years see some frightening possibilities. Unless crime is curbed quickly, they foresee the disappearance of bail and of the probable cause requirement for searches and seizures and a resort to preventive detention and to laws that mete out punishment for conduct that is in and of itself inoffensive, like drug use, loitering, or the possession of potentially dangerous weapons. In other words, they foresee a plethora of ways in which we will disregard our previous moral aversion to purely preventive measures and to disproportionate punishment. Lawmakers who dread the possibility of such draconian laws consider forestalling them by taking somewhat more draconian action now than many people think called for: they would like to pass somewhat draconian laws now—our current drug laws again come to mind—to forestall having to pass even more immoral draconian laws in the future. They would try to preempt, as it were, their own future wrongdoing. This too looks like an intentional foul, an instance of blame-worthiness-reducing blameworthiness.

Price-of-Admission Crimes

Consider the case of the German doctors. Hitler had promulgated the infamous euthanasia decree demanding the involuntary euthanasia of all mental defectives, including both the feeble minded and the insane. Some doctors who worked in the affected mental institutions resigned; some doctors complied reluctantly; still others complied enthusiastically. And finally some stayed on just so they could sabotage it—by encouraging the families to take their relatives out of the sanatoria in time or by reclas-sifying patients so as to fall outside the decree, etc. Needless to say, they also had to participate in some of those indefensible acts of involuntary euthanasia. They were prosecuted for the latter after the war and pleaded the defense of necessity: they had saved more lives than they had taken, they claimed. Alas, the courts said, the defense of necessity did not allow that. They cited approvingly the aforementioned case about shipwrecked sailors who were denied the necessity defense when they ate one of their comrades. (The doctors usually escaped conviction because German law requires an appreciation of wrongdoing, which they were deemed to lack, but that is not an aspect of the case I am concerned with here.)[4]

Now let us compare these doctors with others who did resign and thus avoided the compromising acts as well as the heroic rescues that only thus became possible. Who is better, who is worse? A doctor who stayed, by acquiescing in a variety of indefensible acts of euthanasia, but who was able through all sort of heroic interventions to forestall many more, might well end up with the better overall moral ledger than someone who did not—despite the fact that we would think it impermissible for someone to choose the former course of action over the latter.

There is obviously no dearth of situations in which the commission of a single sin allows us to do a great deal of good down the road—so much in fact that the good swamps the bad and the sinner ends up with a better moral record than the nonsinner—but where we nevertheless would not approve of the initial price-of-admission sin.

It is worth pausing to note just how perplexing a phenomenon intentional fouls are, both in their original form and in their legal incarnation. We are saying that both as a matter of morality and as a matter of law (the two are unusually close in all three varieties of intentional foul we have considered so far), someone should not do something, but if he does, we will regard him as superior to someone who does not. How can that be? Shouldn't we have to choose between either saying that since engaging in the foul gets him a higher moral score, it isn't really a foul or, on the other hand, saying that since we do regard it as a foul, we need to revise his score so that he does not in fact end up with a moral benefit from engaging in it?

What light can social choice theory shed on this?

The Analogy to Counterpreferential Voting

Let's imagine an electoral contest between three candidates to be decided by a plurality vote followed by a runoff. In other words, if none of the three candidates wins more than 50 percent of the votes, there is going to be a runoff election between the two top vote-getters, to be decided by a simple majority vote. Let's suppose that your favorite is the ultraliberal candidate, your least favorite is the ultraconservative, with the moderate falling between the two. You are initially inclined to vote for your favorite, but then it occurs to you that, given the preferences of most voters, if your favorite actually makes it into the runoff, he is likely to be facing the moderate and will probably lose out to him. You therefore decide to vote for the ultraconservative, just to keep the moderate out of the runoff. This kind of voter calculation no doubt sounds completely familiar and commonplace and hardly counterintuitive. But that is true only so long as one looks at it in the way we usually do, from up close.[5]

From a bit of a distance, there really is something extraordinarily strange about the fact that an election system should ever work in this fashion—that counterpreferential voting, or strategic voting, as it is frequently called, should ever work to a voter's advantage. It is certainly not how we would want it to work. Rather, we would want it to be the case that the greater a voter's preference for an outcome, the likelier it should be that it he would vote for that outcome. To be sure, it might not in fact come about despite his vote in support of it, but it seems unbelievably perverse that his voting in favor of something should work out to his disadvantage rather than simply having no favorable impact. "Nonmonotonicity" is the label voting theorists give to this perverse property of a voting system that, on occasion, rewards counterpreferential voting. What one would like to happen is that the eventual outcome should "monotonically" depend on your wishes—that is, be affected favorably, or not at all, but not negatively. Nonmonotonicity is what we call it when that isn't so.

Prompted by such observations, voting theorists set about trying to find a voting system that does not suffer from this particular perversity—nonmonotonicity—and to their astonishment found that there is none, or at least none that isn't unacceptable on other grounds. This is another of those Arrow impossibility theorems, though in fact due to the philosopher Allan Gibbard and the economist Mark Satterthwaite. The original Arrow theorem already gave a hint of this: it told us that all remotely acceptable voting systems are dependent on irrelevant alternatives. That dependence on irrelevant alternatives, however, means that one can often improve one's position by injecting into the mix of choices an alternative one has actually no interest in—like a killer amendment—because it would affect the relative ranking of various other alternatives in a way that might benefit him.

There is a second aspect to my plurality/runoff example in which counterpreferential choices play an even more interesting role. Let's focus for the moment not on what the election looks like to the calculating voter but on what it looks like to the calculating candidate who is courting those voters. Let's assume that the ultraliberal realizes that he is likely to lose a one-on-one contest against the moderate but will probably win against the ultraconservative. He therefore tries to make sure not to take too many votes away from the ultraconservative, so as to keep him around for the runoff. In fact he suspends his campaign early, as soon as he thinks he has secured enough votes to make it into the runoff himself. He doesn't care whether he comes in first or second during the initial round, just as long as he doesn't come in last. What he really cares about is that the ultraconservative get enough votes to make it into the runoff as well. We might call what he is doing counterpreferential campaigning. That it should sometimes not be in a candidate's interest to campaign for as many votes as he can get is at least slightly more counterintuitive than that it isn't always in a voter's interest to vote for his real favorite.

The point of thinking about counterpreferential campaigning is that it seems to have a ready counterpart in sports. Suppose that the way scoring rules work in a certain team sport, every team plays every other team in the first round. A number of the top-scoring teams are then selected for a second round, and the two top-scoring teams from that round are eventually selected for the final round. It might well be in a strong team's interest to deliberately lose a game to a weaker team, hoping thereby to improve that team's position relative to some other team that seems a more serious threat—so as to have that weaker team rather than the stronger one move forward into the next round. In fact it might make sense to actually forfeit a game to the weaker team. Such a forfeit is very much in the nature of an intentional foul. Indeed, I think that understates it: it isn't merely in the nature of an intentional foul. I believe it really *is* an intentional foul. What's more, it is an especially interesting example of an intentional foul, because it allows us to understand why we have them. A foul like this closely resembles counterpreferential voting and arises out of the multicriterial character of the scoring rules, which share most of the paradoxical attributes of voting rules—and like voting rules are likely to give rise to these instances of nonmonotonicity.

Nonmonotonicity in Law

Loopholes in sports, which is what an intentional foul could surely be described as, we now understand to arise out of the multicriterial character of the scoring rules used. Nonmonotonicity is a nearly unavoidable characteristic of most voting rules; hence multicriterial evaluations are going to be prone to it as well. The scoring rules of sports are but one instance of this.

The rules of law and morality are of course another instance. They too, being multicriterial decision-making devices, are going to be prone to this to type of loophole. Still, in the context of legal rules, the manifestations of nonmonotonicity seem singularly paradoxical and hard to swallow. After all, they entail our telling someone not to do something, as a matter of law and morality, despite the fact that if he did so we would regard him, as a matter of law and morality, more highly than if he did not.

It should help to demystify things somewhat if we take note of a fairly familiar situation in criminal law in which a milder version of this sort of thing can happen as well: Think of the insane person committing a crime. We disapprove of what the defendant does, but we don't regard it as worsening his moral (or legal) position, inasmuch as insanity excuses him. Excuses aren't exactly instances of nonmonotonicity, but they come close.

The answers to the three questions with which I began my exploration of loopholes thus are not quite the same with regard to intentional fouls (of the legal variety) as they are with regard to the more ordinary kinds of loopholes with which we began. To be sure, the first two questions have identical answers: we get intentional fouls, for the same reason we get more ordinary loopholes, because of the multicriterial nature of legal decision making, and as long as we remain committed to a multiplicity of criteria, we are going to see both types of loopholes. But the third question—what should we do about such loopholes, freely exploit them or not?—has a somewhat different answer. As to ordinary loopholes, I suggested we should treat the lawyers' actions as being analogous to those of the skilful parliamentarian—in other words, as equally irreproachable. As to intentional fouls, though, the answer quite manifestly is that it's really quite immoral to avail yourself of them. However, if you do avail yourself of them nevertheless, you deserve greater moral approval than if you do not. Absurd? Well, that's nonmonotonicity for you.

Last Thoughts

Social choice theorists like to distinguish between two types of voting manipulation. The first they call agenda manipulation, and its archetypical example is the killer amendment. The second they call strategic, or counterpreferential, voting or, most fancifully of all, the exploitation of nonmonotonicity. As we just saw, each type of voting manipulation has a different type of legal loophole as its counterpart. I suspect, moreover, that by breaking the general archetypes of voting manipulation down into further subtypes, one would find corresponding subtypes of legal loopholes. But that's for another day.

PART III

Why Is the Law So Either/Or?

CHAPTER TEN

The Proverbial Rigidity of the Law

The Man from Sirius

In the early 1980s the highest German criminal court confronted a somewhat unusual case of attempted murder.[1] The case involved a rather naive young woman—let's call her Hilde; the court simply calls her "the Witness"—who became infatuated with a man, let's call him Bruno, who eventually acquired Svengali-like powers over her. She met him in a disco. He was only a few years older than she. Their relationship never became sexual—although it undoubtedly had sexual overtones—but was mostly limited to telephone conversations that would last for hours concerning their common interest in various philosophical and psychological matters. Their contact was intermittent. Months might elapse between their marathon telephone calls. Despite that, Hilde's infatuation with Bruno grew ever stronger. Eventually, we are told, Bruno became her "teacher and advisor in all aspects of her life. She trusted and believed in him unconditionally."

Things took their first really unusual turn when Bruno told Hilde that the time had come for him to reveal to her his true identity. He was not really human, he told her; rather, he said, he was an emissary from the star of Sirius. The Sirians, he explained, were a race that had evolved to a much higher stage than humans and had dispatched him to Earth to find humans worthy of joining them. He had decided, he said, that Hilde was one of the worthy ones. Hilde was ecstatic, but he told her she would have to wait a little. She could not actually move to Sirius until her physical existence had come to an end and her soul was ready to travel unencumbered to its new destination. Bruno was not a lunatic, merely a practical joker seeking to test the limits of Hilde's gullibility. When he first told her the story, he seems not yet to have had any criminal designs.

But soon thereafter things did take a criminal turn. Realizing how convinced Hilde was of his tale, Bruno cast about for ways in which he might exploit that. His first step was to explain to Hilde that her soul was not quite ready yet for its new life. It would need to be suitably prepared. (At this point the court's opinion unfortunately becomes a little too concise, considering what follows.) Bruno explained to Hilde that "she could attain the ability to live on another planet, by having [a monk named] Uliko spend a substantial amount of time in meditation devoted to her. This would allow her to traverse, while she was sleeping, several evolutionary stages and to make the requisite spiritual and philosophical progress. But this would require a payment to the monastery in which Uliko lived of 30,000 DM [Deutsche marks, roughly $15,000]. The Witness [i.e., Hilde] believed the Accused [i.e., Bruno]. Since she did not have enough money, she obtained a bank loan."

When he had used up her money, Bruno decided it was time for a bolder move. At first, whenever Hilde inquired about Uliko's success, which she did often, he told her to be patient. Eventually he informed her that "although the monk had incurred great danger in the course of his efforts in her behalf, he had not had any success so far, because her consciousness contained a block against any further spiritual and intellectual progress. The reason for this appeared to be her particular body. The block could really only be overcome if her old body were destroyed and replaced with a new one." And how might that be accomplished? Bruno explained to Hilde that

> in a red room on Lake Geneva there was a new body ready for her to inhabit, in which she would refind herself [with the new identity of] an artist, provided she left behind her old body. But in this new life she would need money. Such money, he said, she could obtain by purchasing a life insurance policy for 250,000 DM (in case of accident 500,000 DM), naming him as the beneficiary, and then staging an accident by which she would leave behind her old body and enter the new one. Once the insurance company had paid him the money, he would bring it to her. The Witness then bought such a policy per instruction. The policy became effective on the first of December 1979. The monthly premium was 587.50 DM. To the Accused the Witness gave 4,000 DM in cash to hold for her until she reawakened. The money was meant to tide her over until the insurance payments came through.

Now came the final act in Bruno's scheme, the staging of the accident. Bruno told Hilde to get on a certain busy highway, without a divider, and when she saw a big truck coming from the other direction, to head straight into it. She did as she was told. Unfortunately for Bruno, it did not work: her car was totaled, but she walked away unscathed.

Bruno was undeterred, and so was Hilde. He next suggested to her that she seat herself in a bathtub and drop a hair dryer into it. Once again, no luck, or too much luck. Instead of being electrocuted, "the Witness only felt some tingling of her body," the court writes, and "when the Accused, who was nearby, called her and found her answering the phone he was very surprised." But neither Bruno nor Hilde was ready to give up. "For another three hours, he gave her instructions in the course of about ten telephone conversations how such an accident could still be pulled off. When those failed, he finally abandoned the effort, since it seemed hopeless." Later, Hilde mentioned all this to a friend, who passed it on to the police, and Bruno was arrested and charged with attempted murder.

So what makes this case interesting, other than its bizarre facts? Isn't it a straightforward case of attempted murder? After all, Bruno wanted Hilde dead and did what he could to bring that about. The problem is that all the deadly activity was actually carried out by Hilde. Bruno argued that his sole contribution was to persuade Hilde to commit suicide, and that's not a crime. "Yes, but . . . ," argued the prosecution: if you hand someone a glass of water and don't tell her it's poisoned, obviously that's murder, even though in a certain literal sense she is the one killing herself by drinking it. In this case, the prosecution argued, the same sort of thing was going on. Hilde had testified that she would never have contemplated suicide; it was against her religion. Rather, she had been deceived into thinking that she could achieve a higher sort of life by slipping into the body of another person by the methods Bruno was recommending. I suspect you will have no trouble coming up with possible counterarguments the defense might make to that and with possible replies to those that the prosecution might offer in return. The defense might, for instance, compare Bruno to a person who manages to describe the glories of the afterlife so seductively that his listener tries to accelerate the arrival of that moment by suicide. This view of the matter would argue against Bruno's guilt. In support of Bruno's guilt, by contrast, the prosecution might then point out that it was no afterlife that Hilde had in mind, but something very real: after all, she was to awaken in the body of another mortal and live the life of a mortal for a while longer until Uliko, the monk, succeeded in his consciousness-raising meditative efforts.

And so on.

It is a difficult case, and different courts came to different conclusions, each reversing the one below. Although the prosecution did eventually prevail, the initial verdict of the scholarly community was that the highest court had gotten it wrong. More recently, however, legal scholars have come to take an entirely different view of such cases. Let us be clear, they say, as to what exactly makes this a difficult case. It is difficult because it is situated halfway between two easy cases that point in opposite directions. The case of the defendant who hands his victim a glass of poisoned water is one such easy case because it is clear that this is murder. The case of the defendant who persuades his victim to commit suicide is also relatively easy because it is clear that this is not murder. The Sirius case is hard because it is equidistant, as it were, from these two polar opposites. It somewhat resembles the poisoned-water case, and it somewhat resembles the suicide case; the dispute is essentially about which it resembles more. The question scholars have come to raise is why we insist, or rather, why the law insists, on limiting the choice to these two alternatives. Why do we have to pretend that it is like either of these cases when it is really like neither, or like both? Why not acknowledge that this is a hard case because it is *partly* like the first case and *partly* like the second case, and why not provide for a resolution of the case that lies *partway* between these two cases as well, that is, find the defendant *partly* guilty of murder and cut his punishment to half of what the defendant in the poisoned-water case would get?

All hard cases are like this. They wouldn't be litigated otherwise. Indeed just about all cases discussed in a typical law school class are like this. I mentioned a few typical ones in the introduction: If you kiss a sleeping woman and she does not find out about it until a long time after, are you guilty of a battery? If you chase an animal for a long time without actually managing to catch or kill it, do you nevertheless have legal possession of it, so that no other hunter is allowed to interfere?

When beginning law students encounter such cases, they are initially quite nonplussed. A little later they will try to actually resolve them, marshaling precedents, appealing to policy, constructing analogies. But by the end of the first year, or maybe even the first semester, they will often react with an air of frustrated resignation, as if to say: "I understand how this game is played. You've convinced me: all doctrines have borderline cases; everything is on a continuum; everything is a matter of degree. There are clear cases of battery, of legal possession, and of attempted murder and there are unclear cases, and you keep challenging us with cases you pick off the gray zone of the continuum. Why bother making this point again and again? Yes, we've got to draw a line somewhere on that continuum. So let the judge or the jury or whoever is in charge draw it, and let's be done with it. There really isn't much more to say about it."

There is another response, though, which some of them are sometimes tempted to make, and that is the one this chapter will concern itself with. They might say: "That case you gave us about the man kissing the sleeping woman—why do we need to say that it either is battery or that it is not? The fact is it is neither, or both. It is *sort of* a battery. So why not split the difference? Perhaps the thing to do is acknowledge that this is merely a *sort of* battery and therefore calls for only *sort of* the remedy appropriate for a full-fledged battery, a shorter sentence, say, if it's a crime we are talking about, or a lesser damage award, if it's a tort. In other words, since 'batteriness' is a matter of degree, let the remedy for it also be a matter of degree. If we judge the case of the sleeping girl to be halfway between a battery and a nonbattery, cut the sentence or the damage award in half. If we judge the case to be just 25 percent short of being a full-fledged battery, then cut the remedy by 25 percent. The same for all those other seemingly difficult cases involving legal possession, attempted murder, or what have you."

Why is it that the law does not just split the difference? Its refusal to do so is especially puzzling because when people enter into settlements, they end up doing exactly that. If something looks 60 percent like it is a battery and 40 percent like it is not, the parties will probably settle on damages corresponding to 60 percent of what the plaintiff is seeking. (They do so because they figure that there is a 60 percent chance that the judge will find it to be a battery and a 40 percent chance that he will not.) Why then does the law insist on crowning one side the winner rather than splitting the difference in just this way?

The question of why the law is so either/or in its verdicts is not one that has, until very recently, received terribly much attention. If that strikes you as implausible, it might be because you are vaguely reminded of another question that has received quite a bit of attention among legal scholars but that on closer examination turns out to be not really the same, namely the choice between "rules" and "standards."[2] People often think of rules as doctrines that are very either/or and of standards as doctrines that are much fuzzier. And so it might seem as though the debate over when and where and how the law should employ rules as opposed to standards is a debate about the either/or character of the law. But appearances here deceive.

When people speak about rules versus standards, what they usually have in mind is the distinction between what Carol Rose has called "crystals" and "mud"—between doctrines that are crisp and neat and not in need of a lot of litigation before we know what they cover and what they do not—like "first to file wins"—and doctrines that are vague, broad, and easy to grasp but hard to apply confidently, like those employing concepts of reasonableness or good faith.[3] Most bodies of law have both kinds of doctrines. Even tax law, which we think of as mostly rules, contains many doctrines of the latter kind: doctrines easy to grasp but hard to confidently apply like "form over substance" and various kinds of reasonableness requirements. But although superficially a crystalline rule looks more either/or than a muddy standard, in fact they are equally either/or, at least in the sense in which I am using that term here. That is because, however unsure we are whether a defendant has acted in good faith or bad, reasonably or negligently, the law will eventually classify his actions in one of those two bins, good or bad faith, reasonable or negligent. It won't split the difference.

Now, some people might immediately object that in characterizing the law as either/or, I am painting with an extremely broad brush. Look more closely, they will say, and the law will not turn out to be that either/or. What about the provocation doctrine, which reduces a murder committed under extreme emotional distress to manslaughter? Isn't that a way of splitting the difference between a fully excused killing and one that isn't excused at all? Isn't this a way of not being either/or? And what about the doctrine of comparative negligence, adopted in some jurisdictions, according to which the victim of someone else's negligent act will only be compensated for a part of his injury rather than the whole thing if he was negligent himself and thus helped cause the injury? That looks like a way of splitting the difference between making someone's contributory negligence irrelevant (as some places do) and making it a bar to any recovery (as other places do).

One problem with these examples is that they are hardly the norm. At most they force us to temper slightly the question with which I began, "Why is the law so either/or?" to "Why is the law so often, though not invariably, either/or?" But there is another, perhaps more interesting problem with these examples: they represent far less of a split-the-difference solution than they appear to. When facing a case that may or may not be one of provocation or comparative negligence, the law still insists on an either/or approach. If a case fits within those categories, we treat it one way; if it falls outside those categories, we treat it another way. What we do not do is to recognize in-between cases of provocation or of comparative negligence.

On Efforts to Explain and Do Away with Either/Or

The most immediate justification, and the most natural explanation, that suggests itself for the ubiquity of either/or in law are the so-called rule-of-law virtues associated with bright-line rules: we need bright-line rules to give citizens clear notice about what is permitted and what is not and to constrain the ability of judges to make arbitrary decisions.[4] On closer inspection, however, this explanation won't really hold up. Either/or does not necessarily, or even usually, result in bright-line rules. The boundaries of many doctrines are obscure. Yes, there is a fine line, but it is not a bright one—no one can comfortably predict where it lies, and so citizens do not in fact have notice and judges are not really constrained.

In fact, justifications and explanations for either/or have been very hard to come by, and what explanations there are do not serve to justify it. On the contrary, they serve to condemn it. Most of them run along lines given their most recent, vigorous, and ingenious expression by the sociologist Eviatar Zerubavel in his aptly titled book *The Fine Line*.[5] At the root of either/or, he argues, is our irrational dread of everything that lives on a boundary, whether that boundary be real or conceptual—which is why we are repelled by bats, which reside on the conceptual boundary between birds and rats; by "nasty rodents that live in houses yet remain outside the bounds of domestication"; by "insects that dwell in cracks that are zones of separation and that, as parasites, are both part of and separate from us"; by "reptiles that inhabit both land and water"; and by things that are "sticky, which is the intermediate state betwixt and between the solid and the liquid." It is also why we fear witches, revealingly often called "fence riders" between several different realms, and why we are readily made uneasy thinking about other "twilight persons," like embryos and corpses (or even "preinitiates," as anthropologists like to call adolescents, who straddle the boundary between child and adult).[6] As I said, this kind of explanation of either/or does not really aim to lend support to our habit of making either/or distinctions. Instead it means to steer us away from them on the ground that they are the product of little more than phobia, superstition, and cognitive bias.

This skepticism toward either/or distinctions is shared by many legal scholars and has resulted in numerous proposals to "continuize" the law's dichotomous approach by creating intermediate legal categories and embracing split-the-difference solutions. It will be helpful to have some concrete examples of this before us.

Radical Proposal I: Contracts Continuized

In the early part of the twentieth century, an iconoclastic German scholar, Heinrich Hoeniger, tried to recast all of German contract law along such lines.[7] Here is one illustration of how it was supposed to work. German law, like American, distinguishes between bargains, involving a quid pro quo, and mere gifts, but the rules governing each, though perfectly commonsensical, are a little different from ours. For instance, suppose that the thing I gave you turns out to have a problem: it blows up and injures you. Under American law, if I was negligent in not noticing and not warning you about that problem when I gave the thing to you (whether I sold it or gave to you as a gift), I will be liable for the harm I caused. Under German law, I am not—except in really extreme cases of gross negligence.

But whether something is a bargain or a gift is often a murky question, as all first-year law students learn from a famous case about an uncle who promises to pay for his nephew's education if he will only give up drinking and smoking. Is the uncle proposing a bargain, offering to pay money in exchange for the nephew's giving up those pleasures, or is he simply promising to make him a gift but attaching a precondition to it? Hoeniger would say it is neither, or both. It is half gift, half bargain and, according to Hoeniger, should be given the kind of in-between treatment I described earlier: hold the seller liable for something more than simple negligence and something less than gross negligence.

In a related vein, Larry Alexander has recently drawn attention to how unnatural it is to think of the most basic ingredient of consensual interactions—voluntary consent—as an either/or concept, something that is either present or absent.[8] The two factors most responsible for vitiating voluntary consent—coercion and lack of information—clearly are matters of degree. To be sure there are easy polar cases: "Your money or your life," and "Will you agree to a hysterectomy?" when the patient has no clue what a hysterectomy is are easy cases of *invalid* consent. In the first case it is coercion, and in the second case it is lack of information that obviously invalidates the consent. And naturally there are easy cases at the other end as well, cases where the complete absence of coercion or mis-information makes the consent uncontroversially valid. But what about cases in between those two extremes? Surely consent is not invalid in all cases where there is some measure of coercion or misinformation. "Sleep with me or I will not repay the money I owe you, and you will have to go to the trouble of suing me," is an illegitimate threat, but not one that will in-validate the woman's consent if she decides to do so to avoid having to sue for the money. If the consent were invalid, the person making the threat would be guilty of rape, and that does not seem right. "This cosmetic sur-gery will cause your TV career to take off," says the cosmetic surgeon to his patient, who then consents to it. Even if the surgeon is lying, that would not invalidate the patient's consent to the surgery. If it did, the surgeon would be guilty of battery and that does not seem right either.

But if there are cases in which coercion and misinformation vitiate con-sent and other cases in which they do not, where is the line to be drawn? More important, is it likely that there really is such a line? asks Alexander. Isn't it more likely, he suggests, that the validity of consent is something that increases gradually as we move from a complete absence of coercion to the overpowering presence of it and from no information at all to an overabundance of it? And so there is no line; there is only a continuum. Shouldn't the law stop pretending there is such a line when there isn't? Rather than saying that sometimes consent is valid and other times it is not, wouldn't it make more sense to treat consent as only partially valid in most cases, depending on the degree of coercion and misinformation? In practice that would mean that a patient who only partially consented to what the surgeon did to him could recover only part of the damages he suffered as a result.

Radical Proposal II: Good-Faith Purchasers for Value Continuized

Fifty years ago, law professor John Coons first put the either/or problem on the Anglo-American scholarly agenda. In a pioneering article, "Ap-proaches to Court-Imposed Compromise," he proposed reforms to vari-ous parts of law, similar in spirit to those of Hoeniger. His most exemplary proposal involved the problem of the good-faith purchaser for value (sometimes called "the eternal triangle of property law"). The problem is this: a thief steals a radio from its rightful owner. He then sells the radio to someone who has no idea that it is stolen, the so-called good-faith purchaser for value. Sometime later the rightful owner discovers the radio in the hands of the good-faith purchaser and demands that it be returned. What now? Jurisdictions the world over do one of two things. They either require that the good-faith purchaser return the radio, or they allow him to keep it. They rarely do what Coons thinks would be the sensible thing: split the difference between the purchaser and the rightful owner.[9] Obviously, Coons does not have in mind cutting the radio in two. Rather, what he contemplates is letting one party keep the radio but requiring him to pay some money, perhaps half the radio's value, to the other. After all, the two sides are equally innocent, so why shouldn't they share equally in the loss? "Assuming the case where neither [side] has acted foolishly, the equities and policies stand in rough balance," writes Coons. Yet the law "awards the whole pie to one of the parties . . . even though the social interests involved may be in perfect equilibrium and though the parties to the litigation are equally culpable or innocent. . . . [But if] the case favoring one party is no more convincing than its opposite, such a result is [to be] rejected. . . . It [would be] discriminatory to prefer either [side]."[10]

As you can see, Coons limits his split-the-difference proposal to cases in which the merits of the two sides are evenly balanced. But of course one need not be so parsimonious. It would be very much in the spirit of his proposal to treat parties that are not equally balanced differently *only to the extent* that they are not evenly balanced. If the merits stand in a 40/60 ratio, say, rather than a 50/50 ratio, the most natural course might be to split the difference between them on a 40/60 basis as well.

Radical Proposal III: Criminal Law Defenses Continuized

More recently, a criminal law scholar, Douglas Husak, has proposed reforming the law of criminal defenses in a similar way. Husak has raised the issue of what we should do about defendants who partially satisfy the prerequisites of a criminal law defense, such as the person who uses excessive force to fend off an attack, thus almost but not quite meeting the requirements of self-defense. Or the person who is pressured by untoward circumstances into breaking the law, thus almost but not quite meeting the requirements for the defense of necessity or of duress. Or the person who is slightly deranged, thus almost but not quite meeting the requirements for insanity. In all these circumstances, Husak thinks that the defendant should be credited with a partial version of self-defense, or necessity, or duress, or insanity. He points out that this is not nearly as radical a proposal as it sounds: to some extent, we already grant partial insanity defenses—under the doctrines of provocation and diminished capacity. Sentencing practice has long recognized various mitigating factors, and under this rubric judges often recognize what are in effect partial defenses. Husak is asking us to be more systematic, explicit, and consistent about all this.[11]

Radical Proposal IV: The Rest of the Law Continuized

Of late, there have been a flood of proposals to continuize innumerable other areas of law. Michael Moore has proposed continuizing the law of causation.[12] Instead of just saying that something was proximately caused or not, why not treat causal proximity the way we treat spatial proximity—as something that comes in degrees?

Corporate law scholars William Klein, Eric Zolt, and Mitu Gulati have proposed continuizing the distinction between debt and equity on which a variety of tax and corporate law doctrines depend.[13] Whether something qualifies as debt or equity depends on a variety of clearly continuous attributes, such as the degree of risk and the degree of control an investor acquires with a given investment. So why not make the treatment of debt and equity equally continuous? If we did, it would have some dramatic consequences. It would mean, for instance, a radical revision of the corporate income tax code (which makes interest on debt deductible but not dividends paid on stock).

Michael Abramowicz has suggested continuizing the calculation of damage awards to allow plaintiffs who have fallen just short of proving their case by a preponderance of the evidence to recover a fraction of the damages they are seeking: very roughly, if they prove their case up to a 40 percent threshold, say, they should recover 40 percent of the sought-after damages.[14]

Larry Alexander, in his revealingly titled "Scalar Properties, Binary Judgment," presents a plethora of building-block concepts of the law—his discussion of consent I already alluded to above—that he believes are fundamentally scalar and should thus not be forced into an artificially binary framework.[15] He suggests that some of the most notoriously fruitless debates in law, like the one surrounding abortion, stem from our insistence that something like personhood sets in at some magical point rather than coming into existence gradually.

Radical Reform V: Continuization Outside of Law—Personal Identity for Example

Law is not the only domain in which the continuization idea has made inroads of late. One of the most radical instances of it has occurred in the philosophy of personal identity.

What is the philosophy of personal identity? When A's brain is transplanted into B's body, and B's brain is transplanted into A's body, which one is A and which one is B? This does not seem like a hard question: the B-body person now is A and the A-body person now is B. But things get quite a bit harder when we consider some variations. For instance, imagine we transplanted a part of A's brain into B and a part of B's brain into A. What now? Does identity now depend on which body houses most of A's brain? That is, if the A-body still has more than 50 percent of A's brain, then the A-body is A, and if the B-body now houses more than 50 percent of A's brain, then the B-body is A? What if the B-body gets only 45 percent of the neurons, but they happen to be the ones that control the higher cognitive functions, whereas the 55 percent retained by the A-body are mostly involved with motor control? Or imagine that 55 percent of A's brain is kept in a jar, ready to be reactivated in someone's body, while 45 percent is implanted in B's body? Does that mean that the B-body is not really A, whereas it would be if the 55 percent had been destroyed? But how can whether it is or is not depend on exactly what happens to the 55 percent chunk of A's brain?

There are many more variations on this theme. What if someone is "beamed up" or "teleported" from one planet to another, the way it happens in *Star Trek*? Is the person "up there" really the same as the person formerly "down here," even though none of the actual neurons have traveled "up there," only the information needed to reconstruct the person out of new materials? What if someone is cloned but simultaneously killed and some or most of his memories transferred to his cloned duplicate? Is that then the same or a different person? What if someone suffers complete amnesia and a personality transformation that makes him exactly like, let us say, Greta Garbo? And on and on. This is what the philosophy of personal identity contemplates.

One contemporary philosopher, Derek Parfit, has argued that the problem with the way we usually approach these questions is that we are being too either/or. We unreasonably take the position, he says, that whenever someone is subjected to one of these operations—the transplant, the beaming, and so forth—his identity is either preserved or destroyed. One or the other. Either/or. But not both. That, Parfit believes, is a mistake. What we should instead say is that the resulting person is "sort of" identical with the original.—that he is partially identical with the original and partially not. To the extent that he shares the same psychological makeup and some of the memories, he is identical with the original person, but that identity is only a partial affair. That, he says, is the reasonable way to look at the matter.

To sum up, despite its prevalence, either/or has proved hard to justify. Understandably, therefore, there have been numerous proposals to "continuize" it away—to replace existing binary categories with a "scalar" spectrum of intermediate possibilities. Proposals of this sort have been made in many areas of law—criminal law, torts, contracts, property, tax and corporate law—of which I have sampled a few.[16]

Dissenting Voices: Evidentiary Uncertainty

There are occasional defenders of either/or. One of the most striking arguments in behalf of either/or, at least in the way we deal with evidentiary uncertainty, has been offered by the legal scholar and statistician David Kaye.[17] The burden of proof in a civil case is a simple preponderance of the evidence. That means, roughly speaking, that the plaintiff wins his entire sought-after damage award whether he has proved his case with evidence making it just 51 percent likely that he should win, with evidence making it 60 percent likely that he should win, or with evidence making it 80 percent likely that he should win. Conversely, he loses his case even if he comes as close as, say, 50 percent of proving it. As I mentioned before, some people have been troubled by that and have suggested that if a plaintiff proves his case by only 51 percent, then he should get merely 51 percent of the damages he asked for. And if he proves it by 60 percent, then 60 percent of the damages, and if by 80 percent, then 80 percent of the damages. Something analogous could even be suggested for criminal cases. Current practice puts the burden of proof for the prosecutor as "beyond a reasonable doubt," which presumably means the defendant should be acquitted as long as the prosecution's evidence falls short of, say, demonstrating his guilt with a 95 percent probability. It might thus be suggested that if we are only, say, 80 percent confident of the defendant's guilt, we simply reduce his punishment by some suitable amount, rather than decline to convict him altogether.

Kaye reveals, however, a surprising property of the either/or way of treating verdicts. Let's look more closely at a civil case in which the evidence is 80 percent in the plaintiff's favor. What that means is that in eight out of ten such cases the plaintiff deserves to receive all of the damages he asks for; in two out of ten he does not. Let's assume the damages to be $100. Then, under the current regime we are committing judicial errors worth $200, $100 for each of our two "misjudged" defendants. Suppose now we switched to a regime that awards the plaintiff only 80 percent of the damages he asks for. If we do this, every plaintiff will be getting $20 less. What this means, first of all, is that the two "misjudged" defendants now have to pay only $80 each, $20 less per person, than they did before. The liability burden unjustly imposed on them has been reduced by 2 times $20, that is, $40. That's not perfect, but an improvement: we have reduced the extent of the judicial error by $40. But the new system also has a negative effect. It is not just the two "misjudged" defendants who will be paying $20 less than before; the eight guilty defendants who should be paying $100 will also see their liability burden reduced by $20 each. This means an increase in the amount of judicial error by 8 times $20, or $160. So by switching from an either/or fact-finding system to a split-the-difference fact-finding system, we are decreasing the amount of judicial error by $40 and increasing it by $160, a net increase of $120: in other words, under the old system we had a judicial error of $200 and under the new system, $320. That's Kaye's argument for an either/or system of fact finding.

That's a truly insightful and novel discovery concerning the currently prevailing either/or rule of evidence. Unfortunately, it is not one that can easily be generalized to deal with either/or problems in other contexts. The more usual either/or problem arises not because we are lacking in evidence but because we are dealing with imperfect instances of an attempt, a battery, a contract, and so forth. It feels somewhat unjust to treat these imperfect instances as though they were perfect instances of what they are not. If something looks to us like an 80 percent contract, that means, very roughly speaking, that it has 80 percent of the characteristics we look for in a contract, not that we are confident that in eight out of ten such cases we are in fact dealing with a contract, whereas in two out ten we are not.

Dissenting Voices: Color Perception

In a book devoted largely to philosophical problems raised by perception, the philosopher Nelson Goodman suggests, quite indirectly and without meaning to, a very novel and intriguing way of explaining and justifying either/or phenomena. The suggestion arises out of his work with an experimental psychologist, Paul Kolers, investigating the perception of something called "apparent motion."[18]

Apparent motion occurs in its simplest form when a spot flashed very briefly on a contrasting background is followed after about ten seconds by exposure of another such spot a short distance away. "With a shorter time-interval at the same distance, we see two spots as flashed simultaneously; with a longer interval, we see the two spots flashed successively; but within the specified time-interval, we see one spot moving from the first position to the second."[19] This is what allows us to make movies.

With Goodman's guidance, Kolers embarked on an extended exploration of the further ramifications of this phenomenon. Specifically, Goodman and Kolers wondered about "what happens when figures rather than dots or spots are successively flashed." Since a figure is in a sense just a collection of dots, they surmised that it would be seen to move just like a dot, which was indeed the case. Next they wondered, what would happen "if different figures are flashed, say a square first and then a triangle or a circle? Or suppose the two figures are the same in shape but different in size." What they found was that "almost any difference between two figures is smoothly resolved."[20]

Somewhere along the line, Goodman began to wonder, "What happens when the successively flashed displays differ in color?" Previous investigators had said that those changes are smoothed out just like changes in shape or size. Oddly, however, "no one had investigated the *route* of such resolution." There would seem to be many possible ways in which such a smooth transition could happen. It might for instance be that the "route of change from, say, red to green passes through median gray or through the spectral hues orange and yellow or bypasses all of these." Eventually Kolers carried out experiments involving changes in color. "In these experiments, the displays successively flashed were of different colors—sometimes contrasting, even complementary, colors such as red and green, sometimes colors more nearly alike such as red and deep pink. Sometimes the figures flashed were the same in size and shape; sometimes the first might be, say, a small red square while the second was a large green (or pink) circle. As expected," Goodman reports, "the color differences do not at all interfere with smooth apparent transition in place, size, or shape. But what course does the transition in color take?" Over the years, Goodman writes, "Kolers himself and a variety of other psychologists, as well as nonpsychologists like the present writer, made conjectures. What is yours?" Having invited the reader to pause and struggle with the problem a little himself, Goodman continues: "None of us came anywhere near guessing right—and neither did you! Common sense, which surely tells us . . . that the color change will proceed smoothly along some path or other, has here tricked us even worse than usual. The actual result of the experiment is shocking. Flash a small red square and then a large green (or pink) circle, within the specified time and distance limitations, and we see the square, while smoothly moving and transforming and growing into the circle, *remaining red until about midcourse and then abruptly changing to green for pink*."[21]

What could this be due to? Again, Goodman reports on his various speculations. For a while he thought it might be because in everyday life we encounter abrupt changes in shape or size less often than abrupt changes in color. Then he entertained some other possibilities until a sudden realization came to him: that he had "missed the most central and conspicuous consideration of all: *that virtually every clear case of visual motion perception depends upon abrupt shift in color*."[22] What does he mean by that?

Consider a straight row of lightbulbs, each lighting up successively. If they do so in quick succession, we will perceive a dot of light traveling across the row. In the process, each lightbulb flashes very quickly on and off, exhibiting a very abrupt change in color from dark to light and then to dark again. Now suppose we tried to make this change less abrupt, by gradually dimming each lightbulb and equally gradually letting the one next to it grow brighter. Now the interval between the one light going out and the other light coming on would have grown much too long for us to see any kind of continuous motion. We would simply see one light gradually going out and the other gradually coming on. The apparent motion is gone. In other words, by introducing one kind of continuity, in the change from dark to bright and vice versa, we have necessarily eliminated another, the apparent continuous motion of the light spot across the line of lightbulbs.

There seems to be a larger lesson here that goes beyond color perception. The lesson is that sometimes the creation of one kind of continuity—the sense of apparent motion in this case—requires the creation of a discontinuity elsewhere: in this case, the abrupt change in color. Could it be that something like that is going on in law? I think that that is so. In the next chapter, we will see how.

Taking Stock

The law has the reputation of splitting hairs. The reputation is well-deserved. Legal doctrines have sharp and hard-to-justify boundaries. Many people have thought that that is in fact something that cannot be justified and should be changed, although there have been some interesting dissents from that seeming consensus.

In what follows, I will try to show why the law could not possibly avoid being either/or. My point of departure will be one particularly illuminating instance of the either/or problem—the question of why the law treats death as an event rather than a process—and from the answer to that question, I will then proceed to generalize to other manifestations of it. When I say that the law treats death as an event rather than a process, I mean that whereas the law assumes a specific moment of death, in fact a dying man traverses a continuous route in gradually making his way from full-fledged aliveness to total bodily decomposition. Many stages in this process might be (and have been) designated the point at which death occurs. Even more plausibly, however, one might say that death does not occur at any one point. There simply does not seem to be in this gradual process any single moment that deserves to be especially singled out as the point at which the realm of the living has been left for that of the dead. Why, then, does the law insist on proceeding as though there were such a point by putting everyone under one set of rules as long as he is judged fully alive and under another set of rules as soon as he is judged not to be? Why not make the treatment we accord the dying commensurate with the gradualness of the process? Why not have their rights decline as gradually as their membership among the living? In short, why not view death as a matter of degree? The answer to that question—the explanation of why we do not—will then help us understand the either/or character of many other legal concepts: why consent, coercion, self-defense, abortion, intention, attempt, and contract, among others, are not matters of degree either.

Once the principal argument has been laid out, it will help us to deepen our understanding of the issues if we cast a brief look at some relatively recent developments in ethics due to Larry Temkin and Stuart

Rachels, the analysis of the Sorites paradox, due to Roy Sorensen and Timothy Williamson, and in social choice due to Graciela Chichilnisky. These are developments that could, once fully digested (not something I purport to have done), immeasurably expand our grasp on the either/or problem.

CHAPTER ELEVEN

Line Drawing as a Matter of Life and Death

The Largely Unavoidable Pervasiveness of Either/Or

I am not going to defend the either/or character of legal doctrines. I am simply going to show why any efforts to change things are doomed. What I will be arguing is that most of the time either/or can't be avoided, or more precisely, that if we tried to purge a doctrine of it, we would find that either/or has simply migrated to another part of the doctrine or has been replaced by some other, far more troublesome feature. I will do this by looking at a variety of basic legal concepts and doctrines that people have been tempted to continuize away and showing that such attempts could not possibly work—in that we can only affect where a sharp discontinuity will occur, not whether it will occur at all.

I begin with one very special case—the question of why life and death cannot be thought of as lying on a continuum, as occurring by degrees—and will then proceed to generalize from the answer to that question to the larger problem of why it would be difficult to turn every legal boundary into a continuum: why, in Larry Alexander's apt formulation, it cannot be made scalar rather than binary.

In putting forward my argument about life and death, I will adapt for my own purposes an ingenious example created by Larry Temkin, which rivals in its suggestive power some of the most famous intuition pumps philosophers have thought of, from Nelson Goodman's grue-bleen to Judith Jarvis Thomson's violinist.[1] I should caution the reader, however, that I am using it to prove a rather different point than the one for which Temkin initially conceived it (about which I will have more to say later).[2]

Why Death Is an Event and Not a Process

Could we treat death as something that occurs by degrees? At present of course we do no such thing. There is a specific stage—brain death in most contemporary jurisdictions—prior to which one is treated as a living human being entitled to all the rights and privileges our law grants to the living, but upon the arrival of which all of those vanish. What kinds of rights and privileges do I have in mind? There are too many to list, since most everything in our law is for the benefit of the living. It will suffice for our purposes to focus on one of the most elementary: *the right not to be destroyed (as well as not to be exposed to an undue risk of being destroyed).* I use the odd term *destroyed* rather than *killed* to emphasize the discontinuity in our treatment of the living and the dead. Destruction of the living is one thing, and destruction of the dead is another. This is why we refer to the destruction of the living as a killing and the destruction of the dead as the disposition (or possibly mutilation) of a corpse.

As we look more closely at the stages through which everyone passes as he moves from being fully alive to being fully dead, it starts to feel increasingly artificial to designate any one point in this progression as demarcating the boundary between life and death. A person is a bundle of organs, every single one of which can function well, adequately, poorly, barely, or not at all. The brain is just one of these. Not only is brain death not an obvious, indisputable divider between life and death, there is the fact that brain death itself is a matter of degree, of stages, at any one of which someone might linger and languish for shorter or longer periods. Would it not make sense to treat these intermediate stages as intermediate legal categories, during which someone enjoys only a portion of the rights that accrue to him while fully alive and a good deal more than would accrue to him after he is deemed dead?[3] Let's see what would happen if we tried to make good on this.

Imagine, then, a human being at a thousand (or even a hundred thousand, or a million if that seems more plausible) separate stages, ranging from full aliveness at one end to utter cellular decomposition at the other. This is the continuum along which, if we departed from the usual either/or approach, we would gradually reduce someone's rights. Let's call the creature just one notch below a fully alive, regular human being H-minus-1, the creature two notches below a regular human being H-minus-2, and so on. Now suppose we had a choice to make between an H on one side and an H-minus-1 on the other side. What I have in mind here is a choice—any choice—about whether H or H-minus-1 should suffer a certain adverse effect, a choice, for instance, between giving aid to H or to H-minus-1. (Or a choice between helping H by imposing a risk on H-minus-1, or not helping H and therefore not imposing a risk on H-minus-1. But let's stick with the first and simplest of these, the choice of whom to aid.) To sharpen the issue, let us assume that the decision is made by someone with a duty to render aid, an emergency room physician, say, or a lifeguard.

If the choice is between an H and an H-minus-1 and we subscribe to the gradualist approach, we should presumably give the edge, by a narrow margin, to H. Being more fully alive, he has a greater claim to the kind of aid we accord the living. What if the choice is between an H-minus-1 and an H-minus-2? Presumably, by the same token, H-minus-1 should win out over H-minus-2 and so on down the line to H-minus-1,000 (or whatever the number at the far end of the continuum).

Next, however, let us complicate the choice slightly. Suppose the choice is not between H and H-minus-1 but between one H and two H-minus-1s.[4] Now it would seem that the edge belongs to the latter. Two H-minus-1s seem worth more, as it were, than one H. The doubling in quantity seems to more than make up for the slight drop in quality. Let us repeat this process by comparing three H-minus-2s with two H-minus-1's and one H. Presumably the three H-minus-2s beat out the two H-minus-1s, which in turn beat out the one H. Now keep reiterating this process, so that we have a menu of alternatives that contains at one end 1,001 H-minus-1,000s, 1,000 H-minus-999s, and 999 H-minus-998s and at the other end 3 H-minus-2s, 2 H-minus-1s and 1 H. To be painfully explicit, here is the menu:

1 H
2 H-minus-1s
3 H-minus-2s
4 H-minus-3s
. . .
999 H-minus-998s
1,000 H-minus-999s
1,001 H-minus-1000s

Apparently the package in the second row (2 H-minus-1s) should be chosen over the package in the first row (a single H); the package in the third row (3 H-minus-2s) should be chosen over the package in the second row and therefore also over the package in the first row; and continuing all the way down the line, the package consisting of 1,001 H-minus-1,000s should be chosen over the single H as well. More schematically put:

H < 2 H-minus-1s < 3 H-minus-2s < 4 H-minus-3s . . . < 1,001 H-minus-1,000s,

where < of course means "less deserving of help than." But this is absurd! A single H-minus-1,000 is a collection of completely decomposed cells. How can a set of 1,001 such collections possibly trump a single living human being, which is what an H represents? Something has gone wrong. But what?

One or more steps in our chain of inference must be in error. Somewhere in our chain of comparisons, we must have made a mistake. At least one of these inequality signs must not be correct. But what would it mean to say that one of these inequality signs is wrong?

It can mean only one thing: that at some point it must be the case that subtracting an increment in quality from H-minus-n as we go down to H-minus-$(n + 1)$ cannot be made up for by increasing the quantity of such creatures by one. A small decrease in quality cannot be made up for by a small increase in quantity.

Now suppose that as we decrease the quality, we tried to make up for it by a more dramatic increase in quantity. If that were possible, we would then still be able to say that for every H-minus-n there is some number of H-minus-$(n + 1)$s that is more valuable than the H-minus-n. We could then form the same chain of inference as before, according to which some incredibly large number of H-minus-1,000s is more valuable than a single H. But that is just as absurd as the original assertion that 1,001 H-minus-1,000s is more valuable than a single H. The absurdity is not diminished by raising the number of H-minus-1,000s.

How can we avoid this absurd conclusion? Only in one way, it seems: by assuming that there is a point, some particular n, at which no increase in the quantity of H-minus-$(n + 1)$s can make up for the decline in quality from H-minus-n to H-minus-$(n + 1)$. And that point is a *point*. What we have here is a stunningly abrupt transition: suddenly, at the drop of a dime, it is no longer possible to do what was always possible before we reached that point n, namely, to compensate for a drop in quality by vastly upping the quantity of those inferior-grade Hs. This is strange indeed. But what else can one conclude? What else, that is, but that this is the point at which death occurs and that inasmuch as it occurs at such a point, death really is an event and not a process. There is no gentle going into that good night, as it were. Death is a cliff, not a gentle slope. Conceptually it is not possible to be just a little bit dead or a little bit alive. Death is never partial; death is quintessentially an either/or phenomenon.

This analysis raises several questions. The first and most natural of those questions is where exactly that magical threshold is located that is supposed to separate life from death. I am not sure that we are constrained to locate it anywhere in particular. Obviously it cannot be too close to either side of the life-to-death spectrum of possibilities, too close, that is, to the clearly alive end or the clearly dead end. All that this argument demonstrates is that we are constrained to have such a point somewhere and that it needs to be a point. Admittedly, this looks like a somewhat peculiar state of affairs, and perhaps there are constraints I am overlooking that would preclude all but one location for that point (though I doubt it). For now, however, all I am able to conclude is that there is such a point—but that we have discretion about where to put it.

A second question raised by the analysis is this: even if there is a single point of demarcation between the living and the dead, does that necessarily preclude distinguishing between different degrees of aliveness prior to reaching that point? If we suppose that it takes more and more "inferior" lives to outweigh a full-fledged life as we get nearer and nearer to the point of demarcation between life and death, would we not say that such an "inferior" creature is less and less of a human being and should therefore be treated as less and less of a human being, until the moment when it counts for zero? (Note that doing so would not eliminate the discontinuity: it would still be the case that a million "inferior" lives would count for a lot, whereas a million inferior lives minus an increment would count for nothing.)

If we did this, it would have some awkward consequences. There is, to begin with, a problem the philosopher Peter Unger has drawn attention to: we generally feel that the rights granted to all human beings should be the same regardless of abilities and disabilities.[5] The progression from life to death is a progression from ability to disability. If we were to treat the dying differently depending on where they are located on that progression, it seems we ought to also treat the fully alive differently—and remember, we are talking about the most basic rights here, not their eligibility for an NSF fellowship—if they differ in some crucial abilities. And most of us would feel loath to do that.[6]

There is another awkward consequence of treating a life as less of a life as we approach the point of demarcation between life and death. Let us suppose very unrealistically—too unrealistically?—that the mechanisms of pain are among the last to wither away. Next imagine someone at the full-aliveness end of the continuum who is being subjected to severe pain. As the person moves across the continuum, seeing that pain inflicted on him should bother us less and less (even if we imagine ourselves to be the person in question), because it is being inflicted on something that less and less resembles a living creature (and constitutes less and less of "you," if you are that person). To put the point even more forcefully: imagine that when the person is still at the full-aliveness end, he is in fact only suffering from a slight dull pain, and suppose that as he moves across the continuum we gradually increase that pain until, near the life-and-death threshold we have raised it to some horrendous level. If the person becomes less and less human as he becomes less alive, we should then be no more bothered by this horrendous pain than we were by administering a slight dull pain to him when he was still fully alive. But I don't think we feel that way. Our concern about pain will not in fact diminish as we move toward death, whether we are thinking about someone else's pain or our own. Therefore this particular right at least—the right not to be subjected to pain—does not diminish gradually but rather quite discontinuously.

A third question concerns the more general logic of the argument being illustrated by the life-and-death example. What really makes the example work? In brief, what makes it work is this: there is an attribute that all H-minus-n's on the life side of the ledger possess that all the H-minus-n's on the death side of the ledger lack: an increase in their number is considered a good thing. The more we have, the better it is. This holds for all on the life side and does not hold for any on the death side. There is a corresponding attribute that all H-minus-n's on the death side of the ledger have but that all the H-minus-n's on the life side lack: an increase in *their* number is considered a bad thing. Now let's be careful. I don't mean by this that moving people over from the life side to the death side is a bad thing. It is, but that is not what I am alluding to. Rather, I mean that having more of those nonliving H-minus-n's around is basically just an increase in waste—corpses—that needs to be disposed of. This is something that holds for everyone on the death side and for no one on the life side. Something else is crucial to note about these two properties that one group has and the other lacks. They are not possessed by degrees. The properties are either present or absent; there is no in-between. Thus the transition from those who have these properties to those who do not cannot be anything but abrupt.

A final question about my example: is this argument peculiar to the life-and-death context or can it be generalized? The answer is that analogous arguments (some of them strictly analogous, some of them loosely analogous) seem to apply in many other settings, as I will try to illustrate in the following pages.

How the Argument Can Be Generalized to Abortion, the Killing of Witches, and Other Life-and-Death Cases

What goes for the end of life would seem to also go for the beginning. Just about everything said about death can be said, by way of mirror image, about the beginning of life. And therein lies an answer to Larry Alexander and others who question whether there really is any one point at which life can be said to begin.[7]

Indeed it is a straightforward matter to generalize the argument to anything in any way, depending on the distinction between life and death, including the mens rea, or mental state required for a killing to be considered homicide. A verdict of homicide requires a belief on the part of the killer that he is dealing with a human being. (It does not matter whether we are talking about intentional, knowing, or reckless killings. Either way, some belief about the victim is required.) There actually have been cases where the issue of whether the defendant could be said to believe he was killing a human was a difficult and controversial one. The most interesting of these cases involved Sudanese tribesmen who killed other tribesmen, taking them to be witches or ghosts. The courts held that someone who believed he was killing a ghost was like someone who believed he was killing an animal and therefore should not be said to have intentionally killed a human being. Not so, however, someone who believed he was killing a witch. In the belief system of the perpetrators, they reasoned, a ghost is a supernatural being with human appearance, whereas a witch is a human being with supernatural powers. Drawing such a fine line, creating such a sharp discontinuity between such very similar forms of superstition, has struck many people as silly. A straightforward analogy of my argument so far, however, would serve to vindicate the courts' sharply discontinuous treatment of would-be ghost-killers and would-be witch-killers.[8]

Why Consent Is Not a Matter of Degree

Loosely analogous arguments can be made about legal concepts having nothing to do with life and death. Let us return to the issue of consent and coercion. Consent seems a matter of degree (in Alexander's terminology, it seems "scalar") because the factors that can impair the validity of consent—coercion and deception—seem themselves to be matters of degree. And why do coercion and deception seem like matters of degree? Because they in turn depend on things that seem like matters of degree: the more serious the wrongful threat, the more coercive it seems; the less serious the threat, the less coercive it seems. And similarly for deception, but let's limit our attention to coercion. (*Caveat*: The analysis that follows is going to be a bit intricate—not difficult, just intricate. If you are simply interested in getting the general drift of my analysis of either/or rather than its specific applicability to consent, just skip ahead to the next section.)

Is it really true, though, that the more serious a wrongful threat, the greater the coercion and the less valid the consent? To see whether it is, we first need to gain some greater clarity about what makes us regard one threat as more serious—that is, as more blameworthy—than another. One obvious determining factor would seem to be the severity of what is being threatened: threatening someone with death seems more serious than threatening him with the loss of some property. But that can't be all there is to it. After all, threatening to steal someone's property seems more serious—in the sense of being more blameworthy—than threatening to foreclose on his mortgage, even if the theft and the foreclosure would result in equally severe financial losses. The other factor at work seems to be the wrongfulness of the threatened act: stealing is more wrongful than foreclosing, which usually is not wrongful at all, and even when it is, let's say because it violates some provision of the mortgage agreement, it isn't wrongful enough to be a crime. In other words, the more wrongful what is threatened, the more serious is the threat, the greater is the coercion, and the less valid is the consent. Or so it seems.

Now that we understand what we mean when we say that we consider one wrongful threat more serious than another, let's ask why it seems so plausible to say that the more serious the threat, the greater the coercion and the less valid the consent. It is a very seductive intuition, but once we take a closer look at its basis, we will see that it is in fact wrong.

Let's begin by comparing two very straightforward cases of coercion. Case 1 is simply "Give me the $1,000 you have in your wallet, or I will kill you," followed by the victim's turning over the money. A very straightforward case of robbery. The victim consented, but of course the consent is invalid. That's what makes it robbery. We regard robbery as a very serious crime. Compare this with Case 2, an almost equally simple case: "Give me the $1,000 you have in your wallet, or I will destroy your treasured rosebushes." Another straightforward case of robbery. Here too the victim's consent will of course be considered invalid. Let us use these two cases to test the suggestion that as the threatened conduct becomes less wrongful, so does the coerciveness of the defendant's actions and the invalidity of the victim's consent. What exactly makes this a tempting view?

What makes it tempting seems to be an argument that I have never actually seen expressly articulated, probably because most people who have thought about the matter regard it as self-evidently true. It goes something like this: "Robbing someone of $1,000 is a very serious crime. Destroying someone's rosebushes is a less serious crime. When the defendant decides to accommodate the victim's preference for giving up $1,000 rather than having his rosebushes destroyed, he is presumably less blameworthy than if he destroyed the rosebushes outright. Moreover, destroying someone's rosebushes is surely less blameworthy than committing a your-money-or-your-life kind of robbery. In other words, a your-money-or-your-life robbery *is worse than* destroying someone's rosebushes, which in turn *is worse than* accepting $1,000 to not destroy someone's rosebushes. Therefore, the your-money-or-your-rosebushes type of robber is behaving less coercively than the your-money-or-your-life kind of robber."

Something like this logic must underlie the perception that as threats diminish in seriousness, coercion diminishes, and consent gains greater validity. One can imagine adding further cases, in which the blameworthiness of the threat goes down more and more until it has reached zero, at which point presumably the victim's consent has become 100 percent valid.

Let us make this more concrete, by imagining more specifically what such further cases might look like. One such case, let's call it Case 3, might involve the defendant threatening the victim not with a crime but with a mere civil wrong, a tort: "Give me the $1,000 in your wallet, or I will drive around your neighborhood with tortious negligence [negligence enough for a civil wrong, but not a crime], putting you and your family at risk." What is threatened in Case 3 is less serious than the conduct exhibited in Case 2 (robbery), since it is a mere tort, a civil wrong, that carries with it only the obligation to pay damages if harm should ensue. Accommodating the victim's preference to pay $1,000 in lieu of subjecting him to negligent driving in his vicinity is presumably better than not accommodating that preference and proceeding to drive around negligently. Hence it would seem that Case 3 is less bad than Case 2. (In other words, the defendant is less blameworthy.)

Let's extend the argument even further by imagining Case 4, in which what is threatened is not illegal at all but merely immoral: "Give me $1,000, or I will publicize your past relationship with me, which you would find highly embarrassing." Publicizing the relationship would not be illegal—neither a crime, nor a tort—but under the right set of circumstances highly immoral. Being merely immoral, it is less bad than what occurs in Case 3, which involves the extraction of money in exchange for not doing something illegal. Furthermore, accommodating the victim's preference for paying rather than being publically humiliated presumably is better than actually humiliating him. Whence we can conclude, it seems, that Case 4 is less bad than Case 3. Finally, we can imagine a fifth case, in which what is threatened is only very, very mildly immoral, for example, "Give me $1,000, or I will end our friendship," which seems barely coercive at all, so that the victim's payment of $1,000 seems backed by a 100 percent valid consent.

The argument I have just sketched out seems to fully bear out the scalar view of consent: as the threat diminishes, it would make sense to consider the victim's consent increasingly valid and the defendant's extraction of that $1,000 increasingly less objectionable until, as in Case 5, it is no longer objectionable at all.

But as it turns out, this argument, as P. G. Wodehouse might say, is highly peccable. It is not in fact the case that blameworthiness gradually decreases as we move from Case 1 to Case 2 and so on down the line to Case 5. Rather, as we look more closely at those cases, we will discover that blameworthiness stays the same up to and even in Case 4 and then radically drops to just about zero. In other words, the validity of consent is not scalar at all but an either/or phenomenon.

Why does consent's validity changes so suddenly? Cases 1 through 4 (but not 5) are all cases in which a victim is put to a choice between putting up with one of two serious kinds of wrongs: either giving up $1,000 to which the defendant has no legitimate claim or putting up with something else that the defendant is not entitled to do (like killing him, or destroying his rosebushes, or driving around negligently, or publicizing a past relationship). He is not entitled to do these things either as a matter of criminal law (Cases 1 and 2) or as a matter of civil law (Case 3) or simply as a matter of morality (Case 4). To make the argument that Case 1 is less coercive than Case 2, Case 2 less coercive than Cases 3, and so on, we had to presuppose something very elementary and seemingly indisputable, which nevertheless turns out to be untrue. But before explaining what it is we were wrongly presupposing, I will need to provide a bit more background.

Imagine you have to make a somewhat bizarre choice between moving into either of two towns. The choice is bizarre because in Town A there lives a serial killer who is expected to kill five people over the next five years. In Town B, there is a chemical plant run by a rather incompetent manager whose negligence is expected to result in some kind of industrial mishap over the next five years, in the course of which fifty people are expected to die. Which town would you prefer to live in? The question is of course rhetorical. Assuming you are interested in simply maximizing your chances of survival, you would choose Town A, the one that harbors the serial killer. Another rhetorical question: Who is more blameworthy, the serial killer in Town A or the incompetent manager in Town B? Although the manager will end up causing more harm than the serial killer, obviously the latter is the more blameworthy. The manager is not even guilty of a crime. To be sure, he and his company will be liable for the harm they negligently caused, but that does not make them more blameworthy than the serial killer.

All this is very obvious, but it is also quite curious. It is obvious that, since what makes conduct blameworthy depends both on the amount of harm done and the way in which it is done, it will sometimes happen that the person who causes more harm is less blameworthy than the person who causes less, because he causes it in a less objectionable way. To see what makes this so curious, indeed downright paradoxical, imagine the following variation on the two-town scenario. Imagine someone came up to you and said: "I am going to settle in your town, and I am thinking about pursuing one of two career paths. Either I will become a serial killer who in the next five years will kill five people at random, or I will become a negligent chemical plant manager whose incompetence is nearly certain in the next five years to cause the death of fifty people. You choose which of those two careers you want me to pursue." Naturally you will ask him to please become a serial killer instead of a chemical plant manager. And yet if he accommodates your preference, he will end up being more blameworthy than if he does not.

There are two noteworthy lessons in all this. First, sometimes a criminal is more blameworthy when he accommodates his victim's preferences than when he does not. Second, in evaluating the blameworthiness of what the defendant does, we care not about what he threatened to do to his victims (such as killing fifty people by becoming a negligent chemical-plant operator) but what he actually does (such as becoming a serial killer and killing only five people).

Let's now revisit Cases 1 through 4. In order to get to the conclusion that Case 1 is more coercive than Case 2, Case 2 more coercive than Case 3, and so on, we had to presuppose that when the defendant gives the victim the choice between, say, having his rosebushes destroyed or paying the defendant $1,000 and then proceeds to accept the $1,000 from him, he is less blameworthy than if he destroys the rosebushes outright—because that is how the victim prefers it. But our analysis of the foregoing examples shows us that this is not true. To determine how blameworthy the defendant is, we have to ignore the victim's wishes. Moreover, we can be confident that, since in each of those cases the defendant ended up doing the same thing, depriving the victim of $1,000 against his wishes, he is in fact in all of those cases equally blameworthy.

Things change, however, once we get to Case 5. In Case 5, the defendant threatens the cancellation of his friendship unless he gets $1,000. This is hardly different from the ordinary bargaining situation in which the car dealer says, "If you don't pay me $1,000 more than you offered, I will not sell you this car." Here there is no blameworthiness involved at all.

What does all of this have to do with either/or? Well, notice what happens to the defendant's blameworthiness as we progress from Case 1 to Case 5. Blameworthiness stays the same from Case 1 to Case 4 and then suddenly plummets to zero when we reach Case 5, a very abrupt discontinuity. But to say that blameworthiness stays constant from Case 1 to Case 4 is just another way of saying that the defendant behaved equally coercively in the first four and not at all coercively in the last, which means that consent is totally valid in the last case and totally invalid in the first four. Consent, in other words, is either valid or not. It is not a scalar concept after all.

Why Partial Defenses Don't Help with Either/Or

I mentioned earlier Douglas Husak's suggestion that we recognize partial versions of every existing defense—necessity, duress, self-defense, the whole gamut. There is nothing particularly wrong with that, and to some extent we already do it by recognizing mitigating factors during the sentencing process. But one reason it is so tempting to recognize partial defenses is that it seems to do away with the disturbingly discontinuous treatment given to those who qualify for such a defense and those who just barely *fail* to qualify. Does the person who defended himself just a little too aggressively to qualify for self-defense or the person who let himself be pressured just a little too readily to help a criminal with his crime to qualify for the defense of necessity or duress not deserve some kind of break? Indeed, if the latter almost qualified for the defense, should he not be given *almost* the treatment he would get if he did qualify? In other words, only the most token punishment? As we shall see in a moment, recognizing partial defenses will not generally lead to eroding the discontinuity between defendants who qualify and defendants who *almost but do not quite* qualify for a defense. (That does not mean we should not have partial defenses, but it does mean that one of the main aims one might have in creating them cannot actually be attained.)

I will illustrate my argument with the defense of necessity, but it can readily be extended to other defenses as well. The defense of necessity provides that someone who can avert a great harm only by doing something less harmful is permitted to do so. If you can only get a heart attack victim to the hospital by racing your car at breakneck speed down a busy highway in violation of innumerable traffic laws, you might then qualify for the necessity defense. Or even more dramatically, if a gang of bank robbers threatens to kill you and your family unless you give them some minor assistance based on your extensive expertise with bank vaults, you would probably qualify for the necessity defense as well.

But suppose that the threat you face is not quite so serious. What the gang of bank robbers threaten you with is merely that they will use their connections to see to it that a loan you have applied for will be denied and that a school your daughter is trying to be admitted to will reject her and so on. Since the harm you are averting is not nearly as great as the harm in which you are assisting, you would not qualify for the necessity defense. Husak, however, suggests that you should qualify for a partial necessity defense. In other words, you should be treated better than someone who assists in the bank robbery without any other motive than greed. More abstractly put, whenever someone commits a crime, Husak would ask us to take into account the positive purposes for which he is acting and to give him credit for those purposes, even if they are not great enough to warrant complete exoneration. If we do this, it would seem that we will end up with a pleasing continuum of liability: at one end of the continuum we have the defendant who has no justification whatsoever for his crime, and at the other end is the defendant who is completely justified—in other words, qualifies for the defense of necessity. Now let us see why things will not in fact play out that way.

Let's consider a few variations of the case of the defendant who is pressured into helping a gang of bank robbers. Suppose we grant a partial necessity defense to the man who gives such help to avoid the robbers' sabotaging his bank loan application and his daughter's admission to a school. Compare this case to one that is only very slightly different; let's assume that his contribution to the criminal cause is a bit more substantial. The advice he renders is a bit more significant than before, and maybe his sympathy for what the bank robbers are doing is greater as well. Let's also assume, however, that they confront him with more serious threats than before: they will torch his house and blow up his car, although they make it clear that they will try to do so without physically harming him or his family. How does his misconduct compare in blameworthiness with his misconduct in the previous case? On the one hand his contribution to the crime is greater and more willing; on the other hand he faces a more serious threat. One might thus decide that it is a wash, that the increase in the threat and the increase in his participation cancel out. His partial necessity defense is about the same as before: not greater, not less.

Consider a third case. In this variation, the man's involvement in the bank robbery is yet more substantial and willing, but the threats he faces have also grown. The gangsters threaten to physically hurt him and his family unless he cooperates, but not seriously enough for him to qualify for the complete, as opposed to partial, necessity defense. Once again, one might say that on the whole his blameworthiness is no different than before. He is acting somewhat worse, but he has a somewhat better reason for doing so, since he is avoiding physical injury to himself and his family and not mere property damage or denial of a loan or rejection of an application.

Now for the final case. Make the defendant's contribution to the bank robbery slightly greater still, but also increase the threats he is facing somewhat further: serious physical harm to him and his family—to be precise, physical harm just barely serious enough to qualify for the complete, not just the partial, necessity defense. In short, in this last case he will actually be exonerated.

Now notice what is striking about this progression of cases: the fourth case differs only marginally from the third, but the two are treated radically differently. And this occurs despite the fact that we have a partial necessity defense. The reason for this discontinuity is similar to the reason for the discontinuities we have encountered before. Something is true of the last case that is not true of the preceding three. Until we get to a certain critical threshold, we evaluate the defendant's wrongdoing by looking at the harm he does (his contribution to the bank robbery) and the way he does it (enthusiastically? only to avoid the threatened harm, or would he have done it anyway?), the harm he averts (having his loan denied, his daughter rejected, his house torched, his car blown up, himself and his family injured, etc.). But once the disparity between the harm done (the bank robbery) and the harm averted (injury to himself and his family) has grown sufficiently, we completely disregard the manner in which he contributes to the harm. We only care about the degree of the harm averted relative to the harm committed. This kind of either/or effect is going to be ineradicable with regard to all defenses. Making them "partial" will not do away with it.[9]

Why Equity Will Not Mitigate Either/Or

It is natural to think, and has often been suggested, that the rigors of sharply delimited legal rules could be greatly ameliorated by the injection of more "equity" into their application. The most natural illustration of this is the determination of criminal punishment. If the homicide statute seems too rigid, for instance, because it treats a mercy killing just like an ordinary murder, then the sentencing process can allow mitigating factors to bring us closer to a just result. The sentencing process, it might thus seem, serves to "continuize" the law.[10]

But as we saw in our discussion of Douglas Husak's proposal to create more partial defenses—which he noted was similar to the recognition of mitigating factors in sentencing—this will not in fact have the expected continuizing effect, at least not in the context of necessity. But there is nothing special about the necessity context. The fact is that there is nothing about the concepts and maxims of equity that should make them immune to the kind of arguments I have given. Indeed many of the specific concepts already discussed—consent, necessity, bad faith—figure in those maxims and precepts and thus import into equity all the discontinuities associated with them.[11]

Either/Or as the Price of Rationality

At the outset of my analysis of the either/or character of the life-and-death distinction, I noted that I was drawing on an extremely insightful example of Larry Temkin's that he offers to prove a rather different point. It will aid our understanding of either/or if we focus more specifically on Temkin's example and what he hoped to prove with it.

Temkin constructs the example in an essay called "An Abortion Argument and the Threat of Intransitivity." In the course of this essay, Temkin reexamines the most standard conservative objection to abortion, namely the observation that since human beings develop gradually from conception through birth, and since there is no reason ever to treat something that is at a certain point on this continuum differently from something else that is just a little bit farther along on that continuum, there is thus no reason to treat a just-fertilized ovum differently from a freshly delivered baby. The standard response to this argument is that it is a non sequitur: after all, as Temkin puts it, "similar things might be said about the development of an acorn into an oak tree, and it does not follow that acorns are oak trees."[12]

What Temkin realized was that by altering the standard antiabortion argument in a slight but crucial way, he could render the oak-acorn reply irrelevant and restore the force of the original argument. The alteration he proposed was to consider not the usual spectrum of cases: ovum, ovum plus 1 day, ovum plus 2 days, . . . ovum plus 280 days = baby, but rather a modified version of that spectrum in which he added to each of the usual items on the continuum something else.

More specifically, he asks us to think about the following pair of cases. Suppose, he says, you are asked whether it would be worse if

(a) a fetus were killed on day 2 after conception or
(b) a fetus were killed on day 1 after conception *and* a student taking an exam were misled about the timing of the exam.

I take it your answer is (b). After all, killing the fetus on day 2 can only be very slightly worse than killing it on day 1, surely no worse than if a student in an exam is misled about its timing. Consider next the following comparison. You are asked whether it would be worse if

(c) a fetus were killed on day 3 after conception or
(d) a fetus were killed on day 2 after conception *and* a student taking an exam were misled about the timing of the exam.

The answer, as before, presumably is that (d) is worse than (c). Put those two facts together and you are able to conclude that it would be worse if

(e) a fetus were killed on day 1 after conception *and* two students taking an exam were misled about the timing of an exam,

than if

(f) a fetus were killed on day 3 after conception (and no students were misled about the timing of an exam).

You could repeat this argument several times over and would then be driven to conclude that it would be worse if

(g) a fetus were killed on day 1 after conception *and* 280 students taking an exam were misled about the timing of an exam

than if

(h) a fetus were killed on day 280 after conception.

What makes this so paradoxical is that most of us would find it very difficult to swallow the conclusion that (g) is worse than (h). Even abortion foes would presumably find it difficult to argue that if we could prevent either (g) or (h), we should try to prevent (g).

In defusing the standard objection to the conservative antiabortion argument, Temkin's agenda is not, however, to make the case that abortion is impermissible after all. His agenda rather is to prove that there is a fundamental problem with moral reasoning as it is generally practiced. Moral reasoning, he argues, is not transitive. The fact that alternative *a* is morally superior to alternative *b* and alternative *b* is morally superior to alternative *c* does not entitle us to conclude that alternative *a* is superior to alternative *c*. It is in this way that he hopes to avoid the paradoxical conclusion that the killing of a day-old fetus and the occurrence of 280 exam mishaps are worse than the killing of an about-to-be-born (or already-born) infant.

This, however, is not the only conclusion that could be drawn from his example. Temkin himself acknowledges in passing (and critics take him to task for not adequately acknowledging) an alternative possibility: that of a radical discontinuity. That is, one might preserve transitivity and still avert the unpalatable final conclusion by saying that at some point the reiteration of the comparisons between fetus killings plus exam mishaps breaks down; in other words, there is a magic point at which an increase in the number of exam mishaps cannot make up for the decrease in humanity represented by even a single day's worth of decreased fetal development.

The lesson I am inclined to draw from Temkin's example and the arguments of his critics is that we face a stark choice—between transitivity and either/or. If we throw overboard transitivity, we give up on a basic tenet of rationality. But if we accept discontinuity, then things are going to look very weird and artificial at times: important matters—literally matters of life and death—are bound to hinge on fine lines that have to be drawn more or less arbitrarily. When confronted with this dilemma, the law not surprisingly has opted, for the most part, to put up with weirdness, artifice, and arbitrariness as the price of avoiding intransitivity and irrationality.

The Sorites Paradox and Its Relation to What Is Being Argued Here

There is a question that is likely to have been gnawing at the reader from the very moment that I asserted that legal categories have many discontinuous boundaries. How does this differ from the paradoxical claim made by the infamous Sorites argument that all concepts have sharp boundaries—that one hair makes the difference between being bald and not bald, that a millimeter makes the difference between being short and not being short, etc.? Is my argument perhaps just another version of the Sorites argument and therefore equally suspect even if its precise logical defect defies specification in the same way that the fallacy in the Sorites argument has to this day defied a universally accepted explanation?

There are several things to be said in response. It is interesting to note preliminarily that the balance of scholarly opinion on the Sorites paradox has been shifting. In recent times a number of philosophers have made startlingly strong arguments for the proposition that the Sorites paradox is not a fallacy at all but a correct demonstration that concepts like baldness really do have sharp boundaries, that a single hair does in fact separate the bald from the not bald and so on. The argument is in significant part (but not entirely) a negative one.[13] Alternative resolutions to the Sorites paradox turn out to be so fraught with paradoxical implications that accepting the conclusion about one hair separating the bald from the not bald seems like the least of many possible evils.

Fortunately, however, nothing in my argument really hangs on which way one comes out on the Sorites paradox, because it actually is quite different, despite certain similarities. To appreciate the difference, let us imagine the following. Suppose a medical study revealed that as a man's hair grows sparser and sparser, something very abrupt occurs once that sparseness reaches a certain threshold; indeed, astonishingly enough, it occurs at the point at which most people are inclined to first regard him as bald. What the study reveals is that once that threshold is reached, the falling out of a single hair can cause the levels of a certain hormone to drop 90 percent. Just like that. That would be a very interesting empirical finding, a really remarkable and startling discontinuity. But note: nothing about that discontinuity will hinge on how the Sorites paradox is ultimately resolved and whether baldness can be said to set in with the falling out of an extra hair or not. The only similarity between the two issues is that they both have to do with a radical discontinuity involving the number of hairs on someone's head.

The same would be true for other claims of discontinuity, not just in the empirical but even in the purely logical realm. If it were conjectured that a particular set of mathematical functions all exhibited a certain discontinuity at a certain point, then the plausibility, let alone truth, of that conjecture would no more be affected by how we come out on the Sorites paradox than the medical finding about hair and hormones.

Finally, then, consider the discontinuity claims I have been making—for instance that the voluntariness of someone's consent varies discontinuously with the immorality of the threat by which it is obtained. That is a claim similar to the one about discontinuous mathematical functions or about discontinuous hormonal levels. It may be right or may be wrong, but its rightness in no way depends on how we resolve the Sorites paradox.

I do not want to overstate my position. While I believe there is no direct connection between the either/or question in law and the Sorites paradox, in that how one resolves the Sorites paradox does not imply that one needs to explain the either/or phenomenon in a particular way, there are without a doubt more indirect connections.[14] The similarities between the two issues are too great for there not to be. A deeper understanding of the novel arguments and solutions recently generated by Sorensen and Williamson and others about the Sorites problem is bound to turn up further ideas about the either/or character of law. Conversely, I cannot help but think that transposing some of the arguments here made about either/or might be of some use in illuminating the Sorites paradox. Saying this, however, is very different from saying that the either/problem in law is the same as the Sorites problem or that the argument for either/or is the same as the Sorites argument for baldness-by-a-hair's-breadth.

The Social Choice Connection: Chichilnisky's Theorem

The mathematical economist Graciela Chichilnisky several decades ago gave the field of social choice an entirely new turn. She did so by proving a highly counterintuitive new impossibility result, echoing Arrow's famous impossibility result of several decades earlier. What I am claiming about sharp boundaries in law can be better understood and made more plausible if we think about it as a special case of this theorem.[15]

Chichilnisky's theorem is ostensibly a theorem about voting. More specifically, it is a theorem about discontinuity in voting. As is customary in social choice theory, we are to imagine a set of voters each ranking a large set of alternatives in accordance with their individual preferences. Then a voting rule is applied to aggregate all of these individual rankings into a social superranking that somehow reflects, or averages, all of the various individual rankings. If the voting system is to have any claim to being considered fair and rational, we would typically want to insist on its meeting most of the prerequisites of Arrow's theorem: (1) It should respect unanimity. (In other words, if everyone prefers one alternative to another, then the voting rule should also rank that alternative above the other.) (2) It should be transitive. (No ranking a over b, b over c, but then c over a.) (3) It should not be dictatorial. Indeed here Chichilnisky departs somewhat from Arrow in making that requirement a bit more demanding: every voter should have a roughly equal influence over the outcome. (Chichilnisky does not of course require respect for the independence of irrelevant alternatives, since that, we now know, is not to be had.) In other words, everyone's vote gets taken into account to some significant extent.

Any such voting system, Chichilnisky proved, will exhibit a rather surprising kind of discontinuity. Suppose that, having collected every voter's rankings and having calculated from them the social ranking, we learn that we made a slight mistake. With regard to one of the voter's rankings we got two adjacent alternatives mixed up. We misunderstood him to say that he would put alternative n right after alternative b, whereas in fact he meant that he would do the reverse, rank alternative b right after alternative n. Suppose now that we recalculated the social ranking. What would we expect the new social ranking to look like? Not very different from the old one, presumably, since not a lot has changed about the underlying data on which it is based. But that turns out to be untrue. The final social ranking may change dramatically. Something that used to be near the very bottom might now travel to the very top and vice versa. In other words, a slight change in the inputs of the voting system might dramatically change its output. That is the gist of Chichilnisky's startling result.[16]

She illustrates her theorem in a very striking and intuitive way. Consider a beach party, she says, to be held on some spot on the boundary of a perfectly circular lake. Let's now suppose there are two groups of voters, one of which would like to locate the party at Spot a, and the other of which would like to locate it at Spot b. One plausible social aggregation function might pick the spot on the pond's perimeter that is halfway between a and b, namely c. So for instance, if group X would like to put the picnic at a spot corresponding to the twelve o'clock location on a clock face, and group Y would like to put it at the spot corresponding to the two o'clock location, then the compromise spot would be at the one o'clock position. Now let us imagine gradually revising the preferences of the group that chose Spot a by moving it further away from b, let's say in a counterclockwise direction. Initially the effect of doing so will simply be to incrementally move the "compromise" Spot c slightly in the same direction as a. This will continue to happen so long as the spot chosen by group X has not moved sufficiently in a counterclockwise direction to go past the eight o'clock point. If, for instance, it has moved to the 8:01 point, the compromise spot would then be located at around eleven o'clock. But let's next suppose group X moves the spot a smidgeon further in the counterclockwise direction, let's say to the 7:59 location. Now something very dramatic will happen to the compromise spot: it will "jump" from where it was, somewhere around eleven o'clock, to somewhere around five o'clock, because that point is closer to both a and b than the eleven o'clock location. Chichilnisky's result is a generalization of this phenomenon.

As we well know by now, the insights social choice theory provides about voting are not really just about voting. They apply wherever rankings of any kind are aggregated. In other words, they are really insights about multicriterial decision making. Legal doctrines being instances of multicriterial decision making, Chichilnisky's theorem should be applicable to them. Thinking of the discontinuous transition from life to death, one has an immediate sense that Chichilnisky's theorem should have some role in explaining it. My claim about life and death was that it is impossible for the law to treat the seemingly continuous process by which a fully alive human being turns into a collection of decomposed cells as a continuum. Somewhere along the line, I insisted, a point would have to be chosen, prior to which everything would be treated as constituting life, and past which everything would have to be treated as constituting death.

It would not work to try to treat the declining body as gradually less and less entitled to being treated like a human being. In making my argument for this claim, I asked you to think about collections of human beings at various levels of decline: two human beings at the H-minus-1 level, three at the H-minus-2 level, and so on. In order not to run into an absurdity, we were driven to conclude that there is a point—some number n—such that 50,000 H-minus-n human beings are worth a lot (maybe the equivalent of several Hs, i.e., lives in their prime) and 50,000 H-minus-$(n + 1)$ are worth nothing, indeed worse than nothing; they are a simply a collection of corpses, which it might be costly to get rid of.

What we have here structurally resembles the kind of situation Chichilnisky's theorem envisions. There are various alternatives we are trying to rank—the collections of people—and several criteria by which they may be evaluated: the dimension of quality (how far from being in their prime are these people?) and the dimension of quantity (how many of these people are there?). If we focused exclusively on one criterion, we would get one kind of ranking. If we focused exclusively on the other criterion, we would get another kind of ranking. What we were in fact trying to do was to aggregate these rankings into an overall ranking that would take account of both quality and quantity. In the process of doing so, we ran into some radical discontinuities at the point where an increase in quantity could not make up for a further decrease in quality. And that is exactly what Chichilnisky's theorem would predict.

Can we make this more precise? Can we connect Chichilnisky's theorem with legal discontinuities in a way that really allows us to see what is at the bottom of the either/or phenomenon? A good way to do this is to look at Chichilnisky's result in the context of the most basic tool in the economist's toolkit, the indifference curve diagram, which is just about the first thing anyone is taught in even the most introductory of introductory economics courses. The archetypical consumer, whom economic theory here depicts as ranking a series of commodity bundles and arranging them into those familiar indifference curves, is engaged in a multicriterial decision-making process much like the one just described. He ranks the bundles according to their x content. He also ranks them according to their y content. And then he aggregates his x judgments and his y judgments to yield those indifference curves that tell us how different x-y bundles compare.

Now take a look at a typical set of such indifference curves, as depicted in the figure below. In this particular context, Chichilnisky's result focuses our attention on a simple but striking and easily overlooked feature of those familiar diagrams. One way to restate the theorem is to say that comparatively slight change in the inputs—the way in which something is ranked under one or another of the criteria being used—might produce a large change in output, namely the overall rank it is eventually assigned relative to other bundles. In the context of these familiar indifference diagrams, that means that a slight change in the contents of a commodity bundle might have a large effect on how that bundle is ranked, and a large change in a commodity bundle might have a slight effect on how it is ranked. This is obviously true in the context of our diagram. If we look at what is happening near the two axes of the diagram, where the indifference curves start to bunch up, we can see that curves that represent vastly different utility curves come to be very close to each other. In other words, slight changes in a commodity bundle might propel us to a vastly different utility level. Conversely, vast changes in a commodity bundle might simply send us down the same indifference curve, not changing the level of utility at all.

Let us translate this into the setting of legal rules. We can interpret x and y to stand for the attributes, or criteria, that determine the applicability of a legal rule. For instance, x might represent the degree to which a disputed contract satisfies the consideration (i.e., the quid pro quo) requirement and y the extent to which it satisfies the definiteness requirement. Then the higher x and the higher y, that is, the more completely each of these requirements is met, the more "perfect" and uncontroversial an instance of a contract we are dealing with. Let's consider the point (1,000, 1,000), and let's interpret it to correspond to a contract that scores very highly both in the degree to which it satisfies the consideration requirement and in the degree to which it satisfies the definiteness requirement. The other points on the indifference curve passing through (1,000, 1,000) correspond to other contracts that might satisfy either the definiteness requirement or the consideration requirement less well but make up for it by satisfying the other criterion especially well—contracts that are high in definiteness but low in consideration or the other way around. Let's compare with this another indifference curve passing through point (1, 1). That point corresponds to a transaction that does not qualify as a contract because it is very indefinite and does not involve much of a quid pro quo (hence the low scores, 1s instead of 1,000s). The indifference curve passing through (1, 1) consists of other transactions that fall similarly short, either by being more deficient on the definiteness front than the (1, 1) transaction or by being more deficient on the consideration front. Finally consider contracts

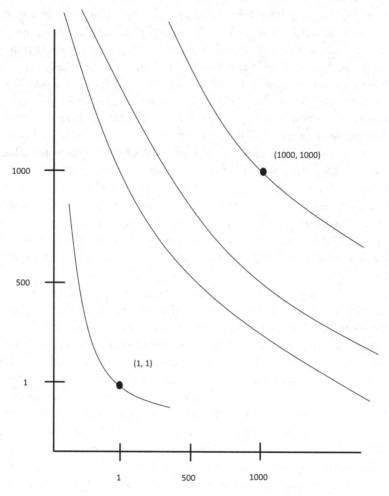

FIGURE 2.

that lie at the far end of either the *x* axis or the *y* axis. Here the (1,000, 1,000) indifference curve and the (1, 1) indifference curve nearly touch. In other words, the slightest difference here can be decisive in turning something that is indisputably a contract into something that indisputably is not. Creating intermediate contract categories, of the sort that Heinrich Hoeniger recommended, for instance, would do nothing to alleviate this. The either/or effect that we can see in action at the end of the *x* and *y* axes is irremediable.

I drew the indifference curves as curves, which is what they usually look like. Still, someone might wonder how much hangs on that. What if we were to think of the trade-off between the consideration requirement and the definiteness requirement as following more of a straight line. It might seem as though the either/or effect would then disappear, since we no longer have the lines bunching up against each other near the x axis and the y axis. But the effect does not disappear; it only grows a little less pronounced. It would still be the case that two points that are quite far from each other spatially are in fact quite close to each other in terms of rankings: For instance, two points lying on the same indifference curve might be quite far from each other, namely at opposite ends of the curve, while of course being ranked identically. By contrast, two points that lie on entirely different indifference curves might be spatially much closer to each other.

What happens if we try to translate some of the other discontinuities discussed in earlier chapters—life versus death, for instance—into this indifference curve setting? In principle, the situation would not look too different from the consideration/definiteness diagram, though they would differ in some important details.

Last Thoughts

The law splits hairs because it cannot do otherwise. Legal concepts synthesize a variety of different criteria for evaluating a transaction—in other words, legal decision making is multicriterial—and this fact in and of itself seems to guarantee discontinuity. I have tried to document this with a variety of interesting legal distinctions, but the argument seems to readily transcend those special cases. What we have here appears to be the legal counterpart of a celebrated result in the theory of social choice concerning the unavoidably discontinuous character of most social choice functions.

PART IV

Why Don't We Punish All We Condemn?

CHAPTER TWELVE

The Undercriminalization Problem

Villainies versus Felonies

*U*ndercriminalization? How could that possibly be a problem? Isn't the problem rather *over*criminalization? Aren't our criminal codes long enough, teeming as they are with an overabundance of crimes, often prohibiting the most harmless kind of conduct? Well, yes and no. As a practical matter, we should of course be more worried about overcriminalization, but as an intellectual matter, we ought to be quite interested in undercriminalization as well. There are a variety of situations in which it seems at once natural and strange that the law should not intervene. We find a nice illustration of this in *Gulliver's Travels*. Among the Lilliputians, Gulliver informs us, "Ingratitude is a Capital Crime, as we read it to have been in some other Countries: For they reason thus; that whoever makes ill Returns to his Benefactors must needs be a common Enemy to the rest of Mankind, from whom he hath received no Obligations and therefore such a Man is not fit to live."[1] This is meant to be funny and absurd, presumably because everyone considers it obvious that although rank ingratitude might qualify as a great villainy, it could not possibly qualify as a felony, or even a misdemeanor. But although the conclusion seems obvious, the reason for it hardly is. Can we find one? *That* is the problem of undercriminalization.

Scandalous behavior among the mighty, the wealthy, or the famous is typically conduct of just this kind—that is, villainies that aren't felonies, iniquities that critics grow red in the face denouncing but that they generally would not even consider criminalizing. A little over a century ago, Lytton Strachey published a book of short, irreverent, exposé-like portraits of some of the most prominent figures of the Victorian age, to which he gave the ironic title *Eminent Victorians*. Florence Nightingale, Cardinal Manning, and Dr. Arnold were among the eminences he took down a notch by exposing their occasional ruthlessness, recklessness, dishonesty, intellectual myopia, and hypocrisy in the pursuit of their various causes, and since then uncovering private sins of the great has become the raison d'être of most all biographies. Something close to a modern-day counterpart to Strachey's book was written just a few years ago by the British historian and journalist Paul Johnson. He titled it quite simply *Intellectuals*, although "Eminent Progressives" might have been more revealing of its true intent, which was do for left-wing intellectuals like Rousseau, Shelley, Marx, Ibsen, Tolstoy, Hemingway, Brecht, Bertrand Russell, Sartre, and Edmund Wilson something similar to what Strachey had done for those "Eminent Victorians": to examine their "moral and judgmental credentials . . . to tell mankind how to conduct itself. How did they run their own lives? With what degree of rectitude did they behave to family, friends, and associates? Were they just in their sexual and financial dealings? Did they tell, and write, the truth?"[2] Let us see what he had to say about the most prominent of the bunch, Karl Marx, because it will serve to make especially concrete the stuff that nonfelonious villainies are made of.

Johnson's essay on Marx, like all the others in his book, is very much a prosecutor's brief. He makes no effort to be judiciously balanced. But for our purpose—which is to find helpful, representative examples of repugnant villainies we would not want to criminalize—that is just as well. As Johnson, the prosecutor, portrays him, Marx was a thoroughly reprehensible human being, someone who shamelessly "exploited anyone within reach . . . in the first place his own family." While still a student, Johnson writes, Marx would pepper his ailing, hardworking, and generous father with insistent demands for more cash and react with outrage to any suggestion of greater frugality. When his father died, he did not bother to attend the funeral; he merely redirected his demands for cash to his mother. Later, Johnson writes,

> Engels was the new subject of exploitation. From the mid 1840s, when they first came together, until Marx's death Engels was the main source of income for the Marx family. He probably handed over more than half of what he received himself. . . . The partnership almost broke in 1863 when Engels felt Marx's insensitive cadging had gone too far. Engels kept two houses in Manchester, one for business entertaining, one for his mistress, Mary Burns. When she died Engels was deeply distressed. He was furious to receive from Marx an unfeeling

letter . . . which briefly acknowledged his loss and then instantly got down to the more important business of asking for money. Nothing illustrates better Marx's adamantine egocentricity.[3]

Johnson sees exploitation even in Marx's treatment of his daughters, whose education and marriage he tried to frustrate at every turn because it suited his personal comfort to keep them at home. But Johnson's most sneering words are reserved for Marx's treatment of his domestic servant and sometime lover, Helen Demuth:

> In all his researches into the iniquities of British capitalism, [Marx] came across many instances of low-paid workers, but he never succeeded in unearthing one who was paid literally no wages at all. Yet such a worker did exist, in his own household. When Marx took his family on their formal Sunday walks, bringing up the rear, carrying the picnic basket and other impedimenta, was a stumpy female figure. This was Helen Demuth, known in the family as "Lenchen" Born in 1823, of peasant stock, she had joined the von Westphalen family [Marx's aristocratic in-laws] at the age of eight as a nursery-maid. She got her keep but was paid nothing. In 1845, the Baroness, who felt sorrow and anxiety for her married daughter, gave Lenchen, then twenty-two, to Jenny Marx to ease her lot. She remained in the Marx family until her death in 1890. . . . [S]he was a ferociously hard worker, not only cooking and scrubbing but managing the family budget, which Jenny was incapable of handling. Marx never paid her a penny. In 1849–50 during the darkest period of the family's existence, Lenchen became Marx's mistress and conceived a child. . . . [I]t was a son. . . . Marx refused to acknowledge his responsibility, then or ever, and flatly denied the rumors that he was the father. . . . [T]he boy was put out to be fostered by a working-class family called Lewis but allowed to visit the Marx household. He was, however, forbidden to use the front door and obliged to see his mother only in the kitchen. . . . [Marx] eventually persuaded Engels to acknowledge Freddy, privately, as a cover-story for family consumption.[4]

Even if one were to accede to all of Johnson's charges, none of this villainy rises to the level of a felony, which makes that much more vivid our problem: whence the reluctance to punish what we are so willing to be outraged by?

A great deal of fiction derives its fascination from our instinctive befuddlement that such villainy should remain beyond the reach of the law. A particularly good illustration is Herman Wouk's splendid novel *The Caine*

Mutiny, known to most through the play and the movie based on it. What everyone remembers about *The Caine Mutiny* is the deranged Captain Queeg rolling those marbles in his hands, the officers who eventually mutiny against him, and the court-martial in which they arduously but successfully defend their actions to a skeptical navy bureaucracy. What tends to be forgotten is that the real villain of the story is not Captain Queeg but one of his subordinates, a budding writer named Keefer who, feeling peeved, insulted, and humiliated by Queeg's crude and petty manner, insinuates in some of Queeg's subordinates the belief that Queeg is not merely unstable—as he manifestly is—but downright insane. That belief becomes a kind of self-fulfilling prophesy. It leads to behavior on the part of Queeg's subordinates that serves to further unbalance the captain and leads him to the actions that then precipitate the mutiny. Keefer's involvement in the mutiny, though pivotal, is sufficiently indirect that he manages to escape even the hint of responsibility during the ensuing court-martial—a perfect instance of nonfelonious villainy and one that dramatically raises the question of why such villainy should remain nonfelonious.

Unsatisfactory Answers

The question of what conduct should be criminalized has a long pedigree. There have been roughly three approaches to it: utilitarianism, the harm theory, and legal moralism. One would therefore think that answers to the undercriminalization problem would not be hard to come by. But none of the existing approaches offers a direct answer to it, although certain answers suggest themselves, which do not, however, seem very convincing.

Let's start with utilitarianism. Not all variants of utilitarianism purport to give guidance on what to criminalize. Some utilitarians for instance take the position that utilitarianism only becomes relevant once we have decided what conduct it is we want to deter. Once we have figured that out, we should then assess the optimal sanctions—sanctions that are severe enough to deter and not so severe that the (marginal) cost of inflicting them exceeds the (marginal) deterrent benefit of doing so. This variant of utilitarianism simply fails to tell us which villainies to turn into felonies and which to leave alone.

But the most traditional type of utilitarianism—the one that instructs us to maximize utility, or some related index of well-being, like wealth— does in fact offer quite unequivocal advice on what to criminalize: all conduct that tends to lower overall utility. As far as this form of utilitarianism is concerned, there are no villainies that should *not* be turned into felonies. Conduct is villainous if it lowers overall utility, and if it does, that probably means it should be criminalized or at least treated as a civil wrong, a tort. The difficulty with this answer is that it is wildly at variance with our commonsense intuitions. It suggests that as a matter of principle, there really would be nothing wrong with criminalizing ingratitude, or "adamantine egocentricity" (one of the main vices Johnson charges Marx with), or exploitativeness (the other main vice Johnson tags Marx with), or extreme manipulativeness of the kind Keefer displays in *The Caine Mutiny*, provided that that is what the balance of utilities suggests. In other words, the utilitarian answer is to ignore our intuitions that some villainies just aren't felony material.

Next there is the harm theory. The original version of this approach to criminalization is John Stuart Mill's: "The only purpose for which [state] power can be rightfully exercised over any member of a civilized community, against his will, is to prevent harm to others. His own good, either physical or moral, is not a sufficient warrant. He cannot rightfully be compelled to do or forbear because it will be better for him to do so, because it will make him happier, because, in the opinions of others, to do so would be wise, or even right."[5] This principle is often taken to exemplify the liberal theory of punishment—liberal, because it does not allow the state to infringe on someone's liberty unless someone else's liberty is being jeopardized by *him*. It makes it difficult to punish a great deal that others abhor, including prostitution, drug use, and gambling, because such activities harm no one but the consenting participants. It is strange to realize, then, that this seemingly restrictive harm principle would put nothing in the way of punishing harmful villainy. Like utilitarianism, this version of the harm theory therefore seems—at least in this respect—deeply counterintuitive.[6]

The harm theory was later greatly refined in Joel Feinberg's four-volume inquiry *The Moral Limits of the Criminal Law*.[7] To begin with, Feinberg supplements the harm principle with a second principle, the "offense principle," which makes it permissible to punish people not merely for *harming* but for *offending* others—typically, by doing a variety of things in public that would be unobjectionable if done in private: relieving oneself, having sex, eating a meal of live insects with pickled animal organs, cursing very graphically, sauntering around in the nude, or defacing a crucifix. However, the offense principle only worsens our problem, because it expands rather than narrows the reach of the law. More promising is Feinberg's proposed amendment of the harm principle, which is to only count something as a harm if it either (a) infringes someone's rights or (b) constitutes a serious setback to his interests, by which he means anything in which one has a real stake. Let us explore what each of these means and how it would affect the treatment of villainies. If Feinberg's approach is to explain why we don't punish villainies, then it either has to be the case that villainies don't infringe anyone's rights or that they don't constitute a serious setback to anyone's interests.

Let's start with setbacks to interests. No doubt there are some things I might have called harmful villainies that Feinberg would declare not to be setbacks to anyone's interest. Interests, says Feinberg, are things in which we have a significant stake, and harm is an incursion that does real damage to those things. For instance, some of what comes under the rubric of bad parenting Feinberg would probably dismiss as a mere "hurt," or the frustration of a "want," because it does not cut deeply enough into the fabric of our existence to count as a harm. (He explicitly draws those distinctions.) He might say the same thing about an epithet-laden, angry outburst. Indeed he might even be able to make this claim about most other of the harmful, nonfelonious villainies mentioned so far (ingratitude, egocentricity, manipulativeness), *but only so long as they are too transient to make the requisite deep and lasting impression on another's interests.* Unfortunately that still allows for the criminalization of really serious cases of ingratitude, egocentricity, and manipulativeness, and that is hard to accept.

Feinberg's requirement that a harm be a rights infringement might seem more helpful. Could it be that this is the reason we do not want to punish ingratitude, egocentricity, exploitativeness, or manipulativeness? This might in fact be what a lot of people would first say when confronted with the suggestion that such conduct should be criminalized. "I don't like it, but the defendants are within their rights"—and therefore not infringing on anyone else's. The problem with this approach becomes apparent once we ask what Feinberg means by a right. A right, he tells us, not implausibly, is a "reason-backed claim against other individuals, for example not to be treated rudely."[8] If that is what a right is, then anyone who is the victim of a harmful villainy can presumably complain of a rights infringement: he has a reason-backed claim that seems no less sturdy than that of the victim of rude treatment. To be sure, there may be a few harmful villainies that could be argued to not constitute rights infringements. Feinberg, for instance, dwells on the fact that conduct to which the victim consents cannot be considered harm. Certain harmful villainies, like Marx's sponging, his refusal to pay his servant a wage, his interference with his daughters' marriage plans, might be declared to be perfectly consensual *folies à deux*. But those are special cases. On the whole, it seems we have a lot more "reason-backed claims" against what people may be doing to us than we would be willing to enforce with a criminal sanction.

A third approach to the question of what to criminalize is legal moralism, sometimes called retributivism. The legal moralist maintains that the criminal law should punish all immoral conduct, generally in proportion to the degree of immorality. On the face of it, legal moralism fares no better than utilitarianism or the harm theory in avoiding the punishment of mere villainy. At least one legal moralist, however, Michael Moore, has spotted the problem and tried to remedy it. He does so in the final chapter of his landmark study on the philosophy of criminal law, *Placing Blame*, in a chapter revealingly titled "Liberty's Limits on Legislation." He begins by readily acknowledging the problem nonfelonious villainies pose for legal moralism. His examples are similar in spirit to those already given but different enough to be worth quoting:

> There are many kinds of parental abuse apart from physical and sexual abuse. Some parents make their favoritism between siblings apparent on a daily basis, making the less favored develop feelings of worthlessness and despair. Some parents, when they divorce, poison their children against the other parent. Some parents make servants out of their children, others spoil them rotten. Some parents dominate their children's ambition, telling them exactly what they will be in all aspects of life. Some imbue them with religious beliefs that can only be described as deranged, and some simply ignore their children emotionally, leaving them to find what warmth they can in this life.... [T]hese are deeply immoral behaviors, yet we tend to think that the state should not use the criminal law to punish such wrongs.
>
> ... [O]r consider free speech.... Revealing a damaging truth from a distant past of a now well-respected and virtuous citizen ... purely for motives of private gain is a plausible candidate for a serious moral wrong, and thus the punishment of such wrong is a legitimate state concern. Despite this, [we don't] think it should be punished....
>
> Suicide is often deeply hurtful to persons other than the actor, persons to whom the actor is bound by many ties and to whom the actor owes an obligation to stay alive.... [Y]et my firm sense is that no one (including the state) has the right to prevent someone from killing themselves.[9]

To explain why a legal moralist might decline to punish such conduct, Moore suggests that legal moralism take on board, as it were, a further principle, beyond the general one calling for the punishment of all immoral acts in proportion to their immorality. It is a principle that would protect what he calls "basic liberties" from state interference. Basic liberties include the liberty to commit what I have called nonfelonious villainies. But how do we know which villainies qualify as basic liberties? Moore makes the intriguing observation that the line of Supreme Court cases descended from *Griswold v. Connecticut,* which invalidated a state law against contraception (and engendering most controversially *Roe v. Wade,* which invalidated laws against abortion) corresponds exactly to this category and that whatever the Supreme Court has said on why the state may not meddle with contraception and abortion can be used more generally to tell us which villainies may not be turned into felonies. In those cases, Moore explains, "the Court has sought to defend a constitutional right 'that a certain sphere of individual liberty will be kept largely beyond the reach of government.' . . . Thus the court has been for thirty years engaged in precisely the kind of political philosophy that is our concern here." To be sure, the Court qua Court has not been very explicit about what that sphere encompasses, but a number of the justices, in dissenting and concurring opinions, have been more forthcoming. Moore finds special merit in Justice Blackmun's idea that certain choices "make us who we are and are in that sense self-defining." Choices that are self-defining should be immune from state regulation because if we are not permitted to make those freely, we are being stripped of an essential ingredient of our human character. "John Stuart Mill had the same idea," Moore writes,

> insofar as he defended liberty on the grounds that we have to be allowed to make [certain] choices about what we shall desire, feel and believe, on pain of our having no character at all. 'A person whose desires and impulses are his own . . . is said to have a character. One whose desires and impulses are not his own has no [more character] than a steam engine. . . .' Our desires, feelings and beliefs are not our own, according to Mill, if they are merely the product of social coercion or mere conforming imitation of social convention. 'He who lets the world . . . choose his plan of life for him has no need of any other faculty than the ape-like one of limitation. . . . But what will be his comparative worth as a human being?'
>
> . . . Mill [is] articulating a version of one of Aristotle's ideals. This is the idea of the self-made individual, in a distinctly non-economic sense of the phrase. It is the idea of each of us choosing our character without undue influence of others (including the heavy-handed influence of state coercion.)[10]

The chief problem with Moore's suggestion is that this concern with "self-definition" does not seem to correlate very well with the line between villainies and felonies. Are suicide, bad parenting, speech that invades someone's privacy, nonfelonious mendacity, selfishness, treachery, greed, cruelty, hypocrisy, manipulativeness, or ingratitude any more intimately connected with the self-definition of the wrongdoer than murder, rape, or theft? Maybe *some* instances of bad parenting are more tied in with "self-definition" than *some* instances of rape, but in general? Or does Moore mean to suggest that because rape is more harmful than bad parenting we can more readily afford to indulge our concern with self-definition when it comes to the latter rather than the former? I can't quite believe that. The difference between felonious and nonfelonious villainies just *feels* a lot more fundamental than this kind of pragmatic judgment suggests.

In sum, none of the major approaches to criminalization seems to me to tell us convincingly how to separate mere villainy from felony. The failure to solve this problem is of more profound significance than it may initially appear. Many of the most basic doctrines of criminal responsibility raise it. Criminal law routinely declines to hold someone responsible whom we are perfectly willing to blame. Take the most basic of all criminal law doctrines, the requirement that before one be punished one must have committed an actual criminal *act*; a mere wicked thought will not do. Imagine someone who has spent years trying to find a way to extirpate certain (perfectly innocent) people he has come to hate. We have no trouble condemning him but wouldn't dream of punishing him: he is a mere villain, not a felon. Or take the doctrine that says that you cannot be held liable if you fail to rescue someone who is about to die, even when you could do so with the most trivial efforts. By and large, we feel disinclined to punish bad Samaritans, however strongly we are willing to condemn them. They seem like villains, not felons. Once one takes a careful look, nearly all the rules of criminal responsibility reveal a dissonance between what we are willing to punish and what we are willing to condemn.

Partial Undercriminalization: The Problem of Comparative Guilt

Actually nonfelonious villainies are but a special instance of undercriminalization. When we don't criminalize what we strongly condemn, that is merely one way in which condemnation and punishment can get out of sync. A milder way for this to occur is when we do punish what we condemn but don't seem to punish it *enough*, at least not when compared to something else we punish much more harshly though it does not seem any worse. To see more concretely what I have mind, consider the following two cases:[11]

> *Scenario 1.* A woman is afflicted with a terminal, highly painful disease. She somewhat ambivalently raises the subject of euthanasia with her husband. Her agony continues, exacerbated, it seems, by her going back and forth on the subject of euthanasia. Her husband eventually decides to cut the agony short by administering a deadly dose of morphine. This would generally be regarded as a case of premeditated homicide, or murder in the first degree.

Compare this with another scenario:

> *Scenario 2.* Two men engage in a drag race. One of them loses control of his car and crashes into an uninvolved driver coming from the opposite direction, thereby killing him. This would generally be regarded as a case of reckless homicide (or involuntary manslaughter), much less serious than murder.

Not surprisingly, many people have questioned whether the law really gets things right here. Is the husband in Scenario 1 really worse than the drag racer in Scenario 2? The husband after all had a pretty honorable reason for doing what he did, even if we judge it ultimately not to be a good enough reason. The drag racer by contrast did not. In fact there are many more pairs of cases that could be constructed according to this blueprint, the blueprint being: Take a case of intentional wrongdoing for which there is some good but not quite good enough reason. Juxtapose it with a case of reckless wrongdoing of the same type carried out for far less defensible reasons. Why is it so easy to come up with cases in which the degree of legal blameworthiness does not match our level of condemnation?

More on Partial Undercriminalization: The Volume Discount Problem

Another striking example of partial undercriminalization is the so-called volume discount for crime. People generally commit more than one crime at a time. The person who sets off a bomb killing several others has in one stroke committed a bunch of murders. The person who steals a bank deposit box containing the deposits of several people has in one fell swoop committed several thefts. The person who in the course of a drunken spree runs over a pedestrian and then tries to elude the police has by this one misadventure committed the three crimes of manslaughter, failure to stop and report an accident, and resistance to an arrest. The man who takes his victim to a secluded place to rape her and then threatens her if she should tell on him has committed a kidnapping, a rape, and an obstruction of justice. The person who breaks into a bank, manhandles the staff, and blows up the vault to get to the money has committed a bank robbery, a number of assaults and batteries, and various kinds of property damage. The person who fires three bullets at his victim, all of which miss their mark, would seem to have committed in that short period three attempted murders. It would in fact be hard to commit only one crime at a time even if one tried.

What should the law do in such cases? The most natural answer would seem to be: punish the defendants for everything they have done—the bomb setter for his several murders; the hit-and-run driver for drunk driving, failing to stop, and resisting arrest; and so on. *But that is not what the law generally does.* Usually people who commit crimes "in volume," as it were, get a volume discount: they are punished less than if they had committed each crime separately. Let's see more concretely what that looks like.

There are actually many different kinds of volume discounts. It will be enough if I list a few of the most important ones. The first type of volume discount is exemplified by the assailant who lands three swift blows on his victim. We would view that as only one battery, not three. Things of course would be different if several days elapsed between each blow. Then there really would be three batteries. We might call this the "quick succession" discount. It applies to a lot of other crimes as well. Several violent acts of intercourse committed upon one and the same victim during one and the same encounter constitute just one rape. Several lies on the witness stand constitute just one case of perjury. Several disruptions constitute just one disturbance of the peace. In sum, if the several iterations of the same crime are sufficiently tightly sequenced, only the first iteration of the crime counts for much; the remaining iterations make no difference to the defendant's guilt.

A second type of volume discount is illustrated by the thief who takes the property he has stolen and destroys it. He meets the requirements of at least two offenses: theft and destruction of property. Nevertheless, the law tends not to punish someone for both offenses in such cases. Or consider the thief who takes the property he has just stolen and resells it. Now he is guilty of both theft and trafficking in stolen property, but again, he would not usually be punished for both. Or suppose the thief offers to sell his loot back to the original owner. Now he is guilty both of theft and of extortion. Again, the law is reluctant to punish for both theft and extortion. Somehow the offenses following the initial theft are treated like some sort of unimportant mop-up operation, so unimportant in fact that they don't get counted at all. We might call this the mop-up discount.

A third type of volume discount is granted for crimes that are committed concurrently. This concurrency discount would apply to the doctor who is careless in carrying out a late-stage abortion as a result of which the patient dies and who has thereby committed both an illegal abortion and manslaughter. Then there is the customer who pays for something with a forged banknote, who has thereby committed both forgery and fraud, or the terrorist who blows up several people with one bomb and thereby commits several murders at once.

This by no means exhausts the kinds of volume discounts granted, but it probably represents the most important ones, enough to get a clear sense of the problem.

Although well established in criminal law, the volume discount seems bizarre. To see just how bizarre, take the most elemental kind of volume discount case, that of the assailant who unsuccessfully fires several bullets at his intended victim. Suppose that after firing the first bullet, the assailant paused and asked himself how bad it would be if he fired a second bullet. The answer we think he should arrive at is that it is as bad as firing the first bullet. He is about to engage in another attempted murder. But if he does fire that second bullet, that is most certainly not how the matter will be looked at in retrospect. In retrospect, the second attempt is going to be combined with the first and the two categorized as just one attempted murder—provided he actually fires the second bullet not too long after the first, thus resulting in a volume discount for attempted murder. If the second bullet would be judged to be as bad as a full-fledged attempted murder, why does our retrospective judgment not reflect that?

This problem arises with every single one of the volume discount cases we have considered. Let's revisit just one more, namely the defendant who kills his victim, throws his weapon into the river, and then tells a witness to the incident that he too will die if he ever breathes a word to the authorities. At first, looking at the matter in a purely commonsense way, the defendant seems guilty of exactly one crime, murder. But suppose we look at the matter in the same incremental way in which we looked at the unsuccessful assassin in our previous example. In other words, having committed the murder, we imagine the defendant asking himself how bad it would be if he covered up his crime by destroying the evidence and intimidating a potential witness. The answer would seem to be that what he is doing amounts to an obstruction of justice and is thus seriously blameworthy. So why does the criminal law's assessment of the situation not reflect that? Why is an obstruction of justice irrelevant if it occurs in sufficient proximity to the crime it is covering up?

Taking Stock

Criminal law seems severely out of sync with our moral intuitions in a somewhat surprising way—surprising mainly because it has been taken note of so rarely: the law fails to punish a great deal that we strongly disapprove of, and even what it criminalizes it often seems to punish much more gently than our intuitive level of disapprobation seems to warrant. Well, that misstates it slightly: we do not after all really want to criminalize everything we disapprove of, but the question is why? None of the so-called theories of criminalization seem to have an answer to this question. Or rather the answer they provide seems unacceptable: as far as the utilitarian, harm, or legal moralism theories of punishment are concerned, nothing should really stand in the way of criminalizing what we strongly disapprove of. So why don't we?

CHAPTER THIRTEEN

Multicriterial Ranking and the Undercriminalization Problem

A Second Look at the Comparative Guilt Question

L et us take a second look at some of the key presuppositions from which our discussion of undercriminalization has proceeded so far. What we have presupposed, because it seemed intuitively so self-evident, is that we do in fact abhor a serious ingrate more than a petty thief, that we condemn a reckless driver more than a conscientious mercy killer, that we consider crimes committed in volume as reprehensible as crimes committed piecemeal. On closer scrutiny, however, none of these presuppositions hold up very well. Let's start with the example illustrating the problem of comparative guilt, the case of the mercy killer.

There are in fact a number of ways in which we might think about the husband in the euthanasia case that will make him appear considerably more blameworthy than he does at first. For instance:

(1) We might ask how much more compelling the husband's reasons would have to be to completely exonerate him on grounds of necessity. The answer would seem to be a lot. To qualify for the necessity defense, the compassionate husband would have to be found to have averted far worse consequences than he actually did: the pain he alleviated would have needed to be much greater and affected many more people, and the assent he obtained for his actions would have had to be a lot less ambiguous, or else the cognitive abilities of the people being asked to give such assent would have had to be a great deal more impaired for us to judge the defendant free of all blame on grounds of necessity. That then would lead us to see the husband's conduct as falling far short of an actual necessity

defense, in that his reasons for the killing were just a tiny fraction of what would be required for complete exoneration. That in turn would lead us to see his blameworthiness for killing only slightly diminished by his desire to help his wife.

(2) Another way of reframing the husband's blameworthiness is to ask how much less serious his conduct would have had to be to be fully justi-fied, on grounds of necessity, by the reasons for which he actually engaged in it. In other words, let us think about a slighter form of wrongdoing—slighter than homicide, that is—that would have been warranted by his desire to alleviate his wife's pain. The administration of an illegal pain-killer might qualify. However, the administration of an illegal painkiller is so much less serious than a killing that the misconduct of the latter starts to look a lot more serious than before.

(3) Yet another way of looking at the matter is to compare the hus-band to a hypothetical defendant who kills involuntarily. After all, to some extent he resembles such a person, in that he acted under extraordinary pressure. Of course the pressure he faced does not come all that close to rendering his action involuntary, but it does move it in that direction. We might in fact judge him to be coming closer to having acted involuntarily than he came to acting under necessity. This would make his actions seem a little less blameworthy than under (1) and (2) but still much more blame-worthy than he appeared at the outset.

(4) We might also compare the husband with someone who acted un-der duress. Proceeding analogously to the way we did with the necessity defense in (1), we might then ask how the defendant's inadequate reason compares to a person who kills for a reason that would be adequate for a duress defense. Alternatively, we might ask what kind of misconduct would be excused under the duress defense by the reason for which he acted. In either case, we would end up judging the husband more harshly than we did at first glance.

Let us now turn to the drag racer and reassess his blameworthiness in a similar fashion. In addition to the way we assessed things at first glance—which was to compare the substantiality of his wrongdoing with the insub-stantiality of his reason for it—there are the following two possibilities:

(1) Once again, ask yourself by how much we would have to increase the good effects of his conduct for his conduct to be judged careful rather than reckless. Probably not by all that much. By this measure, then, the blameworthiness of the racer is very much less than the blameworthiness of the husband, as measured by (1) through (4) above.

(2) Or ask yourself how much less risky his conduct would have had to be to count as justified by the slight reasons for it, namely the thrill of the race. Again, not all that much, at least when compared to the amount of blameworthiness assessed against the husband under measures (1) through (4) above.

On second thought, then, our intuitions about the husband are considerably more mixed than they appeared at first. Something similar will turn out to be true of the case we will turn to next, the volume discount problem.

A Second Look at the Volume Discount

The volume discount is not as peculiar as it seems at first, once one reflects on the ubiquity of the phenomenon. Wherever one looks, one finds that when certain phenomena are tightly squeezed together—in other words, when they appear to occur "in volume"—they are evaluated differently than if they are spread out over time. I am no longer just talking about cases in which the defendant is committing several offenses "in volume." Rather I have in mind something like the following: A person begins to rescue someone and then interrupts himself midway through; let's say he has started to drag the drowning victim out of the lake and then decides to drop him back into the water (maybe because he recognized him to be his mortal enemy). Or he has thrown a life preserver to the drowning man and at the last minute yanks it back. If he does all this before the drowning man has actually reached shore or taken hold of the life preserver, then what he is doing is probably OK, legally speaking. Only once his efforts have somehow passed out of his rightful sphere of influence—perhaps once the drowning victim has actually been deposited on shore or once he has actually grasped the life preserver—does he lose the ability to reverse course. In other words, so long as the reversal of course is sufficiently tightly sequenced, or closely bundled, with the start of the rescue, the defendant escapes liability.

Or consider a similar "tight sequencing" effect in the area of self-defense. Compare these two cases. Case 1: Someone attacks me and I kill him. Case 2: Someone attacks me, and I am mortally wounded and will die unless I get a heart transplant. I therefore kill my attacker to utilize his heart. In both cases I cause the death of my attacker to save my own life. But in one case the killing was sufficiently "tightly sequenced" with the attack that I escape liability, and in the other case it was not.

Or consider a simple case of an abandoned bank robbery. The defendant has broken into the bank, has opened the vault, has taken the money, then changes his mind and puts it back. He has abandoned his crime and is not guilty of anything. But if he first took the money out of the bank building, not merely the vault, perhaps kept it for a day, and only then decided to give it back, he no longer would have such a defense. In other words, he only gets the defense if his abandonment is sufficiently closely bundled with the crime he is abandoning.

Indeed the phenomenon seems to transcend law. There is a well-established psychological effect, already discussed at some length in William James's *Principles of Psychology*, which goes by the name of Weber's law.[1] (The Weber in question is not Max Weber but the psychologist Eugen Weber.) What it says is this: Suppose you are lifting a one-pound weight and you add to that another pound—you will have no trouble telling the difference. Indeed you will probably be able to tell that what you have added is roughly another pound. Now suppose you are lifting a ten-pound weight instead and you add that same extra one pound on top of it—you will have a much harder time telling the difference. It won't feel to you as though you have added an extra pound. It will seem like much less. That's an illustration of Weber's law. This effect holds across the board. It applies to all kinds of sensations and judgments. Increase the brightness of a light by a given amount, and it will be harder to tell that it has been increased the brighter the light was to begin with. Increase the loudness of a sound, and it will be harder to tell that it has been increased the louder the sound was to begin with. Increase the height of an object, and it will be harder to tell that it has been increased the taller the object was to begin with. Increase the size of an object, and it will be harder to tell that it has been increased the larger the object was to begin with. And so it appears that as we add one crime on top of a pile of crimes the defendant has already committed, it will seem to increase his blameworthiness by less and less the higher the pile of crimes to which it is added. There is some work in criminology, most notably Thorsten Sellin and Marvin Wolfgang's famous study, *The Measurement of Delinquency*, that would support this application of Weber's law to our perceptions of crime.[2] Their work suggests that if we view the rapist who commits a rape on top of an already committed robbery as less serious than the rapist who has not committed a robbery, we may be doing the same thing as when we view the pound lifted on top of several already lifted pounds as lighter than it actually is.

There is a problem, however, with explaining or justifying the volume discount in this way: that is, Weber's law seems to be something in the nature of an optical illusion. After all, the one-pound weight we lift after we are already carrying ten pounds only *seems* lighter; it isn't really. So perhaps the rape committed on top of the robbery only seems less serious, but it isn't really. And if the criminal law grants a discount for that rape, it would seem to be falling prey to an optical illusion. And if that's the case, does it make sense for the criminal law to try to reflect that optical illusion? If anything, Weber's law might seem to suggest that a volume discount for crimes is quite inappropriate, intuitions to the contrary notwithstanding.

But it's not that simple. Weber's law looks like a sort of optical illusion only so long as we apply it to physical attributes like weight or height or loudness or brightness. But when applied to other, nonphysical attributes, like blameworthiness, it may not be an illusion at all but an aspect of our everyday morality, which the law needs to reflect. Let me make what I have in mind a little clearer by talking briefly about another nonphysical attribute, utility. Everyone has heard about the principle of diminishing marginal utility, the fact that the first apple is tastier to us than the third, the fact that the first million earned is more important to us than the third million, the fact that the first third of a lecture is more enjoyable to us than the last third. Such diminishing marginal utility is surely not just an illusion. To say that something is more pleasurable than it seems doesn't make any sense when it comes to utility. It may be like that with blameworthiness as well. If the third crime the defendant has committed seems to add less wickedness to his moral ledger than the first, does it really make sense to say that it actually adds as much blameworthiness as the first but we just don't realize it? I am inclined to think not. When it comes to physical things like weight or height or loudness or brightness, Weber's law may be a sort of illusion. When it comes to nonphysical attributes like utility or blameworthiness, the story seems to be different. If the third crime seems less blameworthy, then it seems more reasonable to conclude that it really is less blameworthy.

A Second Look at Nonfelonious Villainies

Finally, let us cast a revisionist glance at nonfelonious villainies. Let's begin by revisiting the case of Marx, of whom Paul Johnson drew such an unflattering portrait based on his insensitive sponging off friends and family, his infidelity, and his emotional tyranny over his children. He seems by Johnson's account much worse than a petty thief, and yet the law does not so view it. But that only holds true when we do a purely binary comparison between Marx's situation and the petty theft. Once we bring in other cases, our perceptions are apt to change. Think of situations like the ones we have been talking about, in which someone harms others either by petty property crimes (e.g., purse snatching) or by emotional tyranny, but add one additional feature: imagine a victim who fights back, using actual physical force. In other words, he tries to directly interfere with the actions of the domineering father and the petty thief. It seems intuitively clear that physical force is only warranted against the thief, not the tyrannical father. Why should that be? It comes back to something stated at the very outset of this book. Our claims against would-be invaders of our interests can be thought of as a series of concentric circles. The innermost circle is the boundary that surrounds our body, invasions of which count the heaviest, which is why we can defend against them with deadly force. The next circle, moving outward, is the one that surrounds our property. We are allowed to defend it with a significant measure of physical force, but not deadly force. Next there are weaker kinds of claims, like those arising out of a contract. Those cannot be defended with any kind of force. Legal recourse is all one gets. And still further out is our interest in emotional health, dignity, etc. The strength of our claims depends on which of these circles the defendant is penetrating, not on how much we actually value that interest. When we compare just the situation of the villain Marx and the felon thief, all of this tends to be obscured, as the only thing that seems to matter are the preferences of the victim, and most people would prefer being subject to a petty theft than the kind of personal misconduct Marx inflicted on his intimates. But when we take a more global view of the matter, things start to look rather different.

The Social Choice Connection: Three Suggestive Analogies

Where does that leave us? Our intuitions regarding condemnation are obviously more mixed than we thought. Criminal law necessarily has to make a choice about which intuitions to respect and which to violate, and whatever that choice, it is going to look questionable in light of the intuitions it violates. But what accounts for this welter of conflicting intuitions? And what accounts for the particular choices criminal law has made among them? Social choice ideas here again prove quite suggestive, as one might well expect, since the undercriminalization problem is fundamentally a problem of ranking—the ranking of wrongful acts according to their levels blame-worthiness. The paradoxical feel of each of the three undercriminalization problems we have looked at turns out to mirror one or another paradoxical phenomenon from social choice theory. Let us see how.

Comparative Guilt and the Clash of Aggregation Principles

One of the broadest lessons one can draw from voting theory is this: we know that the same set of voter preferences can result in vastly different outcomes depending on which of many perfectly plausible alternative voting systems one uses. I mentioned earlier Donald Saari's example of an election among five candidates, in which one candidate would have won under a simple plurality vote, another would have won under a plurality vote with a runoff among the two top vote getters, a third candidate would have won if we were looking for the so-called Condorcet winner (the candidate who would beat every other one in a two-person race), and each of the remaining ones would win under some other, less familiar, but no less reasonable voting methods. Something completely analogous is true for multicriterial decision making. Perfectly plausible alternative ways of aggregating the same criteria will yield radically different outcomes. Each outcome will thus seem intuitively fairly compelling, because it is the product of some extremely reasonable-looking aggregation methods.

The problem of comparative guilt is a pretty good illustration of this. We have several eminently plausible aggregation rules for synthesizing the same set of criteria—the criteria being the harm done and the mental state of a defendant—producing divergent rankings. There is the aggregation approach we used initially, simply comparing the harm, according to which the mercy killer and the reckless driver were identical, followed by a comparison of their reasons, according to which the mercy killer looked more benign than the reckless driver. But then we encountered other plausible-looking aggregation rules—by considering, on the one hand, how much more compelling the husband's reasons for killing his wife would have had to be to exonerate him (under the doctrine of necessity), next considering how much more compelling the reckless driver's reasons for driving that fast would have had to be to exonerate *him* (under the doctrine of negligence), and then comparing those two. When we do that, the relative blameworthiness of the two actors is likely to be reversed. (We considered some other possible aggregation rules as well, but these two should be enough to make the point.) Our inconsistent intuitions about comparative guilt are thus a mirror image of our inconsistent intuitions about who should be considered the "real" winner of an election: the winner of the plurality vote, the Condorcet winner, or someone who prevails under any number of other plausible voting rules.

The Volume Discount and Nonmonotonicity

When considering intentional fouls, we encountered another odd property of many voting rules, nonmonotonicity: the possibility that sometimes some voters raising an alternative in their individual rankings can actually result in an overall lower ranking of that alternative. We saw that this phenomenon had interesting legal counterparts, in which someone's choice of the morally and legally wrong course of conduct could actually improve his moral and legal ledger. Intentional fouls were instances of such morally profitable "immoral" conduct. When considered side by side with morally profitable immoral conduct, the volume discount looks a lot less peculiar. We can think of the volume discount as a milder version of it. In a volume discount case, the defendant's immoral conduct does not actually improve his overall moral position; it simply fails to have an effect that is commensurate with the seriousness of the immorality. The person who fires a second bullet at his target is engaged in conduct that is as immoral as a single freestanding attempt, but when aggregated with the first shot he fired, it has a much smaller impact on his moral ledger. Here, then, the effect of one's misconduct is simply smaller than expected, rather than—as happens with morally profitable immoral conduct—being the direct inverse of what is expected.

Nonfelonious Villainies and Menu Effects

Finally, it is worth reminding ourselves of those ubiquitous "menu" effects, the influence of irrelevant alternatives: the possibility that removing an alternative from a set may well end up reversing the relative ranking of the remaining alternatives. (Removing the fish from the menu might cause us to chose the steak over the chicken, whereas before we had preferred the chicken.) The Borda count is a good illustration of this: in the case of the three candidates who were ranked Alain, Bertrand, Cecil. When Bertrand dropped out, the relative ranking of Alain and Cecil switched. Something like that seems to be at the heart of the problem of nonfelonious villainies.

When we rank blameworthy conduct, we might picture ourselves as taking a vast number of cases and then organizing them according to a plausible pattern such as the one I described earlier: intentional infractions of the most serious interests (bodily integrity) ranking above intentional infractions of less serious interests (property, followed by less tangible interests like emotional well-being and so on). When the interest is sufficiently minimal, we draw a line and declare everything below that line to be too de minimis to deserve criminalization. Now suppose that having done this, we then pluck just two from the set of alternatives and eye them very intensely, performing a purely binary comparison. Even applying the same aggregation principles as before, there is a good chance that we will now reverse their ranking—or at least this is what the connection with multicriterial decision making suggests.

We can make this more precise by focusing on our judgments about ingratitude versus petty theft. We have ranked, let us suppose, all wrongful conduct using a mix of relevant criteria, including the nature and extent of the harm done, or attempted, the mental state with which it was carried out (intentionally? recklessly? accidentally?), the presence or absence of a sufficiently direct causal link, the degree of involvement (as a principal or a mere accomplice?), the availability of defenses, and so on. Next we pluck out two cases, say, accidental killing and petty theft. As soon as we focus on these two cases side by side and to the exclusion of all others, something mildly strange will happen. We will hesitate whether we really want to continue to place accidental killings lower on the blameworthiness scale than petty theft, especially if I invite you to think about those cases by posing the following hypothetical: Someone tells you he is thinking about pursuing two career paths. One of them has a high probability of his accidentally (not intentionally, not recklessly, though possibly with tortuous negligence) killing you, and the other has an equally high probability of his stealing a small amount of money from you. Naturally you will prefer his doing the latter rather than the former. And that will at least tempt you to declare accidental killing more blameworthy than petty theft. It won't seriously tempt you because it is so preposterous to blame anyone for a purely accidental killing. But if the defendant's conduct were just a smidgen less innocent—perhaps he acted with the kind of negligence required for a civil case—you will now find it irresistible to say that if the victim prefers the one course of action to the other, especially if somehow, magically the perpetrator actually put him to the choice, then the course of action he preferred and perhaps even pleaded with the perpetrator to choose, then that alternative must be less blameworthy. It is a simple but hard-to-swallow consequence of the fact that we weigh more than just harm in assessing blameworthiness, that sometimes we would prefer to be victimized by a greater rather than lesser wrongdoer. It is the same way with ingratitude and petty theft. We might well prefer to be the victim of a minor theft than of devastating ingratitude. But if multicriterial assessment is what is required for ranking blameworthy conduct, then such cases will arise because in ordering the universe of wrongdoing, as the criminal code tries to do, we are not going to be exclusively focused on harm but on all aspects of wrongdoing.

Last Thoughts

The problem of undercriminalization appears to arise out of a set of highly conflicted intuitions. These conflicting intuitions are precisely the ones that give rise to several of the social choice paradoxes we have already seen. This in a way should not be surprising, since we are dealing with a ranking problem here: how to rank various blameworthy actions relative to each other.

Each of the three types of undercriminalization problem we have considered reflects one or another of the ranking paradoxes we have already encountered. The *comparative guilt problem* reflects the surprising possibility that a set of alternatives can plausibly be ranked in just about any way, meaning that a plausible set of aggregation principles can be found that produces that ranking. The *volume discount problem* reflects the odd feature of nonmonotonicity that plagues virtually all voting systems.

And the most basic of the undercriminalization problems, the one we started out with, the *problem of nonfelonious villainies*, reflects the menu effect to which many voting systems are subject, whereby the same rule when applied to a smaller subset of the available alternatives might completely rerank them relative to each other. Against this background it should no longer be so astonishing that when two types of wrongdoing, such as ingratitude and petty theft, are ranked in the context of every other kind of wrongdoing, ingratitude should end up in the de minimis range and petty theft much higher, but that on being reconsidered in juxtaposition and isolation from every other offense, we should end up taking a different view of their relative degrees of wickedness.

Final Thoughts

A few years ago I heard a story on National Public Radio, which has since become quite famous. Called "A Plate of Peas," it is the rueful recollection by Rick Beyer of a key episode in his childhood. Eight-year-old Rick is out on a shopping trip with his mother and grandmother. They stop for lunch, and to his great horror the dish he orders includes a food that revolts him beyond anything—a plate of peas. Upon noticing that he hasn't touched his peas, his grandmother orders him to eat up. But Rick hates peas, his mother reminds her. Undeterred, his grandmother whips out a five-dollar bill: five dollars if he will eat his peas. That's quite a fortune for Rick, and he digs in. His mother, however, is furious—furious with Grandma for offering such a deal and furious with Rick for letting himself be bought. Rick doesn't care. He wolfs down the peas, fighting his revulsion all the while, and collects the five dollars. And that, he assumes, is that.

But of course it isn't. The story continues:

That night, at dinner, my mother served two of my all-time favorite foods, meatloaf and mashed potatoes. Along with them came a big, steaming bowl of peas. She offered me some peas, and I, in the very last moments of my youth, declined. My mother fixed me with a cold eye as she heaped a huge pile of peas on my plate. Then came the words that were to haunt me for years.

"You ate them for money. You can eat them for love." . . .

. . . Did I eat the peas? You bet I did. I ate them that day, and every time they were served thereafter. The five dollars were quickly spent. My grandmother passed away a few years later. But the legacy of the peas lived on, as it lives on to this day. If I so much as curl my lip when they are served (because after all, I still hate the horrid little things), my mother repeats the dreaded words one more time.

"You ate them for money," she says. "You can eat them for love."[1]

The logical structure behind the argument that so defeats Beyer should seem vaguely familiar. "How can you refuse to eat those peas for love when you were willing to do so for five dollars," his mother in effect argues. It is quite similar to the argument that recurs throughout our discussion of the first perversity taken up in this book, the limitations on consent. It resembles, for instance, the argument the emergency room doctor makes to Al when he refuses to go along with Al's request that he treat Chloe's finger before treating anyone else. "How can you insist that Bea give up her one leg so that you can get treated, when you then squander that treatment opportunity on Chloe and her finger?" (If we wanted to make the resemblance painfully explicit we might put the argument by Rick's mother thus: "How can you insist that I swallow my hurt at seeing you spurn my cooking, supposedly because it would just be too hard on you to do otherwise, and then throw away my emotional sacrifice for the sake of five dollars?") The argument also resembles the one we used to explain the law's refusal to let that happy-go-lucky employee assume the risk of doing a hazardous job without proper protective gear: "How can you insist that the people with whom you interact outside of your work life take extensive precautions to avoid injuring you when you are perfectly willing to then let yourself be injured for some pitiful increase in your wages?" It also resembles the argument we used to explain the law's ban on drug use and other self-injurious behavior. What the law is in effect saying to the would-be drug user is "How can you insist on imposing all those costs on the rest of us for the sake of your health, your body, and your life—how, in other words can you call on us to sacrifice the equivalent of Bea's leg—if you are willing to surrender them for frivolous thrills (boxing, drugs, Russian Roulette), which are the equivalent of Chloe's finger?"

There is something going on in all of these cases that judges and lawmakers perceive dimly but cannot put their fingers on. It has to do with the fact that we are dealing with three-way relationships and our view of the relationship between two things often changes when a third is thrown into the mix. Judges and lawmakers sense this, but they don't quite see it. It is because they *sense* it that they limit the assumption of risk, the sale of bodily organs, prostitution, indentured servitude, and unorthodox property rights. And it is because they don't *see* it that they (and their critics) feel they are doing something perverse.

The chapters dealing with the second perversity—loopholes—are a further variation on this theme. The gist of the strategy pursued by exploiters of loopholes, I argued, is the introduction of a seemingly *irrelevant* alternative that somehow manages to reverse the relationship between the *relevant* alternatives. What a lawyer does, I claimed, is the equivalent of telling the collectivity, as it is about to choose chicken over steak, that there is also fish on the menu, which then causes it to choose steak instead. I sought to establish this equivalence by drawing an elaborate analogy between loophole exploitation and the manipulation of voting rules. The reason we cannot get rid of loopholes, or even convincingly criticize their use, is thus related to Arrow's theorem, which proved, among other things, that agenda manipulation (the formal name for what the waitress does when she mentions fish) is a logically ineradicable—and hence probably unobjectionable feature—of any plausible voting system. To take lawyers to task for availing themselves of this fact of logic is like calling a chess player unethical for making a strategic sacrifice.

To come back to "A Plate of Peas," however, notice how the heart of my argument is the odd three-way relationship between steak, chicken, and fish—namely that our judgment about the relationship between the first two will depend on the presence or absence of the third.

The fourth of my perversities, undercriminalization, I explained as being at least in part another manifestation of the steak, chicken, and fish phenomenon. The comparison of two offenses will yield very different results depending on which other offenses are implicitly included in the comparison. Nonfelonious villainies are misconduct that does not seem so very immoral against the background of a wide range of immoral conduct but often looks that way when compared exclusively to certain specific offenses.

In my discussion of the third of my perversities, the either/or character of legal rules, the "plate of peas" phenomenon takes a little more teasing out. Recall the argument that we need to draw a hard-and-fast line between life and death—no continuum allowed. If we only look at the two polar ends of the life-and-death continuum, it isn't evident why lots of intermediate categories should not be allowed to exist, why the treatment we accord people as they move from one end of the continuum to the other should not vary perfectly continuously with their descent down that continuum. It was the relationship of life and death to a third thing that revealed a discontinuity: an accumulation of impaired lives will outweigh a single unimpaired life; an accumulation of corpses will not. That forces us to mark the transition from the diseased to the deceased by a cliff rather than an incline, even if the place where we need to put that cliff is somewhat arbitrary.

"Of the Magic Number Seven, Plus or Minus Two" is the title of a famous essay by the psychologist George Miller. It may be best known for its title, which refers to the fact that seven (plus or minus two) is the number of distinct items most of us can hold in our working memory at any one time. For our reasoning capacity, the magic number may be three. It is when we go from two to three that relationships grow sufficiently complex for us to find them perennially surprising—and perverse.

Notes

Introduction

1. I am putting to the side concerns about rehabilitation and incapacitation. If we object to torture, it surely is not because of its failure to achieve those things. In other words, even if we thought that the deterrent effect was so powerful as to make the need for rehabilitation and incapacitation irrelevant, we would object to it.

2. Wrongly credited to Condorcet. See Keith M. Baker, *Condorcet: From Natural Philosophy to Social Mathematics* (Chicago: University of Chicago Press, 1975).

3. I say "vaguely democratic" because a monarchy would in fact meet these conditions. If the monarch is rational, then (1) his preferences will be transitive, (2) he will never choose something in the face of unanimous disapproval (if it is unanimous, then he too would disapprove), and (3) he will not be like that diner choosing steak over chicken and fish.

4. Matthew L. Spitzer, "Multicriteria Choice Processes: An Application of Public Choice Theory to *Bakke*, the FCC, and the Courts," *Yale Law Journal* 88, no. 4 (1979): 717–80; Frank Easterbrook, "Ways of Criticizing the Court," *Harvard Law Review* 95, no. 4 (1982): 802–32. For a good collection of the research-agenda-setting contributions of the pioneers in this field, see the reader by Maxwell Stearns, himself one of those pioneers, *Public Choice and Public Law: Readings and Commentary* (Cincinnati: Anderson, 1997).

5. Lewis A. Kornhauser and Lawrence G. Sager, "Unpacking the Court," *Yale Law Journal* 96, no. 1 (1986): 82–117; Lewis A. Kornhauser and Lawrence G. Sager, "The One and the Many: Adjudication in Collegial Courts," *California Law Review* 81, no. 1 (1993): 1–59. This insight was then developed further in a variety of imaginative ways by Bruce Chapman, Christian List, and Philip Pettit and soon sparked work by others as well, which is being tracked on a Web site maintained by List on judgment aggregation (see "Judgment Aggregation: A Bibliography on

the Discursive Dilemma, Doctrinal Paradox and Decisions on Multiple Proposi-
tions," http://personal.lse.ac.uk/list/doctrinalparadox.htm). Among the strictly
legal contributions, a particularly interesting one is Edward Rock's application of
the discursive paradox to corporate law: "The Corporate Form as a Solution to the
Discursive Dilemma," *Journal of Institutional and Theoretical Economics* 162, no. 1
(2006): 57–71.

6. Kenneth J. Arrow and Hervé Raynaud, *Social Choice and Multicriterion
Decision-Making* (Cambridge, Mass.: MIT Press, 1986).

7. Spitzer's approach is laid out in "Multicriteria Choice Processes." Bruce
Chapman's presentation and extraordinarily original elaboration of this approach
are to be found throughout his work, most prominently perhaps in the following:
"Law Games: Defeasible Rules and Revisable Rationality," *Law and Philosophy*
17, no. 4 (1998): 443–80; "Law, Incommensurability, and the Conceptually Sequenced Argument," *University of Pennsylvania Law Review* 146, no. 5 (1998):
1487–1528; "The Rational and the Reasonable: Social Choice Theory and Adjudication," *University of Chicago Law Review* 61, no. 1 (1994): 41–122; "More Easily
Done Than Said: Rules, Reasons and Rational Social Choice," *Oxford Journal
of Legal Studies* 18, no. 2 (1998): 293–329; "Rational Aggregation," *Politics, Philosophy and Economics* 1, no. 3 (2002): 337–54; "Rational Choice and Categorical Reason," *University of Pennsylvania Law Review* 151, no. 3 (2003): 1169–1210;
"Preference, Pluralism and Proportionality," *University of Toronto Law Journal*
60, no. 2 (2010): 177–96. Unfortunately, many of the treasures in Chapman's path-
breaking work are still awaiting proper notice and fuller exploration by the rest of
the academic community.

Chapter One

1. Each of these recognized exceptions, however, contains within it a hornets'
nest of difficult and unresolved issues. Among important recent explorations of
these are Joel Feinberg, *Harmless Wrongdoing* (New York: Oxford University
Press, 1988); Joel Feinberg, *Harm to Others* (New York: Oxford University Press,
1984); Barbara Fried, *The Progressive Assault on Laissez-Faire: Robert Hale and
the First Law and Economics Movement* (Cambridge, Mass.: Harvard University
Press, 1998); Margaret Jane Radin, *Contested Commodities* (Cambridge, Mass.:
Harvard University Press, 1996); Stephen Schulhofer, *Unwanted Sex: The Culture
of Intimidation and the Failure of Law* (Cambridge, Mass.: Harvard University
Press, 1998); Detlev Sternberg-Lieben, *Die objektiven Schranken der Einwilligung
im Strafrecht* (Tübingen: Mohr Siebeck, 1997); Alan Wertheimer, *Consent to Sex-
ual Relations* (Cambridge: Cambridge University Press, 2003); Alan Wertheimer,
Exploitation (Princeton, N.J.: Princeton University Press, 1996); Alan Wertheimer,
Coercion (Princeton, N.J.: Princeton University Press, 1987); Peter Westen, *The*

Logic of Consent: The Diversity and Deceptiveness of Consent as a Defense to Criminal Conduct (Aldershot, UK: Ashgate, 2004).

2. Perhaps the most sophisticated form of this variant of paternalism is what goes by the name of "false consciousness." Elizabeth Anderson, for instance, argues for it in "Is Women's Labor a Commodity?" *Philosophy and Public Affairs* 19, no. 1 (1990): 71–92, citing as the paradigmatic case a woman selling her services as a surrogate mother.

3. Wertheimer, *Exploitation*.

4. Radin, *Contested Commodities*, 138.

5. John Harris, "The Survival Lottery," *Philosophy* 50, no. 191 (1975): 81–87.

6. Robert E. Goodin, "Selling Environmental Indulgences," *Kyklos* 47, no. 4 (1994): 573–96.

7. Thomas Merrill and Henry Smith, "Optimal Standardization in the Law of Property: The Numerus Clausus Principle," *Yale Law Journal* 110, no. 1 (2000): 1–70; Thomas Merrill and Henry Smith, "The Property/Contract Interface," *Columbia Law Review* 101, no. 4 (2001): 773–852; Bernard Rudden, "Economic Theory versus Property Law: The Numerus Clausus Problem," in *Oxford Essays in Jurisprudence*, 3rd ser., ed. John Eekelaar and John Bell (Oxford: Oxford University Press, 1987).

8. See Kenneth W. Simons, "Assumption of Risk and Consent in the Law of Torts: A Theory of Full Preference," *Boston University Law Review* 67 (1987): 213–87; Kenneth W. Simons, "Reflections on Assumption of Risk," *UCLA Law Review* 50 (2002): 481–529. The problem I am here considering involves what is usually put under the heading of the "express" and the "primary" assumption of risk rather than the so-called secondary assumption of risk. The main puzzle raised by the secondary assumption of risk is this: the defendant engages in an activity despite the fact that he knows full well that it is very risky. He never actually consents, and the question then arises whether his actions are to be deemed as tantamount to consent. In the cases I am considering, no one disputes that the defendant consented, and meant to consent, but we nonetheless have doubts about the validity of his consent.

Chapter Two

1. Some readers have wondered whether in making the judgment that a two-leg injury is worse than a one-leg injury I am not simply smuggling in some kind of objective welfare judgment. Why is it, they ask, that I automatically assume that Al's two-leg injury is more serious than Bea's one-leg injury, when it seems logically quite possible that Bea derives more utility from her one leg than Al does from two? It must be, they say, because I think that any two-leg injury is objectively worse than a one-leg injury, regardless of how the victim judges the matter. But if

I am relying on objective welfare judgments, as they imply, then it is unremarkable that in intermixing such objective welfare judgments with subjective welfare judgments (like Al ranking Chloe's finger above his legs) we should end up in a cycle.

I am not, however, relying on any objective welfare judgments here. I do not assume anything about the comparative welfare of Al and Bea when I assert that he has more of a claim to help with his two-leg injury than she does to help with her one-leg inquiry. There is no particular connection between claims and welfare. Talking about claims is not just a roundabout way of talking about welfare. To see this more clearly, note that it will often happen that Person A has a stronger claim to something than Person B, but B would derive greater welfare from it (whether assessed objectively or subjectively) than A. The simplest example of this are claims to property. Obviously, Person A may have a stronger claim to a piece of property than Person B by virtue of the way in which he acquired it (perhaps it is the fruit of his own labor), despite the fact that it would do more for B's welfare if he, instead of A, were to own it. In a later section in which I discuss the logic of claims more extensively, I will offer other examples of how comparing the strength of claims has little to do with comparing welfare or utility.

It is an important feature of my argument that I am not relying on any ideas about objective welfare, since many people find such ideas eminently resistible. What I say about claims, by contrast, seems much harder to resist.

2. Some people might find this example more convincing if what your friend wanted to do was not something as frivolous as going on a cruise but something more "heroic," like climbing Mt. Kilimanjaro.

3. Some readers might find the following variation on the foregoing argument illuminating. The doctor might reason to himself thus: "What is the cost of acceding to Bea's claim to have her one-leg injury treated? Is it that I cannot treat Al's two-leg injury, or is it that I cannot treat Chloe's finger injury? It cannot be both, since I could not possibly treat both. Well, let us say I regard the treatment of the finger as the cost of treating the one-leg injury. Then I clearly should go ahead and treat the one-leg injury, since Bea's claim to her leg is stronger than Chloe's claim to her finger. Now let me try the alternative supposition on for size. Let me suppose that I regard the treatment of Al's two-leg injury as the cost of treating Bea's one-leg injury. Then, of course, I should decline to treat the one-leg injury, since Al's claim is clearly superior to Bea's. But in that case what I ought to do is treat the two-leg injury. If I do not, then why am I considering it (rather than the finger) as the cost of treating the one-leg injury? *Either way I should not be treating Chloe's finger.*"

4. Thomas Nagel, *The View from Nowhere* (New York: Oxford University Press, 1986).

5. Ibid., 166–67.

6. Ibid. (italics mine). Nagel is echoing an equally famous passage from an article by Thomas Scanlon, in which he writes: "The fact that someone would be will-

ing to forgo a decent diet in order to build a monument to his god does not mean that his claim on others for aid in his project has the same strength as a claim for aid in obtaining enough to eat." T. M. Scanlon, "Preference and Urgency," *Journal of Philosophy* 72, no. 19 (1975): 659–60.

Some readers will be tempted to conclude from Nagel's and Scanlon's examples that when they speak about claims, they are really just making a paternalistic judgment about what someone ought to desire (if he were only enlightened enough), namely, the stuff he really needs. But that is just an unfortunate feature of the particular way in which Nagel and Scanlon choose to illustrate their point. In fact, there is nothing paternalistic about the judgment that someone who desires something intensely has a low claim to it or that someone who desires something only slightly has a strong claim to it. The example I gave earlier, when explaining why talking about claims is not just another way of valuing welfare objectively, involving property rights, is equally relevant here. Another example might serve to further elucidate my point. When a defendant causes harm to Victim A, let us say by not helping him escape some harm like drowning, or by inflicting on him a purely accidental injury, he is infringing only on a very modest set of A's claims. By contrast, when a defendant causes harm to B by injuring him intentionally, he is infringing on B's very strong claim. The harm caused to A may be much greater than the harm caused to B. But A's claim to be free of such harm is nonetheless much weaker than B's claim to be free of such harm. Once again, it is evident that this judgment about the comparative strength of claims has nothing to do with paternalism.

7. Readers well versed in the theory of social choice may be bothered by a seeming incompleteness in my analysis of the triage cycle, as was one early reader of this book. In terms of social choice, the question presented by the case is how to distill a final ranking from a variety of possible rankings based on the preferences of the individuals involved—namely, the patients and the doctor—and other considerations unrelated to their preferences. Many more distillation possibilities (the technically more correct term would be aggregation possibilities) seem to exist than the two that I consider. For instance, someone might wonder why I don't use a two-stage aggregation process that reverses the process described in the text: namely, one that first ranks the three patients on the basis of the win-win principle and thereafter ranks them based on their medical needs. In other words, what about saying: To begin with, in the choice between Al and Chloe, Chloe should be chosen under the win-win argument? If we next compare Chloe with Bea, the latter should be chosen based on the medical necessity criterion. But there are many more complicated possibilities. One might, for instance, use versions of majority or plurality voting to count up the preferences of the three patients and the doctor and thereby obtain an entirely different ranking.

What I would claim for the possibilities that I do consider in the text is that they are really the only plausible contenders. Let's divide all possible aggregation methods into two groups, the first group consisting of those that satisfy the win-win principle and the second group consisting of those that do not. All aggregation methods satisfying the win-win principle are vulnerable to the same critique as the most prominent and plausible member of that group, the win-win-based ranking that I consider in the text. The aggregation methods that do not satisfy the win-win principle are vulnerable to attacks based on the win-win principle, to which they are unable to offer the claims-versus-desire-based response that I offer in behalf of the ranking I argue for in the text.

Chapter Three

1. Goodin, "Selling Environmental Indulgences," *Kyklos* 47, no. 4 (1994): 575.

2. Michael Sandel, "It's Immoral to Buy the Right to Pollute," op-ed, *NY Times*, Dec. 15, 1997.

3. Cass Sunstein, "Moral Heuristics," *Behavioral and Brain Sciences* 28, no. 4 (2005): 531–42.

4. Merrill and Smith, "Optimal Standardization in the Law of Property," *Yale Law Journal* 110, no. 1 (2000): 27. See also their "The Property/Contract Interface," *Columbia Law Review* 101, no. 4 (2001): 773–852.

5. I say "usually" because there are some very narrowly circumscribed circumstances—under a doctrine aptly titled "intentional interference with contractual relations"—under which I might have some limited recourse against the interferer.

6. There are actually numerous priority rights that arise here. There is the simple priority right that allows the driver not to have to pay any damages to me. But there is also a more profound kind of priority right at work; it has to do with the way we assess whether the driver drove carelessly or not. That will depend on our weighing the costs and benefits of his driving behavior. Risks he imposes on caterers and their ability to keep their contracts probably need not figure in that weighing process, but risks he imposes on property owners of course will.

7. Larry Alexander, "Consent, Punishment, and Proportionality," *Philosophy and Public Affairs* 15, no. 2 (1986): 178–82.

8. This should give one a new perspective on all kinds of social contract arguments and surely deserves more extended treatment elsewhere. Social contract arguments usually refer to a person's *ex ante* consent (sometimes actual, more often hypothetical) to a vast range of things, including many that would constitute invasions of the body. What I have said casts a large shadow over such arguments.

Chapter Four

1. Amartya Sen, *Collective Choice and Social Welfare* (San Francisco: Holden-Day, 1970), chap. 6.

2. The critique is restated particularly well in Howard Chang, "A Liberal Theory of Social Welfare: Fairness, Utility, and the Pareto Principle," *Yale Law Journal* 110, no. 2 (2000): 173–235.

3. Louis Kaplow and Steven Shavell, *Fairness versus Welfare* (Cambridge, Mass.: Harvard University Press, 2002).

4. A few qualifications. There are several ways in which they do not actually ignore or recommend ignoring fairness. To begin with, they believe the Pareto principle is a principle of fairness, albeit one that precludes adherence to just about any other. Second, they would accommodate fairness in certain very limited ways. They leave open what one wants to incorporate into the welfare conception: Distributive justice could be built in, so that a dollar taken from the rich but yielding only fifty cents for the poor might count as a gain if the welfare function weighs the gains of each group appropriately. And if people derive pleasure from seeing certain fairness principles observed, that too could be counted as part of welfare. But that is far from adopting the fairness principles that are invoked for the bulk of legal cases: those based on corrective justice in private law and those based on retributivism in criminal law.

5. See Chang, "A Liberal Theory of Social Welfare."

6. Kaplow and Shavell, *Fairness versus Welfare*, 347n106.

Chapter Five

1. See generally Douglas G. Baird, *The Elements of Bankruptcy* (Westbury, N.Y.: Foundation Press, 1992), 24–54.

2. See Boris Bittker and Lawrence Lokken, *Federal Taxation of Income, Estates, and Gifts*, 2nd ed., vol. 3 (Boston: Warren, Gorham, and Lamont, 1991). See generally chap. 75, "Assignments of Income," and specifically sec. 75.3.5, "Gift-Leasebacks of Income-Producing Property."

3. See Paul H. Robinson, "Causing the Conditions of One's Own Defense: A Study in the Limits of Theory in Criminal Law Doctrine," *Virginia Law Review* 71, no. 1 (1985): 1–64.

4. See Joachim Hruschka, *Strafrecht nach logisch-analytischer Methode*, 2nd ed. (Berlin: Walter de Gruyter, 1987), 353.

5. T. Alexander Aleinikoff and David A. Martin, *Immigration: Process and Policy*, 2nd ed. (St. Paul: West, 1991), 777–79.

6. Lynn LoPucki, "The Death of Liability," *Yale Law Journal* 106, no. 1 (1996): 1–92.

7. See generally Joseph Isenbergh, "Musings on Form and Substance in Taxation," *University of Chicago Law Review* 49, no. 3 (1982): 859–84.

8. Steve Bundy and Einer Elauge, "Do Lawyers Improve the Adversary System? A General Theory of Litigation Advice and Its Regulation," *California Law Review* 79, no. 2 (1991): 313–420.

9. David Weisbach, "Ten Truths about Tax Shelters," *Tax Law Review* 55 (2002): 222.

10. See Frederick Schauer, *Playing by the Rules: A Philosophical Examination of Rule-Based Decision-Making in Law and in Life* (New York: Oxford University Press, 1992), and Larry Alexander and Emily Sherwin, *The Rule of Rules: Morality, Rules, and the Dilemmas of the Law* (Durham, N.C.: Duke University Press, 2001).

11. The example here is based on Ian Ayres's ingenious analysis of a parallel problem in corporate law, the right of corporate officials to lie about merger negotiations. See "Back to Basics: Regulating How Corporations Speak to the Market," *Virginia Law Review* 77, no. 5 (1991): 945–99.

12. Larry Alexander, "The Gap," *Harvard Journal of Law and Public Policy* 14 (1991): 695–701, quote on 695 (italics mine).

13. Fred Schauer, who launched this line of argument in *Playing by the Rules*, put it thus: "In every case of rule application . . . we can imagine . . . the possibility that the rule-maker (the authority) were she present, would herself have a view about whether this application did or did not reflect her justifications in setting forth the rule." Schauer then goes on to list several possibilities. First, "The subject will believe that in this case the rule should not be followed, and the authority, if present would disagree." Second, "The subject will believe that in this case the rule should be followed, and the authority, if present, would disagree." Then, he posits, "Suppose the authority predicts that the incidence of the first [possibility] will be greater than the incidence of the [second possibility], that from the perspective of the authority there will be more cases of mistaken non-following than of mistaken following." In other words, "the authority predicts that the cases of erroneous disobedience [will] outweigh . . . the cases of justified obedience." That being so, "the rule-maker will wish to stifle disobedience simpliciter. In other words, even accepting that it is irrational rule-worship to follow rules when it is best, all things considered, not to follow them, it is still rational for the authority, in advance, to encourage (by sanctions or otherwise) the very rule-worship she would avoid were she the subject. Rule-worship, however irrational from the standpoint of the subject, is something the rational authority may seek to inculcate" (131).

Chapter Six

1. See generally Blaise Pascal, *The Provincial Letters*, trans. A. J. Krailsheimer (Baltimore: Penguin Books, 1989), and Jacob Katz, *The "Shabbes Goy": A Study in Halakhic Flexibility*, trans. Yoel Lerner (Philadelphia: Jewish Publications Society, 1989).

2. James C. Scott, *Weapons of the Weak: Everyday Forms of Peasant Resistance* (New Haven, Conn.: Yale University Press, 1985); James C. Scott, *Domination and*

the Arts of Resistance: Hidden Transcripts (New Haven, Conn.: Yale University Press, 1990).

3. Scott, *Domination and the Arts of Resistance*, 140.

4. Jörn Kalkbrenner, *Urteil ohne Prozess: Margot Honecker gegen Ossietzky-Schueler* (Berlin: Dietz Verlag, 1990).

5. *Bronston v. United States*, 409 U.S. 352 (1973).

6. The seminal article that drew attention to this phenomenon is Christian Boorse and Roy Sorensen, "Ducking Harm," *Journal of Philosophy* 85, no. 3 (1988): 115–34. There are less artificial analogues of this. Indeed, they abound. A particularly striking version of it occurs in Harry Mulisch's novel *The Assault*, in which the Dutch resistance kills a Nazi collaborator in front of the house of the Korteweg family, who decide to deflect certain-to-ensue indiscriminate German re-taliation by moving the corpse in front of another house, occupied by the Stenwijk family. Our assessment of what the Kortewegs do is rather different than it would be if they had instead avoided German retaliation by simply fleeing their home, even if they could expect with certainty that this would simply lead the Germans to take out their wrath on their neighbors, the Stenwijks.

7. For a fuller rendition of this argument, see my *Ill-Gotten Gains: Evasion, Blackmail, Fraud, and Kindred Puzzles of the Law* (Chicago: University of Chicago Press, 1996), part 1.

Chapter Seven

1. We would calculate Cecil's rank thus: we add together 40 times 1, because 40 voters put Cecil first, plus 30 times 2, because 30 voters put Cecil second, plus 30 times 3, because 30 voters put Cecil third; we divide the total by 100, which is the number of voters, to obtain 1.9 as the overall "average" rank for Cecil. We proceed analogously for Alain and Bertrand.

2. Donald Saari, *Decisions and Elections: Explaining the Unexpected* (Cambridge: Cambridge University Press, 2001), 40.

3. See Donald Saari, *Disposing Dictators, Demystifying Voting Paradoxes: Social Choice Analysis* (New York: Cambridge University Press, 2008), chapter 3, "Voting Dictionaries." For a classic report of how two voting theorists actually put this into practice, see Michael E. Levine and Charles R. Plott, "Agenda Influence and Its Implications," *Virginia Law Review* 63, no. 4 (1977): 561–604.

4. Samuel Issacharoff, Pamela S. Karlan, and Richard H. Pildes, *The Law of Democracy: Legal Structures and the Political Process*, 3rd ed. (St. Paul, Minn.: West, 2007); Larry Alexander, "Still Lost in the Political Thicket (or Why I Don't Understand the Concept of Vote Dilution)," *Vanderbilt Law Review* 50 (1997): 327; Larry Alexander and Saikrishna Prakash, "Tempest in an Empty Teapot: Why the Constitution Does Not Regulate Gerrymandering," *William and Mary Law Review* 50, no. 1 (2008): 1–62.

Chapter Eight

1. Arrow himself explores this connection in a book coauthored with Hervé Raynaud, *Social Choice and Multicriterion Decision-Making* (Cambridge, Mass.: MIT Press, 1986).

2. The precise extent of the analogy between voting and multicriterial decision making is a subject of some heated controversy. For good introductions to this literature, see Susan Hurley, *Natural Reasons: Personality and Polity* (New York: Oxford University Press, 1989); Amartya Sen, "On Weights and Measures: Informational Constraints in Social Welfare Analysis," in *Choice, Welfare, and Measurement* (Cambridge, Mass.: MIT Press, 1982), 226–63, especially 251–56; Allan M. Feldman and Roberto Serrano, "Arrow's Impossibility Theorem: Two Simple Single-Profile Versions," Brown University Department of Economics Working Paper No. 2006-11, 2008.

3. These are the kinds of situations Thomas Schelling deals with at great length, most famously in *The Strategy of Conflict* (Cambridge, Mass.: Harvard University Press, 1960).

4. See, e.g., *Barber v. Superior Court*, 147 Cal. App. 3d 1006; 195 Cal. Rptr. 484 (1983).

5. Amos Tversky and Daniel Kahneman, "The Framing of Decisions and the Psychology of Choice," *Science*, January 30, 1981, 453.

6. Louis Kaplow and Steven Shavell, *Fairness versus Welfare* (Cambridge, Mass.: Harvard University Press, 2002), 347n106.

7. The points I have just made are actually made by Arrow himself in the second edition of *Social Choice and Individual Values* (New Haven, Conn.: Yale University Press, 1963), albeit in very elliptical fashion. Arrow there discusses a specific instance of multicriterial decision making. He discusses the case of a decision maker who has to distribute a set of goods among a variety of recipients. He imagines his doing so in a very traditional utilitarian fashion, by evaluating how much utility each recipient would derive from a given package of goods and then distributing them in such a way as to maximize the sum of their utilities. This presumably is the way one might generally go about dealing with the need for multicriterial decision making—score each item on an appropriate-seeming scale and then add the scores up for a final ranking of the alternatives. Arrow claims that this violates the irrelevance of independent alternatives and proceeds to demonstrate how.

He considers a specific method for assessing utility devised by Goodman and Markovits. The method uses

> just noticeable differences as interpersonally valid units. [Goodman and Markovits] argue that no individual can make indefinitely fine comparisons of alternatives. Hence, it may be supposed that each individual has only a finite number of levels of discrimination; a change from one level to the next represents the minimum

difference which is discernible to an individual. Goodman and Markovits then make the basic ethical assumption that the significance of a change from one discretion level to the next is the same for all individuals and independent of the level from which the change is made.

The consequence of this assumption (in conjunction with other, more usual conditions, Collective Rationality, the Pareto principle, and Equality) is that social choice is made according to the sum of individual utilities, where the utility of any individual for any social state is the number of discrimination levels below the level in which the individual places the given social state. . . .

[However, in such a system] the ranks [of the different goods' distributions] can easily depend on the choice [set]. Suppose, for example, that a new commodity becomes available but is prohibitively expensive. If [the choice set] is expanded by adding distributions of commodities including the new one, it may contain elements more desirable than any of the old ones, as well as some less desirable than some old ones. The additional components of the social state vector will increase the possibility of discrimination, so that it is to be expected that the enlargement of the [choice set] will introduce new discrimination levels whose ranks lie between some of the old ones. Then the perceived ranks . . . of the original alternatives will be altered by the introduction of new alternatives which may not be technologically feasible.

This objection is, of course, simply another illustration of the argument for the principle of Independence of Irrelevant Alternatives. (115–16)

Chapter Nine

1. In Judith Jarvis Thomson, "The Trolley Problem," in *Rights, Restitution, and Risk: Essays in Moral Theory* (Cambridge, Mass.: Harvard University Press, 1986), 94–116, a scenario along these lines is taken up, though analyzed rather differently.

2. William Manchester, *American Caesar: Douglas MacArthur,* 1880–1964 (Boston: Little, Brown, 1978), 38.

3. Frank Jackson and Robert Pargetter, "Ought, Options, and Actualism," *Philosophical Review* 95, no. 2 (1986): 235. See also the superb discussion of this issue in Michael Stocker, *Plural and Conflicting Values* (New York: Oxford University Press, 1989), 96–109.

4. See Willi Dreßen, "NS—'Euthanasie Prozesse' in der Bundesrepublik Deutschland im Wandel der Zeit," in *NS—"Euthanasie" vor Gericht: Fritz Bauer*

und die Grenzen juristischer Bewältigung, ed. Hanno Loewy and Bettina Winter (Frankfurt: Campus Verlag, 1996).

5. For an exhaustive look at the Gibbard-Satterthwaite theorem and the literature that grew out of it, see Alan D. Taylor, *Social Choice and the Mathematics of Manipulation* (New York: Cambridge University Press, 2005).

Chapter Ten

1. Sirius Fall, BGH, Urt. V. 5.7.1983, 1 StR 168/83, BGH 33. Translations of excerpts are mine.

2. For an authoritative discussion of rules versus standards, see Mark Kelman, *A Guide to Critical Legal Studies* (Cambridge, Mass.: Harvard University Press, 1987).

3. Carol Rose, "Crystals and Mud in Property Law," *Stanford Law Review* 40, no. 3 (1988): 577–610.

4. Not that it never works. For a very successful use of this approach, see Peter Schuck, "When the Exception Becomes the Rule: Regulatory Equity and the Formulation of Energy Policy through an Exceptions Process," *Duke Law Journal*, 1984: 163–300.

5. Eviatar Zerubavel, *The Fine Line: Making Distinctions in Everyday Life* (New York: Free Press, 1991); Paul Fussell, *The Great War and Modern Memory* (New York: Oxford University Press, 1975), 75–113.

6. Zerubavel, *The Fine Line*.

7. See Heinrich Hoeniger, *Untersuchungen zum Problem der gemischten Verträge* (Mannheim: J. Bensheimer, 1910), 306–8. Discussed in detail in Detlef Leenen, *Typus und Rechtsfindung* (Berlin: Duncker & Humblot, 1971), 134.

8. Larry Alexander, "Scalar Properties, Binary Judgments," presented at the University of San Diego School of Law, 2005, http://papers.ssrn.com/s013/papers.cfm?abstract_id=829326.

9. John Coons, "Approaches to Court-Imposed Compromise: The Uses of Doubt and Reason," *Northwestern University Law Review* 58 (1963–64): 750–94. For more legal, historical, and economic background on the good-faith purchaser problem, see especially Saul Levmore, "Variety and Uniformity in the Treatment of the Good-Faith Purchaser," *Journal of Legal Studies* 16 (1987): 43–65.

10. Coons, "Approaches to Court-Imposed Compromise," 765.

11. Douglas Husak, "Partial Defenses," *Canadian Journal of Law and Jurisprudence* 11 (1998): 167–92. See also Stephen Morse, "Undiminished Confusion in Diminished Capacity," *Journal of Criminal Law and Criminology* 75, no. 1 (1984): 1–55.

12. Michael S. Moore, *Placing Blame: A General Theory of the Criminal Law* (New York: Oxford University Press, 1997).

13. G. Mitu Gulati, William A. Klein, and Eric M. Zolt, "Connected Contracts," *UCLA Law Review* 47 (2000): 887–948.

14. Michael Abramowicz, "A Compromise Approach to Compromise Verdicts," *California Law Review* 89 (2001): 233; Gideon Parchomovsky, Peter Siegelman, and Steven Thel, "Of Equal Wrongs and Half Rights," *New York University Law Review* 82 (2007): 738–89.

15. Alexander, "Scalar Properties, Binary Judgments," http://papers.ssrn.com/so13/papers.cfm?abstract_id=829326.

16. Similar approaches have been touted outside law. See, e.g., Robert Nozick, *The Nature of Rationality* (Princeton, N.J.: Princeton University Press, 1993), 41–63 (a split-the-difference solution to Newcomb's problem); Derek Parfit, *Reasons and Persons* (Oxford: Clarendon Press, 1984), 199–350 (a split-the-difference approach to concepts of personal identity); and, in law, Lothar Philipps, "Unbestimmte Rechtsbegriffe und Fuzzy Logic," in *Strafgerechtigkeit: Festschrift für Arthur Kaufmann zum 70. Geburtstag*, ed. Fr. Haft. W. Hassemer, U. Neumann, W. Schild, and U. Schroth (Heidelberg: C. F. Müller, 1993), 265; Lothar Kuhlen, *Typuskonzeptionen in der Rechtstheorie* (Berlin: Duncker & Humblot, 1978).

17. David Kaye, "The Limits of the Preponderance of the Evidence Standard," *American Bar Foundation Research Journal* 7, no. 2 (1982): 487–516.

18. Nelson Goodman, *Ways of Worldmaking* (Indianapolis: Hackett, 1978), 72.

19. Ibid.

20. Ibid., 74, 75.

21. Ibid., 83, 84.

22. Ibid., 88.

Chapter Eleven

1. Nelson Goodman, *Ways of Worldmaking* (Indianapolis: Hackett, 1978), 128; Judith Jarvis Thomson, "A Defense of Abortion," in *The Rights and Wrongs of Abortion*, ed. Marshall Cohen, Thomas Nagel, and Thomas Scanlon (Princeton, N.J.: Princeton University Press, 1974).

2. Larry Temkin, "A Continuum Argument for Intransitivity," *Philosophy and Public Affairs* 25, no. 3 (1996): 175–210; Larry Temkin, "A Spectrum Argument for Intransitivity," in *Well-Being and Morality: Essays in Honour of James Griffin*, ed. Roger Crisp and Brad Hooker (Oxford: Oxford University Press, 1999); James Griffin, *Well-Being: Its Meaning, Measurement, and Moral Importance* (Oxford: Clarendon Press, 1986), 85–89; Ken Binmore and Alex Voorhoeve, "Defending Transitivity against Zeno's Paradox," *Philosophy and Public Affairs* 31, no. 3 (2003): 272–79; Bruce Chapman, "Rational Choice and Categorical Reason," *University of Pennsylvania Law Review* 151 (2003): 1169–1210; Kaye, "Limits of the Preponderance of the Evidence."

3. For sympathetic discussions of such an idea, see Christos Mylonopoulos, *Komparative und Dispositionsbegriffe im Strafrecht* (Frankfurt am Main: P. Lang, 1998).

4. Let me resolve a possible ambiguity here: When I speak of aiding H-minus-1 (or H-minus-2 or H-minus-300 or H-minus-whatever), I do not mean restoring him to being an H but simply making possible his continued existence as an H-minus-1 (or whatever) rather than letting him be destroyed altogether.

5. Peter Unger, *Identity, Consciousness, and Value* (New York: Oxford University Press, 1990), 211–55.

6. And there is something else. Reflection will show that the creation of such subcategories of aliveness would not in fact increase our sense of continuity, because the distinction between two adjacent members of such subcategories is itself a function of several different criteria (different bodily organs that may malfunction).

7. To make this painfully explicit, let us transpose the argument just given from the end of life to the beginning of life. Imagine, to begin with, a perfect baby. And consider a spectrum of cases, consisting at one end of that perfect baby, right next to it a baby just like it but one day younger (i.e., one day before being born), then an identical baby but two days younger (i.e., two days before being born), and so on down to the day of conception, some 280 days earlier. Each "baby" in this progression is exactly one day behind the next one in its stage of development. Suppose, then, we went along with the commonsense view that there is no one point at which this creature becomes human—that rather what we have is a continuum that starts with a mere assembly of cells that then gets progressively more human up until the moment of delivery.

Now imagine having to make the same kind of choice previously considered: whether to give crucial help to the neonate (i.e., the perfect recently delivered baby) or the fetus one day before delivery. Someone who thinks of the spectrum of partly formed babies as a continuum of value would presumably say that the neonate deserves to be aided slightly more than the neonate-minus-one-day and that that creature in turn deserves to be aided slightly more than the neonate-minus-two-days and so on. Let us modify the menu of choices in the same way we did before. Let us imagine we had to choose between aiding a single neonate or two neonate-minus-1s. Again, it would seem that the decrease in quality (one day less of development) is made up for by the increase in quantity (two creatures instead of one), and therefore the group of two gets priority over the one. Now repeat this process over and over as before, so that, once again, we get the following chain of judgments regarding eligibility for aid: 1 neonate < 2 neonate-minus-1s < 3 neonate-minus-2s < . . . < 281 neonate-minus-280s.

But this, too, is absurd. It cannot be that 281 just-conceived fetuses are more eligible for help than a full-fledged baby. (If that seems controversial, the argument can be pushed back a few increments further, into the very process of fertilization, considered, as it were, in slow motion, without changing its logic in any way.) The only way out of this absurdity is to conclude that someone's status as a human being begins at a particular point rather than emerging gradually over time.

Once again it will be natural to ask where that point is. The answer is the same as before. It does not seem as though there are any considerations that would dictate putting it at a specific place. There are considerations that preclude putting it very near the point of delivery or very near the point of conception. Beyond that, however, it seems we have discretion to put it in lots of places. What we do not have discretion about is that there will have to be such a point and that it must be a point and not anything more extensive or gradual than that.

And once again it will be natural to wonder whether one might not still take the position that human life gets gradually less valuable as one recedes from the moment of delivery up until one gets to the point at which it begins. The answer would seem to be that in doing so we work running up, probably much less egregiously than before, against precepts that grant the same rights to the disabled as to others.

8. Just imagine a series of hypothetical defendants, each intending to kill one of a spectrum of creatures ranging from the completely human to the completely supernatural. Now imagine each of those defendants having to make a choice much like the ones involved in our death and abortion examples—that is, a choice between killing one perfect human or killing a large number of "spectral" creatures. While it may seem plausible that as we move by increments away from the completely human we get gradually less human, it seems preposterous to say that someone intending to kill a very large number of totally supernatural creatures could be said to be on a par with someone intending to kill one complete human. And so there must be a kink, a cliff, a sharp line, an either/or moment separating the imagined victims—something like the ghost/witch line that the Sudanese courts drew.

The other point made about the human being category also carries over. If humans are not to lose their basic rights (such as the right not to be killed) based on disabilities, then presumably they ought not to lose them on grounds of supernatural, or parapsychological, abilities either. For the case law on these matters, see Krishna Vasdev, *The Law of Homicide in the Sudan* (London: Butterworths, 1978), and Leo Katz, *Bad Acts and Guilty Minds: Conundrums of the Criminal Law* (Chicago: University of Chicago Press, 1987), 165–74.

9. Not everyone will be interested in this, but some will undoubtedly wonder about an issue I raised at the outset of the either/or discussion. This note is for them.

In his original article on court-imposed compromise, as he called this problem, John Coons suggested that the law was being unduly either/or in not splitting the difference between the original owner and the good-faith purchaser for value in the classic stolen goods scenario. The thief who stole the goods from the original owner and then sold them to the good-faith purchaser is the only guilty party here. Since the other two are both innocent, why should they not share the burden of the loss among themselves, perhaps by letting one of them retain possession of the good and requiring him to make some partial compensatory payment to the other?

Coons's original proposal was intended only for the case in which the two parties were literally equally innocent. He did not take a strong position with regard to the case in which the two parties were not equally innocent (say, because one of them was less careful than the other in forestalling the mishap—the original owner, perhaps, in leaving his goods carelessly accessible to a thief, or the good-faith purchaser in being too trusting). If we construed Coons's recommendation narrowly, we would simply be replacing one discontinuity with another: we would now have introduced a new discontinuity between the cases in which the relative innocence of the parties is equal and in which they are slightly lopsided. The objective of reducing discontinuity would thus not have been accomplished. But suppose we set things up so that the loss from the stolen goods is distributed in proportion to the relative fault of the two parties. In other words, we might introduce something like the comparative negligence regime, whereby each party contributes to a loss in proportion to its own negligence. That would at first glance seem to do away with all disturbing discontinuities. But certainly not at second glance. *For if one of the parties exhibits even a tiny amount of fault, whereas the other party exhibits none, then suddenly we would switch from dividing the loss equally among them to putting the entire loss on the party at fault.*

In other words, even in what might have looked like the easiest and most compelling cases in which either/or cried out for reform, it is not easy to see how it could possibly be done away with.

10. William Simon, *The Practice of Justice* (Cambridge, Mass.: Harvard University Press, 1998).

11. And what about the question of why personal identity is either/or? In other words, how should we think about cases in which a new "you" has somehow been created from an old "you"—if your brain is taken out and put into a new body, or if it is cut up and most of it is put into one new body and the rest into another, or if you are cloned and the old you is destroyed altogether, and so on. The hard question in each of these cases is whether the new you is identical to the old you—whether it is in fact still you.

Common sense would seem to tell us that there has to be a definitive yes or no answer to that—that the transformed you either is or is not you. Derek Parfit, as we saw, makes the bold claim that that is nonsense. He backs this claim with some powerful arguments, simple at their core, but subtle and ingenious in their development. One such argument is a clever variation of what lawyers call the slippery slope argument. Suppose, he says, someone were to gradually "transform" you into Greta Garbo. Initially just a few cells, then a few more. Very gradually your memories, personality, looks would change into hers. Suppose now you were asked at which point the resulting person is still you. Indeed, suppose the question were made more meaningful to you by the added threat that that person will be subjected to a painful procedure. When would you feel that you were being threatened by that painful procedure and when would you feel that it was someone else who was being threatened? It seems clear that there is no clear answer—no magic number of cells past which it no longer is you but Greta Garbo. Therefore, Parfit concludes, our personal identity is not in fact an either/or matter. It is a matter of degree. As he sees it, the question whether the transformed you is still you is rather like the question whether today's Iraq is identical to antiquity's Mesopotamia. There is a partial geographic overlap. There are probably quite a few Iraqis whose bloodlines go back all the way to the inhabitants of Mesopotamia. Does that mean that Mesopotamia is identical to Iraq? This looks not like an either/or matter but like a matter of degrees. It is true *to the degree that* there is geographical and biological continuity between the two. It's the same, Parfit maintains, with personal identity.

If Parfit is right, this has many startling consequences. For instance, it means that if I tell you that before subjecting you to some extremely painful treatment I will first subject you to some partially identity-destroying transformation, you should dread what I am going to do to you that much less. But I venture to guess that you are going to dread it just as much.

But is Parfit right? An extension of the arguments already given suggests he is not: Imagine a spectrum that has you on one end and someone you regard as a human monster (pick your favorite historical villain) on the other end. Once again, contemplate the possibility of administering gradually increasing amounts of pain as we move across the spectrum from you to the monster. If there is no discontinuity—as Parfit insists—then you should dread the administration of such great pain being administered to the monster as much as you should dread the administration of the lesser pain to yourself. But do you?

12. Larry Temkin, "An Abortion Argument and the Threat of Intransitivity," in Crisp and Hooker, *Well-Being and Morality,* 268.

13. Indeed, the most ingenious contributions to this literature offer some truly remarkable affirmative explanations for the validity of the Sorites argument. The main sources here are two books by Roy Sorensen, *Blindspots* (New York: Oxford University Press, 1987) and *Vagueness and Contradiction* (New York: Oxford University Press, 2001), and two books by Timothy Williams, *Identity and Discrimination* (Oxford: Blackwell, 1990) and *Vagueness* (New York: Routledge, 1996). Their work has spawned a large follow-up literature. Among the most interesting recent legal treatments of Sorites-like problems, see Eugene Volokh, "The Mechanisms of the Slippery Slope," *Harvard Law Review* 116 (2003): 1026–1134.

14. There is for instance this connection: Temkin's construction can be used to show that a standard way of trying to solve the Sorites paradox will not work. In other words, we can think of it as a supersophisticated version of the Sorites paradox that resists the standard way of coping with it. (Thinking of it as a supersophisticated version of the Sorites paradox should not, however, detract from the originality of his insight. After all, one can think of a sculpture as a supersophisticated slab of rock.) This standard way is to say that the paradox is built on

the failure to realize that imperceptible differences can add up to perceptible differences. The fact that a given fetus is virtually indistinguishable from one that is one day older and that fetus in turn is virtually indistinguishable from one that is another day older does not mean that the first is virtually indistinguishable from the last. Virtual indistinguishability is not a transitive relationship. Nothing of the sort can be said about Temkin's examples. In comparing the various fetus-killing-plus-exam-cheating cases, we are not overlooking imperceptible differences. On the contrary, the cases are all clearly distinguishable, and the argument *depends* on the fact that they are clearly distinguishable.

15. Graciela Chichilnisky, "Social Aggregation Rules and Continuity," *Quarterly Journal of Economics* 97, no. 2 (1982): 337–53.

16. My summary of Chichilnisky's theorem in a way somewhat distorts its import. Its contribution to the theory of social choice is not merely, indeed not even principally, the substantive result regarding discontinuity but the spawning of an entirely new approach, the topological one, to this subject. But that does not require discussion for our purposes. For more on the approach, see the recent survey article by Nicholas Baigent, "Topological Theories of Social Choice," in *Handbook of Social Choice and Welfare*, vol. 2, ed. Kenneth J. Arrow, Amartya Sen, and Kotaro Suzumura (Amsterdam: Elsevier/North-Holland, 2010), and, also by Baigent, "The Beach Party Problem: An Informal Introduction to Continuity Problems in Group Choice," presidential address of the Central European Program in Economic Theory Annual Workshop, 2002.

Chapter Twelve

1. Jonathan Swift, *Gulliver's Travels*, ed. Robert Greenberg (1726; repr., New York: Norton, 1970), 39.

2. Paul Johnson, *Intellectuals* (New York: Harper & Row, 1988), ix, 2.

3. Ibid., 74–75.

4. Ibid., 79–80.

5. John Stuart Mill, *On Liberty and Utilitarianism* (1859; repr., New York: Bantam, 1993), 12–13.

6. What was Mill thinking? Surely this objection must have occurred to him. The closest he comes to addressing this possibility, however, is this: "The acts of an individual may be hurtful to others, or wanting in due consideration for their welfare, without going the length of violating any of their constituted rights. The offender may then be justly punished by opinion, though not by law" (ibid., 97). This sounds a lot like the line Joel Feinberg pursues and that I critique in the next few paragraphs. This is just one problem with it. The other is his puzzling insistence elsewhere that the same criteria determine not merely someone's eligibility for punishment but also his eligibility for social disapprobation. He prefaces the state-

ment of his famous principle by saying, "The object of this Essay is to assert one very simple principle, as entitled to govern absolutely the dealings of society with the individual in the way of compulsion and control, *whether the means used be physical force in the form of legal penalties, or the moral coercion of public opinion*" (ibid., 11, italics mine).

7. Joel Feinberg, *The Moral Limits of the Criminal Law*, 4 vols. (New York: Oxford University Press, 1984–88).

8. Ibid., vol. 1, *Harm to Others*, 110.

9. Michael S. Moore, *Placing Blame: A General Theory of the Criminal Law* (New York: Oxford University Press, 1997), 763–64.

10. Ibid., 772–73.

11. Based on Model Penal Code's commentary on the homicide section.

Chapter Thirteen

1. William James, *The Principles of Psychology*, vol. 1 (New York: H. Holt, 1918), chap. 13.

2. Thorsten Sellin and Marvin Wolfgang, *The Measurement of Delinquency* (New York: John Wiley & Sons, 1964), 268. See also George A. Gescheider, *Psychophysics*, 2nd ed. (Hillsdale, N.J.: Lawrence Erlbaum Associates, 1985), 227–67.

Final Thoughts

1. Rick Beyer, "A Plate of Peas," read on National Story Project with Paul Auster, *Weekend All Things Considered*, NPR, http://www.npr.org/programs/watc/storyproject/2000/001203.story.html.

Index